RIPENING HARVEST, GATHERING STORM

Ripening Harvest, Gathering Storm

What is the relevance of the Christian faith in a world sliding into crisis?

MAURICE SINCLAIR

MARC
STL Books
Church Missionary Society
Evangelical Missionary Alliance

Biblical quotations are from the New International Version
© International Bible Society 1973, 1978, 1984

Front cover photo: Zefa Picture Library

British Library Cataloguing in Publication Data

Sinclair, Maurice
Ripening harvest, gathering storm.
1. Christian missions
I. Title
266

ISBN 0–86065–648–9 (MARC)
1–85078–046–3 (STL Books)

Co-publishers

STL Books are published by Send The Light
(Operation Mobilisation), P.O. Box 48, Bromley,
Kent, England.

Church Missionary Society, 157 Waterloo Road,
London SE1 8UU

Evangelical Missionary Alliance, 186 Kennington Park Road,
London SE11 4BT

Printed in Great Britain for MARC,
an imprint of Kingsway Publications Ltd
Lottbridge Drove, Eastbourne, E Sussex BN23 6NT by
Richard Clay Ltd, Bungay, Suffolk.
Typeset by Watermark, Hampermill Cottage, Watford WD1 4PL

To my Father and Mother
whom I remember with love and
gratitude

Acknowledgements

The book has been five years in the making and many people have helped me in bringing it to birth. More than fifty have responded to particular questions about mission in their part of the world. To the valuable material they have given me, I have added more from written sources, as indicated in the bibliography. Much encouragement and practical assistance has been given me by colleagues in the Church Missionary Society, South American Missionary Society, Evangelical Missionary Alliance, and Consultative Group for Mission, among other mission agencies. Those with whom I work in Crowther Hall and in the Selly Oak Colleges' Department of Mission generously covered for me during a term's leave for study and writing. Here I specially thank Joanna Cox, and at the same time pay tribute to Jane Barnett, my secretary. Henry Tyler, Stanley Davies, and Pat Harris are among those who read the manuscript and made very helpful suggestions for improvements. Within my own family and relations I want to thank my cousin, Hugh Butterworth, and most of all my wife, Gillian. Tony Collins, for my publisher, has cut through the verbal undergrowth and let the light into dark corners. I record many thanks to many friends in Christ.

Maurice Sinclair

Contents

1

World of Promise: World of Menace

Mirror images

Untroubled by stresses building up in the wing components, the jet-set executive settles back in his seat and enjoys the powerful thrust of take off... Unable to believe her eyes, an Ethiopian nurse wakes to see through her window the huddled forms of a thousand refugees, some of their children coughing and crying but otherwise gauntly silent in the morning light... In an immaculately furnished town house sitting-room a ten-year-old hides his face in his hands as the home-hired video reaches its climax of hideous violence... After the rains a Nepali farmer gazes down into a gaping crater: a gash in the eroded mountainside just where he had cleared the trees to make a field... Lunch is over at an old people's home at Hornsey Rise. A tabloid newspaper is draped over the head of a drowsy resident. He hasn't read it, but even if he had it would have told him little of substance about the world outside.

It would be possible to choose a thousand different images to reflect the world we live in. Our selection could highlight the breathtaking opportunities and the awe-inspiring potential of our present situation: the brilliant technology, the human creativity and heroism, the profound insights and the imaginative schemes. However, whatever balance of optimism or pessimism we prefer, and whatever direction a day's headlines may propel us, we have to try at least to face both the menace and the promise which hover over us. Can we come to terms with the fact that we live in days of accelerating change and accumulating crises? And what in global and personal terms does this mean?

Accelerating change and accumulating crises

In a series of four dramatic upward-soaring graphical illustrations the *Gaia Atlas of Planet Management* shows the global changes in population, energy consumption, information distribution and human mobility.[1] Levels reached in all these indicators of world development in our present century completely dwarf anything which was known before. Not only that, the massive changes of the twentieth century are still speeding up, and some of them are of a kind our planet cannot long sustain.

Because some of the rapid changes taking place in our modern world have a destructive quality, we are also experiencing a series of crises. 'Suddenly—virtually overnight when measured on a historical scale—mankind finds itself confronted by a multitude of unprecedented crises: the population crisis, the raw materials crisis, the environmental crisis... New crises appear while the old ones linger on, with effects spreading to every corner of the earth.'[2] Tom Sine quotes this passage from *Mankind at the Turning Point* in talking about the humanly uncertain future of development projects. This situation has wide implications in several different spheres. These we must look at in turn.

Economic crises Economics is literally to do with housekeeping. In some parts of the world it has never been easier to keep house; in other parts of the world it has never been harder. While the privileged and affluent are guiding smooth-running, heavy-laden trolleys a short distance through the supermarket carpark, their under-privileged counterparts may be trudging miles to collect a few litres of contaminated water or a few sticks of increasingly scarce firewood. The house in which the housekeeping is done may reflect the same extreme contrast: a miracle of construction technology, comfort and convenience, on the one hand, or a makeshift shelter, lacking space, security, weather proofing, or hygiene, on the other.

For the housekeeper these may be the realities behind the global statistics on distribution of wealth. The destabilising imbalance in the global economy is shown in the relative positions of the wealthiest and poorest fifths of the world population. On the one side over one billion affluent people follow lifestyles and patterns of consumption which impose a grossly disproportionate strain upon the earth's resources and environment. On the other hand the number of those who live in absolute poverty is also approaching one billion. All these people are so poor that their health standards and life opportunities are seriously impaired. Nearly all are illiterate and lack adequate housing. Half suffer the effect of a diet below the minimum calorie requirement. Forty million starve to death each year.

Tragically there are a number of indications that world poverty is worsening and inequalities are widening. In 1983 per capita grain production throughout the world decreased. The gross national product for the world as a whole has not improved since the late '70s. GNP per person in the rich countries of the West is now forty times higher than in the low income countries. In the last three decades average increases in income per head in the rich countries have amounted to nearly $4,000 in real terms whereas the equivalent figure for the poorest countries is $50, no doubt largely absorbed by their more privileged minorities.

The result of these trends is summed up in a stark sentence in the *Gaia Atlas*: 'Half the world's nations have economies on the point of bankruptcy or indeed collapse.'[3] The international debt burden for many countries has grown to the point at which their only means of covering interest payments is by taking out yet more loans. To the material scarcities and inequalities in the world there is added a financial crisis producing acute strains in the international monetary system.

Population crises Economists who study world trends are

right to speak of a poverty bomb threatening the future of both rich and poor. The fuse set to detonate the bomb is all too short. It is not a simple fuse, though. It has a number of strands, the most obvious of which is population growth. In the last 150 years the world population has increased almost 5 times over. The acceleration in growth, however, is such that in less than a decade we may expect to add to our total now as many as lived throughout the world in the 1830s: one billion people.

An overcrowded ship may take on extra passengers without sinking but the further this process continues the more important it becomes that the passengers should be distributed evenly and that their movements be carefully restrained. No such conditions apply now on the overcrowded earth. In recent years one billion people have moved from rural areas into the cities. At least fifteen million people are displaced from their native areas and live as refugees. While population numbers are stabilising and the proportion of old people is increasing in the North, annual increases remain as high as 3 and even 4 per cent in the South, and nearly half the people are young and have their reproductive lives ahead of them. There is the prospect of the Third World population increasing to 90 per cent of the total. These imbalances, on the ship analogy, suggest the imminent danger of capsizing!

Environmental crises Any attempt to describe the environmental crises (another thread in the fuse to the poverty bomb) suffers from similar depressing, fatigue-producing statistics: on present trends one fifth of all arable land will be lost by AD 2000; one third of tropical forests will be destroyed; and the world's deserts will have been increased by two thirds. Crudely numbing facts do not tell the whole story. As the *Gaia Atlas* points out, 'Human survival is intertwined with the survival of genetic diversity and thus with the fate of every natural system.'[4]

The environmental crisis is, therefore, also a genetic crisis. Whereas at the beginning of the century it is claimed we were destroying one natural species per year, now we are destroying one species per day. Because of uncontrolled destruction, erosion, and pollution, natural cycles are becoming seriously distorted. Human activity has already altered the nitrogen cycle by 50 per cent, the carbon by 20 per cent and the sulphur cycle by 100 per cent.

Long-term effects of such changes are not yet fully known. Some already appear bizarre. Widespread soil erosion on the Nepali slopes of the Himalayas is building up deposits which may form a massive island in the Bay of Bengal. Higher temperatures resulting from the greenhouse effect from higher levels of carbon dioxide in the atmosphere may lead to the partial melting of the polar icecaps, the raising of the ocean levels, and so the threatened flooding of the new Bengali mega-island together with low-lying coastal areas thoughout the world.

Crises of security Although all kinds of economic activities and population changes put severe strains upon the environment that supports us, a breakdown in security threatens the whole of life on earth yet more abruptly and destructively. The militarisation of our planet represents one more accelerating change producing yet more crises. Since 1960 military expenditure throughout the world has absorbed all the increase in economic growth. The civilian world economy is actually smaller now than it was at that time when population was substantially less. Since 1980 arms exports to developing countries have grown to exceed the value of economic aid.[5]

The nuclear dimension to the security threat and the arms race give it a wholly new and potentially catastrophic character. Existing nuclear arsenals in East and West could produce the equivalent of one million Hiroshima explosions. A single submarine can deploy weaponry with a firepower which far exceeds, at one despatch, all expended throughout World War II. The devastation produced by these horrific weapons is well known: the heat, the blast, the short-term and the long-term radiation effects are all documented. Eye witnesses of what happened in those Japanese cities in 1945 have also told their harrowing, excruciating story.

Since that time, although there have been 120 wars, all have been fought with conventional weapons—none with nuclear weapons. As a result the damage and loss of life has been regional and bitterly grievous rather than global and totally catastrophic. The situation of global menace, however, remains. Levels of peacetime armament in country after country are quite unprecedented. The overkill capacity of the weapons developed in each upward spiral of the arms race become, by any rational criterion, more and more ludicrous. As observed by the authors of *The Church and the Bomb*, 'The military endeavour, with its huge world-wide industrial base, absorbs an immense fund of human energy.' And we could add brains. Only 1 per cent of research conducted in the North is directed to the amelioration of poverty; 32 per cent is focused upon defence and space. We are constantly spending on war weapons resources in excess of those needed to remove the deprivations and grievances which produced the war situation in the first place.

Into this paradoxical and gloom-laden scene the signing in Washington of the Intermediate Range Missile Treaty has brought a most welcome intermission. At the time of writing it is impossible to know the full outcome of this step in nuclear arms reductions. Even though the diplomatic and political difficulties have been overcome, the technical problems are by no means easy: we are told that it will take three years to neutralise and dismember the weaponry involved—8 per cent of the superpowers' atomic arsenals.

Crises of perception In editing the *Gaia Atlas of Planet Management,* Norman Myers considers the danger of planetary breakdown. In this context he singles out one crisis which he thinks might determine the outcome more than all the others: 'National leaders, with honourable exceptions, have been slow to recognise the new sources of conflict: there is in short a crisis of perception which could prove most critical of all.'[6]

The Church and the Bomb takes up this theme: 'The existence of these (atomic) weapons induces a paranoia in the states owning them which distorts their judgement... The war machines often seem close to controlling their creators.' Leaders are guilty of projecting the 'blind dehumanisation of the prospective adversary'.[7] Ruth Sivard, in *World Military and Social Expenditures*, points out: 'An atmosphere of permanent emergency is indispensable for militarism and its huge budgets.'[8] Even as long ago as 1961, President Eisenhower was warning against the 'misplaced power' of a military establishment of unprecedented size. Now again we can be thankful that in the Washington summit of 1987 the power of the media, at least for the time, ran counter to the power of the arms manufacturers and their political lobbyists. We ask ourselves, 'Will the crisis of opportunity be seen and grasped, or will the powers revert to blind reliance on massive overkill?'

At a stage in history when clarity of perception and breadth of vision are most urgently needed, any narrowing of sympathies, distortion of values, and surrender to vested interest needs to be most vigorously resisted. At a time when media of communication have a versatility and scope far in excess of anything previously conceived, it should be noted that the control of mass communication both in East and West is concentrated in dangerously few hands. With the population movements, people of different cultures and religions are living alongside each other on a scale unknown before, yet in many places there is a way of viewing each other which makes personal relationships across the divides particularly difficult.

Christians in the crises

For Christians the crises of the modern world point up some very sharp questions. The gospel of Jesus Christ was born out of a crisis; it came at the critical point in human history. Christian faith, if it is true to its own character, should function, even flourish, in crisis. So we would expect that at a crucial juncture in human affairs, a time of judgement and decision, Christian witness should be particularly strong and Christian perceptions particularly penetrating. At other moments in history this has been so. In some parts of the world it is so today. But what about our part of the world?

If we live in the West we find ourselves on the 'comfortable periphery' of the world,[9] but it is only the periphery. We may bask in a patch of sunlight, but it is only a patch. How carefully are we watching the storm clouds of worsening poverty, escalating violence and the fluctuating threat of nuclear catastrophe? Ostrich-like, are we burying our heads in parochial concerns and ignoring the problems of the many poor which threaten to engulf the privileged few. Is it our inclination to pull down the shutters and narrow our horizons to safe limits? Or dare we not only look out at the world's physical and social problems but also see its lostness and spiritual malaise?

As a Western Christian I want to frankly admit to a crisis of perception which many of my Western brothers and sisters share. I do not see a commitment to local and global mission in our churches which responds to the insistent call of the God we serve or the crying needs of the world we occupy. 'But what is this about "mission"?' someone will ask. 'Aren't we talking about world crises?' Here, though, we are near the heart of the matter. This is the blind spot. Many Christians do not see a vital connection between world mission and the confrontation of world problems. Most Westerners have their minds divided into compartments. The mission compartment is a small one next to the archives. Christians can fail to relate the mission of Jesus Christ to the headline news. They assume that if secular problems have solutions at all, then they are only secular solutions. Too many who profess to follow Christ do not align themselves effectively with his missionary purpose for the world. They have neither adequately grasped the nature of that purpose, nor seen its wide extent.

Sweeping criticisms these may be, but in our precipice situation do we have the luxury of excuses? We are accountable to God as stewards of his gospel of redemption, and this crisis-ridden, precarious, potentially magnificent yet distorted world is where this missionary stewardship must be discharged.

An agenda for mission

A renewed Christian obedience, required of this writer as much as anyone else, must, I believe, be a missionary obedience. Only commitment to Christ's mission, pursued in Christ's way, is a sufficient life purpose and lifestyle. Uniquely it measures up to every criterion, including the extremity of the worst crises today. Within my limitations, I want to base this missionary solution to our contemporary dilemma upon an unfolding plan revealed in Scripture. I want to trace some threads in the missionary story of the church from Pentecost to the present. Having returned to our own time with some lessons learnt, I want to try to see our world afresh through missionary eyes. My aim will be to sketch it continent by continent: a kind of global doodling. Then I want to match a picture of six continents with six localities. A world-view informed by Christ's mission is needed for Christ's mission. So is partnership making the links between his people in different places. Another concern: can the whole body of the church of Christ make a wholehearted response to his call to mission? Can a band of enthusiasts become a mainstream movement? Can mission be rescued from the specialists and given back to the people of God? What will shake their repose and stir their spirits? Lastly, what of the future? Can we look ahead in mission and combine confidence with realism, a balanced perspective with abounding zeal?

These questions will follow, but now in conclusion here I ask, 'Can the blind see?' I have no doubt that underlying this crisis of seeing, already described, and indeed all the other accumulating storms, is a spiritual crisis. Some of the blindness to the political follies, the military dangers, the human injustices and the environmental irresponsibilities can have no full explanation apart from Satan's work. Yet even darkened in this way the human picture has some remarkable highlights. There is a secular voice pleading for respect for the natural order. Earth, our 'blue pearl in space', is being seen as something not to plunder but to cherish. Norman Myers puts the challenge thus: 'We have the chance to live in final accord with our spaceship earth and hence in final harmony with each other.'[10]

This vision evokes many echoes of the kingdom of God, promised in the matchless words of Scripture. The modern crisis situation is compelling more people to look to the contrasting features of the kingdom. May they also see the King!

2

The Master-plan of the Servant

God's voice obeyed and disobeyed

A voice of irresistible power rang out in the void: 'Let there be light!' A massive ball of fire erupted, and was flung apart in a thousand galaxies. The newborn cosmos passed through aeons of time, adjusting, differentiating and expanding. Then God spoke another creative word: 'Let there be living creatures!' In response, even on a single planet, there developed a staggering multiplicity of organisms: plants and animals, wonderful in the beauty of their form and the intricacy of their working.

The same voice spoke again, and in a new way: 'Let us make creatures who can delight in our friendship, and who can freely choose to share our purpose of love, conceived from eternity. Let us make humankind!' Thus our first, fully human parents took their being. God's word came to them not in irresistible creative power but rather in acceptable or refusable relationship. Herein lay both the potential and the risk of creation; the man and the woman could say 'Yes!' to God and enter with him into the fullness and the blessing he had prepared, or they could refuse to co-operate in his good purpose.

In the event, the pioneers of humanity took the wrong road. As a result they retained the splendid image of the Creator, but it was tarnished. They had a longing for the Being who made them, but it was unfulfilled. They were alienated from

God and in a degree from one another. This alienation, stemming from the disobedience of the Fall, bit deeply into the created order. Tension became evident amid the harmony: cruelty mingled with the beauty; growth and life were interspersed with decay and death.

If we are to understand the mission of God as it relates to his world, then we must begin with his work of creation. At once we start to see the universality of Christian mission. It was by Christ that all things were created.[1] He was the Word who spoke that creative word in the beginning. So all humanity has to do with him. People's present religious adherence or ideological preference cannot make God's creative purpose in Christ irrelevant to them. No one can safely say, 'It is no concern of mine.' God's mission in creation applies to all his creatures without exception. In every case their destiny is bound up in its fulfilment.

We turn now, though, from the broad and inclusive base of God's plan in his creation, to a narrow and humanly precarious channel, through which his persevering love would flow to a world at odds with him. Can we picture a next episode in this creative and redemptive mission of God?

God's friendship restores purpose

A business man, well into middle age but bronzed and fit, was sitting on the sunroof of his house in the Eastern city where he had made his home: a prosperous, sophisticated centre of commerce. Because it was siesta time the street traffic had subsided, and in the sultry stillness of the afternoon the reclining figure was settling more comfortably on his couch. The surroundings would have induced pleasant thoughts, but the business man had been saddened by his father's recent death and was anxious because he had no son of his own. 'Who will inherit my business?' he wondered.

Without warning, a voice broke the drowsy silence. 'Leave your country, and go to the land I will show you! I will make you into a great nation. You will be a blessing, and all peoples on earth will be blessed through you.'[2] This voice was none other than God's voice, the man who heard it was Abraham, and the city from which he set out in obedience was Haran.

God broke into Abraham's privileged but anxious world and revealed himself to him as the God of personal relationship and universal purpose. This 'Almighty', 'Eternal', 'Most High' God, possessor of heaven and earth, 'Righteous Judge of all the earth' befriended this particular man. Such a friendship meant a total transformation for Abraham. Life in the Fertile Crescent was a cyclical affair, following the seasons, and lacking any ultimate purpose. Nevertheless, Abraham was carried bodily into the straight-line purpose of God. God demanded that he should set out on a journey with an end in view: blessing, as we have seen, not only for himself but for all humankind. He set off, and God challenged him again: 'Look into the distance as far as you can see, north and south, east and west.' 'Look at the stars in the sky and see if you can count them.' 'Consider the grains of sand on the seashore.'[3] 'My purpose for you,' said God, 'is as wide or wider than these objects of my creation.'

God's power brings freedom

God intervened in the life of that Middle Eastern business man and gave him a profound revelation of his character as God. Another crucial self-disclosure of God came about 500 years later and involved another unlikely recipient.

A 'drop-out' from powerful political circles in Egypt had made a new life for himself as a ranch manager in Midian. In some ways he was over qualified for the job; as a young man he had had a personal tutor and attended an elite college of further education. Still he liked the open-air life and soon adopted the slow drawling speech of the outback. He seemed to have found contentment away from the intrigue and dangers of the Egyptian power struggle. Being from immigrant stock, he felt at home again in the arid grassland region frequented by his forebears. On one occasion when the regular pasturage was exhausted, he took the flocks westward and grazed them below the massive red granite outcrops of 'God's mountain'. As the evening sun dipped lower, bathing the thorn scrub in its light, one bush shone with a special brilliance. While the natural light faded, the supernatural light gathered in intensity. Eyes accustomed to the desert scene were irresitably drawn to the bush glowing bright with a fire that needed no fuel. And then the voice spoke: the same voice that his ancestor Abraham had heard. Moses found himself in the awesome presence of God, the Lord: terrible in judgement and tender in compassion.[4]

It is scarcely possible to exaggerate the significance of that encounter in the Midian outback, and the events that were soon to follow. Abraham's tribe, suffering as exploited immigrants in Egypt, would be roused from abject submission. Those who had oppressed them faced humiliation and defeat through a unique display of power. The liberated Hebrew slaves were to be welded together into a God-fearing nation and Moses was to become not only their law-giver but also a figure of central importance in the history and religion of Israel.

The events of the Exodus are dramatic and pivotal; the figure of Moses towers above his contemporaries. But what stands out in this critical period is the sternly compassionate nature of God and his unfolding purpose for man. 'I have heard the groaning of my people,' said God to Moses. 'I have witnessed their suffering. I have seen their oppression.'[5] It was because God cared so passionately that he acted so decisively. In God's holy and loving purpose the tyranny of evil must not forever hold people in its grip. Its power must be challenged and broken.

God acts in terrible judgement upon those who refuse his warnings and persist in the cruel exercise of tyrannical power. Sharp punishment for the oppressors brought with it profound freedom for the oppressed. The Israelites were certainly liberated politically; Pharaoh and his taskmasters no longer dominated their lives. More than that though, their freedom was enlarged through the worship of the living God, whose presence and glory accompanied them on their desert journey. Again, strange though it may seem, they were free in so far as they were obedient; the law given at Mount Sinai represented for them the revealed and liberating will of God.

Trough of sin: peak of glory

God entered into Abraham's life and experience as someone personal and purposeful, making a deep relationship with him. God entered into Moses' life, judging and saving, rescuing and redeeming. We pass over another 500 years and see how God breaks into the stream of history and a man's consciousness in a substantially new way again. The person concerned in this instance was perhaps a little more predictable; the surprise element was in the timing.

It was the year after the death of one of Judah's most powerful and prosperous political leaders. This buffer state had for a time flourished exceptionally because its powerful neighbours were in decline. There had been territorial gains, an impressive strengthening of the nation's defences, prosperity and even luxury for the privileged and a great show of religion. The faith of Abraham and of Moses appeared to be alive and well in Judah, at least on the surface.

A young theology student was growing up among the privileged and influential in Judah's capital. This young man had a rare gift for words and often found himself at the centre of a noisy joking crowd at one of the city gates. These were heady days when the rich were still rich, when there was big money to be made in the market, when the high-born women dressed in fine style. The men loved to gather, especially on feast days, and boast of their tough business deals, their shrewd political manoeuvrings, and to watch the smart young women pass by with their flashing armlets and anklets and gauzy garments and veils, half hiding and half revealing what especially fascinated the male onlookers.

And this young man also boasted, and watched and commented as wittily as any of his peers. He enjoyed the sophistication and the gaiety, but he was uneasy within himself. It wasn't just that the political climate was changing, with a powerful northern state rearming and menacing Judah and her neighbours. The young man understood the politics well enough, but he sensed something even more serious: a spiritual vacuum. He was aware of the hollowness in the life of the nation, and in his own life as well. The disturbing thought may already have crossed his mind that his powerful Judean friends were treating the poor among God's people no better than their Egyptian taskmasters had done centuries ago.

Soon it was time for him to attend a major religious festival. The solid square edifice of Solomon's Temple stood resplendent in the winter sunshine. Worshippers crowded its courts. The massive pillars of its portico towered high above the human throng, apparently immovable. Then suddenly there sounded out the voice of God. Not this time a whisper in a man's ear; not now a glowing bush and an echo in the desert wind; for Isaiah it was a mighty voice which shook the Temple to its foundations. God's presence filled the dark interior with a dazzling bright cloud. And God's prophet saw God's form: the beauty of his holiness, the majesty of his glory. Just when the earthly throne was empty, the heavenly throne was filled.

Isaiah cried out, 'I have seen the King! The Lord of Hosts!' It was a cry of terror. He was overwhelmed with this vision of God's holiness and his own sinfulness. Every shred of his complacency was stripped away. Exposed and vulnerable, he stood before God. Knowing himself to be as unclean as his companions he waited to receive God's wrath and condemnation. Instead, by a miracle of grace, he received God's forgiveness and his commissioning. The coal from the altar cleansed his lips. The voice from the throne asked, 'Who will now share my mission?' 'Whom shall I send, and who will go for us?' With every fibre of his being Isaiah answered, 'Here am I! Send me.'[6]

Tracing God's missionary plan

To understand God's new revelation to Isaiah we must look again at the earlier steps in God's missionary intervention, with Abraham and Moses. God called Abraham out of the manipulative, ultimately purposeless and dehumanising fertility religion of ancient Mesopotamia into a personal and purposeful relationship with himself. He was to be God's man through whom fulfilment, well-being, and blessing should come to all people. Abraham's family and immediate descendants were the bearers of this momentous assignment. Yet they scarcely knew what they were about. They proved as fallible as other peoples. Their very existence as landless nomads was precarious in the extreme. But they never lost their belief in the different God who had made himself known to their tribal leader. When famine drove them to Egypt they believed that the God of Abraham had guided them there.

So far this purpose of God, however faintly perceived, appeared intact. At first the Hebrews multiplied in Egypt. Perhaps God's people would one day become as numerous as the stars in the heaven. But then the foreign gods of Egypt and their human representatives began to exert their power. Abraham's people were reduced to helpless slavery. Worse still they were forced to become unwilling tools in building monuments to human vanity and idolatry while all the time their true destiny was to be willing agents in serving the universal rule of the living God.

What had happened? Had God's purpose failed even at this early stage in its fulfilment? Not at all. As we have already seen, through Moses, God's purpose was to be carried further. The Israelites marched out of Egypt free people. God had acted in judgement leaving their oppressors and their oppressive gods impotent. God's mission was now seen to be a rescue mission: rescue, release, redemption for his people, the agents of his mission; restraint, rebuke and ultimately retribution for those who perversely and determinedly opposed it.

The Exodus opened up to Abraham's people a vastly greater opportunity in realising their God-given calling. God guided them through their desert journey with a luminous cloud, giving visible evidence of his glorious presence at the head of their columns. God gave the nation in the making his law to make its social relationships harmonious and fruitful. The relationship with God himself, far from being weakened, was constantly to be reinforced through the worship of the Tabernacle. God pitched his tent with his people; their journey was his journey, their mission was his mission too.

Beyond the desert lay the Promised Land. The occupation of this land was intended to give a wider opportunity for these people: God's special instrument. There was land to be shared out fairly among every family and held in trust for children's children. There was a city to be built: a city of peace; a place where God would make his name dwell, a place of pilgrimage, an altar of sacrifice, a house of prayer for all nations. God was to rule this land. He would raise up Spirit-filled leaders and righteous monarchs. The nation of Israel was to be an example and an inspiration to every other nation in the world.

All this was God's intention. He had sketched this outline from the beginning. What was painted in by his chosen people, however, was a different picture. The kingdom of Israel, by Isaiah's day long partitioned into two rival kingdoms, was depressingly similar to other small states sandwiched between Egypt, Assyria and Babylon. There had already been a long history of religious compromise. The very survival of Israel and Judah had appeared to depend upon political alliances, which in those days involved the accommodation of foreign gods as well as foreign diplomats. The introduction of the cult of the Baals alongside the worship of Jahweh not only weakened the people's grasp on the truth that their God was the universal and only God, it also led to many dehumanising features in Judean and Israelite society: sacred prostitution, child sacrifice, cheapening of the value of life, and a cold disregard for the rights of the poor.

It was against these evils, which threatened to frustrate God's purpose and obscure God's design in and through his people, that God's prophets repeatedly raised their voices. Isaiah was one of a long line of protesters: people who said No! to compromise; people who refused to place Jahweh, the God of Abraham and Moses, on a level with other gods. Even so, the whole nature, destiny, even survival of God's chosen community was again in the balance. Could these two divided, corrupted and compromised nations fulfil a promise of blessing even for themselves, let alone to all nations besides? Weren't foreign armies on the point of invading and devastating them, scattering their populations and deporting them to other lands? Would these invaders not desecrate their holy places, notably the Temple of Solomon, and abruptly break their royal and priestly dynasties? With all this in prospect the prophet spoke words of warning which were timely indeed.

Isaiah saw as clearly as other prophets the 'deep darkness' in which the people walked. He stood alone, though, in seeing the quality and the radiant power of the light that was to shine upon them. Isaiah gave an inspired and uniquely comprehensive answer to the question of God's continuing missionary purpose through his erring but still chosen people.

Because Isaiah had seen 'the King in his Beauty', his eyes had also 'beheld a land which stretched afar'.[7] He had perceived both the beauty of God's holiness and the breadth of God's purpose. Like Abraham he had entered into this great purpose and could see even more of its extent. 'This is the purpose that is purposed concerning the whole earth,' he overheard God saying. 'And this is the hand' (God's hand) 'that is stretched out over all the nations.' 'For the Lord of Hosts has purposed and who will annul it? His hand is stretched out and who will turn it back?' 'I work,' says God, 'and who can hinder it? My counsel shall stand, and I will accomplish all my purposes.'[8]

What could be more emphatic: a comprehensive, prevailing, divine purpose. Yet it appeared in ruins! How could God's salvation be affirmed when the descendants of those who under Moses had experienced it so dramatically now were on the brink of national disaster? We can imagine messengers bringing Isaiah news of the Assyrian advance deep into Judean territory, and in later years, the prophet bluntly telling King Hezekiah that Babylonian invaders would strip his capital bare, and carry all his royal sons into captivity.

Light in the darkness

Here was the deepening darkness and the impending doom. Yet into this situation Isaiah spoke an inspired word of glorious light. Yes, the nation would fall. Yes, her line of kings would be cut off, but a new king would rise like a green shoot from a felled tree. A new people would be gathered; a remnant would be snatched from the jaws of extinction. Not only would God's purpose be upheld; it would be enlarged. Not only would God's salvation be vindicated; it would actually extend in breadth and depth as never before. In Moses' day God punished an idolatrous and oppressive nation in order to save a people sinned against. In Isaiah's day the people were actively the sinners, and their own leaders were oppressive and idolatrous. Now they would not be rescued from a godless nation but actually defeated by one. Now God would go further in punishment because he would also go further in salvation. He would now begin to say not only 'Blessed be Israel my heritage,' but also 'blessed be Egypt my people,' and (even more amazing) 'Assyria the work of my hand.'[9]

Isaiah had good news to tell the nations. He was supremely the evangelist of the Old Testament. His very name meant 'God is salvation'. His whole ministry had depended on hearing for himself God's word of salvation: 'Behold, this coal has touched your lips; your guilt is taken away and your sin is forgiven.' And so, through Isaiah, God articulated his impassioned appeal to the whole alienated humanity: 'Turn to me and be saved, all the ends of the earth! I was ready to be sought by those who did not ask for me; I was ready to be found by those who did not seek me. I said, "Here am I, here am I" to a nation that did not call my name. I spread out my hands all the day to a rebellious people.' 'Why do you spend your money for that which is not bread, and your labour for that which does not satisfy? Come, buy wine and milk without money and without price.' 'I am He who blots out your transgressions for my own sake.' 'Though your sins are like scarlet they shall be as white as snow.' 'I have swept away your transgressions like a cloud and your sins like mist; return to me for I have redeemed you.'[10]

An appeal so breathtaking in its scope, in its depth of emotion, in its sublime generosity, had never been heard before. All the world ought to have heard words such as these, but as far as we know few did. The lives of Isaiah's hearers ought to have been totally transformed, but all we know is that the decline of Judah was not halted. And the pain continued: the trail of pain left by devastating armies, the misery of exploited and oppressed peoples. No salvation for them it would seem! Where then was the solid core of this hope that promised so much more than it had actually demonstrated?

The Servant King

Isaiah's hope of salvation was invested in the promise of a new King. This Anointed One, the promised Messiah, gave substance to the hoped-for deliverance. This King would be different: not a warmonger, but a Prince of Peace, not a puppet king but one whose government would extend beyond the bounds of any kingdom, not an oppressor of other men but one who would champion the weak and the poor. He would be like none of his predecessors in David's line. He would bear the divine name: Mighty God, Everlasting Father. The Spirit of God would rest upon him.

The work of God's Spirit in God's Messiah is profoundly significant and quite beyond human invention. Because God's Spirit will rest upon him his delight will be in reverently obeying God. This Spirit is a spirit of obedience and has a quality of gentleness. He will neither break a bruised reed nor extinguish a dimly burning wick. Such gentleness is not weakness though: 'He will not fail or be discouraged.'[11] In fact it has a quality of steel; it stems from an awesome obedience. The Messiah becomes the Servant.

And so in Isaiah's writings the King is designated the Servant King. But there is more besides; the nature of his service is strange and costly. His ear will be awakened to a summons, from which any mortal man would shrink in horror. Instead, he is to embrace it, setting his face like a flint. The pathway by which the Servant will assume his kingly rule is to be one of shame and suffering. This young shoot from David's interrupted line will be more like a 'root out of dry ground'. There will be no eye-catching attraction, no flattering courtiers, no favourable environment for him. On the contrary, he will be asked to offer his back to the smiters and his face to those who would spit at him. The one whose name is 'Wonderful, Counsellor' will himself be despised and rejected, oppressed and afflicted. The 'Mighty God' will become the 'Man of Sorrows'; the Servant King will be the Suffering King.[12]

For whom will the Messiah bear this weight of suffering? He will do no violence; it will not be for his own sins that he will be punished. In Isaiah's day it was not just one nation or people who were clearly sinful and oppressive. Isaiah knew that there were many sinners and many oppressors (actual or potential) and that God's own people were among them. His answer was that the Servant will bear the sins of many. Indeed the Lord will 'lay upon him the iniquity of us all'. The Messiah will not only be stricken for the transgression of God's people but also many nations will be startled by his amazing act of sacrifice. They will see a unique sin-bearing love in action; they will understand that he has suffered and died for them.[13]

When in glorious self-revelation God broke into the life of the young Isaiah that festival day in the Jerusalem Temple, he set in train a process of inspired thinking, preaching and writing. This book of prophecy has a certain completeness. The Most High Creator God, known to Abraham as a God of personal relationship and universal purpose, is known by Isaiah as the One who has an intimate bond with his Servant, in whom his soul delights, and through whom his purpose is fulfilled. Moses had met with God who is terrible in judgement and tender in compassion. Isaiah, and those who learnt from him, began to see into the heart of God and discern how these two opposite things might be expressed together to open a way of justice, healing and salvation for all people. In the person of a defenceless man, the Mighty God would take upon himself the pain, the futility, the enslaving sin of a whole rebellious world. His judgement would be executed, his compassion would bring its healing fruit, the travail of his soul would be satisfied, the world would be saved. Here set out was the complete answer to the plight of man, for Isaiah's time and for all time.

A remnant survives

The scrolls were written and history continued. The Babylonian army breached the walls of Jerusalem. The last pathetic survivor of David's proud dynasty was captured with his fleeing army. King Zedekiah was forced to watch the cruel execution of his sons and then his eyes were put out. The people of Judah who had not died of starvation in the siege, or violently in the ensuing battle, were carried captive into Babylon.

Another empire superseded that of Babylon and a remnant of the deported Jews were allowed to return to the ruins of Jerusalem. Then followed periods of heroic reconstruction and more intense religious zeal interspersed with times of cowardice and compromise. Even with the best efforts, Jerusalem and its surrounding enclave was only a shadow of its former state. Its independence and survival were more precarious than ever. God's people were living on the neglected fringes of other people's empires: the Persian's, the Greek's and then the Roman's. They knew the mean poverty and the bitter violence that such a situation brings.

Where, then, in these sordid and disappointing circumstances was the fulfilment of that brilliant prospect set forth by Isaiah and succeeding prophets? Where was the new King who would inaugurate the new Jerusalem, promulgate the new law, and usher in the new age with new heavens and a new earth? What natural or supernatural person would intervene to transform a situation which was so bleakly unpromising? Above all, who had grasped that truth about redemption through suffering about which Isaiah had spoken? Who would fulfil the role upon which depended the true salvation of a tortured world?

One thing at least was already realised from Isaiah's prophecy; there was a faithful remnant among the people: those who like their hero Daniel would have no truck with idolatory and went on believing in God's power to intervene. 'But if not' and he didn't act, then they would still not give in. They resolutely kept themselves as a law-keeping people among the Gentiles. They celebrated God's presence among them. God was present among these his people and they were present, though inconspicuously, among all mankind. This was their God-given mission, to worship, to obey, to be a presence, to suffer and to keep a greater hope alive.

Jesus: special agent of mission

Into this modest, but noble, inheritance both Mary and Joseph were born: unknown people living devout, though humdrum, lives in an obscure village in Gentile Galilee. Mary, perhaps in her late teens, would have lived the more sheltered and uneventful life of the two of them. But now she was looking forward to a great event: her marriage with Joseph. Before this could take place though an immeasurably greater event overtook her. She was amazed and profoundly troubled when an angel messenger appeared before her eyes, gave her a solemn greeting, and announced that she would bear a son who would be the promised Messiah. Her baby would occupy David's throne; his kingdom would be without geographical boundaries, nor limits in time. Then the blurted question, 'How can this be?' to which came the assured reply, 'By the Holy Spirit's power.' Finally comes Mary's surrender: 'I am your servant, Lord, do with me what you have said.'[14]

The great service that Mary gave was to bear, nurse, and cherish Jesus, the Servant Son. With her carpenter husband she took him to give thanks to God in the Temple. There an old man, Simeon, took the baby in his arms and declared him to be the Saviour of all peoples and a Light to the nations.[15] The hidden years of his boyhood, youth and early manhood were a time of self-discovery. With a dawning realisation he knew who he was: the one of whom Isaiah the prophet had spoken. At his baptism God spoke again, affirming him as his dear Son. In his desert temptations he deliberately chose that way of suffering through which the world's salvation would be wrought. Thus prepared, he steps into the brief span of his public ministry, to do what had been written of him and to willingly accomplish the Father's purpose.

Those who were to record this earthly ministry saw with crystal clarity that Jesus, as Messiah, was the perfect embodiment and principal agent of God's redemptive mission. For Mark this mission is centred upon Jesus, who bears the vital message, demonstrates the needed authority, enters the unavoidable conflict and even though harassed by hostile opponents still expresses God's tender compassion towards those in need. Far ahead of his disciples on the road to Jerusalem Jesus walks resolutely into the armed camp of his enemies and their oppressive overlords. In Gethsemane, with the horror of crucifixion now staring him in the face, he weeps tears of anguish but still clings to that way of obedience which takes him to Calvary. Mark shows forth Jesus, Son of God and Son of Man: one who 'came not to be served but to serve, and to give his life a ransom for many.'[16] Those who recognise him for who he is, Jesus invites to share his mission of costly sacrificial service.

If Mark's Gospel is the Gospel of Christ the Servant, then Matthew's Gospel is the Gospel of Christ the King. Even to the infant Jesus, great men of other nations pay homage. Neither King Herod nor Prince Satan can have any power over this King, who from the mountain of temptation looks out over all the kingdoms of the world, who from the mount of teaching proclaims a new law of love, and from the Mount of Olives surveys the royal city and descends to it in lowly pomp acclaimed by a loyal crowd. The throne of this King of the Jews proves to be a cross, and his crown one of thorns, but his death only enlarges his kingdom. On the mountain in Galilee the risen Jesus confidently tells his followers that all authority in heaven and on earth is his. He commands them to make people of all nations observe his law and accept his rule. This great missionary commission is a royal commission.[17]

The special emphasis in Luke's Gospel is upon Jesus as the Saviour, Spirit-filled and universal. With his words and works he brings in a new era of salvation. Jesus tells a surprised audience in the synagogue at Nazareth that with his coming Isaiah's prophecy is fulfilled: the captives will be released, the oppressed will be set free and the poor receive good news at last. Because the Spirit rests upon him he is able to be a true champion of the poor, one who can sensitively and effectively raise the status of women, and a person who reaches out to the despised members of society, giving them a sense of self-value and hope. Luke, himself a Gentile, took a special delight in recording the courtesy with which Jesus treats Gentile individuals who approached him. Luke gives us the fullest account of Christ's own deep concern for those who are lost. That inspired utterance of Simeon, declaring Jesus to be the Saviour of all peoples, is recorded by Luke. More than any other, this doctor evangelist inspiringly communicates Jesus, the Saviour-Healer, whose therapy has such depth and scope.[18]

Mark tells us most about the sacrifice of Jesus the Servant. Matthew underlines the unique authority of Jesus the King. Luke emphasises the wide embrace of Jesus, the Saviour, and John dwells upon the glory of Jesus, the only begotten Son. Jesus reveals this glory through the miraculous signs that John describes in his Gospel. Above all, though, it is through the shameful cross that Christ's greatest glory is made known. Indeed the darker the darkness, the brighter the glory shines.[19]

It is remarkable how the principal features of the person and work of Jesus Christ as recorded in the four Gospels are anticipated in the messianic prophecies of Isaiah. Isaiah had foreseen the costly sacrificial service and spoken of its meaning. Mark describes for us vividly and starkly how that service was rendered and how that sacrifice was made. Isaiah had seen the King; so did Matthew. Isaiah spoke of a Mighty Saviour, filled with God's Spirit; Luke recounted his doings among the rejected, the poor and the lost. Isaiah paid eloquent tribute to the majesty of his glory; John saw the glory of God in the face of his Incarnate Son.

Grasping God's purpose now

To trace the story of God's missionary purpose from creation and then through Abraham, Moses and Isaiah to Jesus Christ, prompts us to see its breathtaking scope and generosity. From the beginning he is planning blessing for all families. His purpose encompasses release from every kind of hardship and oppression, forgiveness for all sins and an invitation to all people that they should be reconciled to him. His intention is to bring meaning where there is loss of meaning, friendship where community has broken down, and a quality of holiness and glory where, because of sin, life is devalued and impure. God's missionary purpose is very great, and, like his work of creation, very good.

On the basis of what God has revealed through his Son and what is recorded for us in Scripture, I affirm that missionary obedience is the only sufficient response to life's imperatives. There is no other way of aligning ourselves with God's purpose or adequately confronting the world's problems. Mission is basic to God's relationship with humankind. Anyone who tries to understand God's dealings with a rebellious world should recognise him as a God of mission whose purpose is to reach out ever more widely in salvation. From our review of Old Testament passages and Gospel emphases we can clearly see that God's mission through his Messiah is global in its scope. The Bible in fact goes further and reveals a saving purpose for the whole of creation. This saving mission of God is so big it can never be shunted to the sidelines and dismissed as of secondary concern. Where both local and global mission do not head the churches' agendas, then they have dismally failed in reading God's agenda. To ignore mission is to show oneself unaware of the central movement in the whole of his-

tory. To minimise it is to belittle God; to trivialise mission is
to insult him.

I am talking of God's mission, conceived from eternity,
worked out through human history and to be consummated at
the end of the age. This design can only evoke our deep
respect and reverent praise. Our amazement at what God has
done, is doing, and will do increases though when we
remember that it has been patiently, sacrificially pursued in
the face of defiant opposition from human and demonic powers, and constant disobedience and betrayal from God's own
people. In these circumstances we marvel too at the frailty of
the human agencies God uses in his mission. Even God's Son
takes frail flesh. God's mission, it seems, is a powerful way of
weakness.

Our next objective must be to trace that way of power and
weakness in its outworking from the Day of Pentecost to the
present. But meanwhile suppose there should be another of
those divine encounters with some unlikely individual or
group of people. It might take place on a crowded bus, or during an office lunch-hour, or in a queue in a job centre, or in a
daydream during a lecture, or under arching trees along a
country lane. Wherever it happens there will be the voice of
conviction saying, 'Be ready to go anywhere in the world to
share the good news about my remedy for its pain. In the
spreading circle of my kingdom you are to be among my witnesses. Don't be afraid! You won't be alone!' The unlikely listeners to this voice might include your neighbours or mine, it
might be you and it might be me. God invites us also to
become servants in his master-plan.

3

God's Mission Makes History

Small beginnings: great results

It must have seemed a matter of small importance to his neighbours that a member of the business community in Haran should collect his assets and leave for the less civilised regions of Canaan. The mass exodus from Egypt of Abraham's descendants did evidently cause a greater stir. Even so, this collection of Semites crossing the Sinai desert might not have appeared so very different from other migrants during those troubled years. Though they recorded Isaiah's prophecies, not even his own countrymen seemed to grasp the significance of that prophet's sublime utterances. The Galilean who fulfilled them gathered big crowds during a brief public career, but was despatched without too much political disturbance by his powerful opponents. He gained only a passing mention by contemporary historians, except those who were his followers.

How then did a movement with such small beginnings produce an active membership which now numbers 1,000 million? By what means has a religious stirring in one restricted area of the Middle East by now achieved a unique penetration throughout the world? Mission history tells the story. It is worth tracing from Pentecost to the present day, because in doing so we understand more fully how we have arrived where we are. This cannot be a cold understanding; the heroism and sacrifice of the missionary saints and the cruelty and the folly of the missionary sinners can scarcely leave us unmoved.

Action at Pentecost

The streets of the old city are packed with people, as politically volatile as they are religiously fervent. Detachments of the security forces eye them warily. They will be glad when the festival is over and the pilgrims go home. Suddenly men and women come staggering out through the doorway of one of the houses and begin shouting excitedly. This kind of political demonstration is always liable to erupt. The bearded leader of the group looks every inch an activist, if not a revolutionary.

But then the incident takes on a wholly unpredictable and dramatically new dimension. The faces of those at the centre of the crowd have a special radiance and intensity. Their speech reaches through to the understanding and the hearts of their listeners whatever their native language. It is as if all the barriers of communication are broken down and people long separated by different customs and forms of speech are enabled to focus upon the one all-important message. Even the soldiers sense that something of great moment is taking place; they remain discreetly in the background.

The announcement concerns a man executed seven weeks before, and no more than half a mile away. Peter, the spokesman, declares that he is alive. He and his friends have seen him. Peter names his man: 'This Jesus whom you crucified, God has made both Lord and Christ.' No one escapes responsibility for the unjust death, but no one need miss the free pardon and the new beginning that that death and resurrection have achieved. Those who respond will be filled by the same Spirit of God which is empowering Peter and his companions.[1]

The pattern is set: Spirit leadership, satanic resistance

Three thousand do respond and this first powerful impulse and initiative by the Holy Spirit is under way, setting a pattern for every subsequent phase in missionary advance. God takes the lead through his Spirit. It wasn't that Peter was incapable of taking an initiative; when it came to a decision about fishing Peter would say the word. But on this Day of Pentecost a power beyond Peter's power was at work. With the other apostles, he was literally blown out of the house and catapulted into that inspired announcement to the bewildered crowd.

Everything about that initial 'launch' of Christ's church bears the stamp of the Spirit's influence and power: the wise boldness of the apostles, the many conversions, the unity of heart and mind among the new believers, their willingness to share possessions, their joyful hospitality. Jesus had promised the Spirit's enabling for the first phase of mission in Jerusalem, and the promise was faithfully fulfilled. But even in the fulfilment we see another and very different process coming into view. A movement stamped with God's power and love begins to be marred by man's weakness and sin and quickly suffers a counter-initiative from the Evil One. In part it is a problem of success; administration fails to keep pace with church growth. Some needy people get neglected in the welfare programme and resentments surface. More seriously, an attempt is made to counterfeit the generosity of so many of the new converts. Behind a 'holy' smoke-screen Ananias and Sapphira set a terrible precedent for deception, and receive an exemplary punishment.

In this instance even the setbacks provide opportunities for further Spirit initiative: men wisely appointed to supervise the distribution of relief to needy widows contribute such a vital new dimension to the leadership of the church that, 'the number of disciples in Jerusalem is greatly increased, and a large number of priests make their submission to the faith'.[2]

Once again, though, the success of this missionary movement sparks off a reaction. The Jewish leaders are rapidly discovering that this Jesus of Nazareth sect is likely to gain a massive following. There is no time to lose; drastic counter-measures must be taken. The first thing to do is to destroy the new generation of leaders.

Stephen, the foremost among these leaders, is dragged before the Jewish council. There in front of that hostile audience he makes a speech, the like of which the Sanhedrin has never heard before. He recounts to these powerful men the history of their nation and then tells them that in their judicial murder of Jesus they have acted like many of their forebears. They have defied the Holy Spirit of God. Truth or treason? This devastating accusation raises the assembly to fever pitch. Lynch law takes over from Torah: they sweep Stephen out of the council chamber, through the streets of Jerusalem and out of the city. The mob hurls stones at their defenceless victim until his pulverised body is left lifeless. Scarcely have Stephen's friends time to bury him before the most systematic and ruthless persecution yet experienced by the infant church is unleashed.[3]

Masterminding this mopping up operation is a young man who no doubt heard Stephen's speech besides witnessing his death. He is going to put an end to this most dangerous heresy even if it means search and arrest house by house, street by street, city by city. In the event, Saul the persecutor doesn't reach beyond Damascus. The Holy Spirit has never lost the initiative and already this latest and fiercest resistance he is turning into a missionary advantage. Persecuted refugees prove to be powerful preachers. The gospel message brings joy in Samaria, Judea and even Antioch, and many converts. The most important convert of all, however, is stopped in his tracks a few miles short of Damascus. Saul could no longer resist the Spirit of Jesus, echoing in Stephen's remembered words, shining through Stephen's stone-bruised face, and then descending like a lightning shaft upon the Damascus highway.[4]

Wide opportunities: high obstacles

The Spirit's way of missionary advance is to turn fierce opposition into far-reaching advantage, and high obstacles into wide opportunity. What a formidable obstacle for mission in those early days after Pentecost was the barrier between Jew and Gentile! Why, the Jews wouldn't even sit at table with Gentiles! Neither would Peter, still a Jew, though leader of the apostle band. Could it be that even this pioneer of mission was resisting the missionary spirit in this respect? Looking back on a chain of events that produced in him a radically new attitude, Peter ruefully said, 'Who was I to withstand God?'

Cornelius, a senior non-commissioned officer in the Roman occupation army based at Joppa, deeply influenced by the Jewish faith, received a visitation. A messenger from God appeared to him and instructed him to summon Peter who would have a message for him and his friends. Simultaneously, through a dream, Peter was convinced that Christ's sacrifice cleansed all people and so he was prepared both to receive Cornelius' representatives and then accompany them back to the official's house. There awaiting him was the most responsive congregation a preacher could wish for: 'We are all here in the sight of God,' said Cornelius, 'to hear all that you have been commanded by the Lord.' So Peter preached, the Spirit fell and the Gentile listeners were baptised.[5]

With this precedent enacted before the astonished gaze of Peter's Jewish companions, it was a natural sequel that those preaching Jesus in Antioch should address themselves directly to Gentiles. In fact Antioch was to gain a new and special importance in the Spirit's emerging mission strategy. Here followers of the way of Jesus, Jews and Gentiles alike, were blended together and became the first to be called Christians. In this most Gentile of the churches there was no question of Jewish members being excluded from the leadership. Both Barnabas, the encourager, and Saul, now Paul the convert, were held in high esteem. They were the chosen messengers to bring relief to believers in famine-affected Jerusalem. And they were numbered among those sent out in the next major initiative prompted by the Spirit.

Antioch Church Missionary Society

Deliberate and organised overseas mission began in a church

prayer meeting in Antioch in AD 46, thirteen years after
Pentecost. Then the Holy Spirit spoke distinctly to all present:
'Set apart for me Barnabas and Paul for the work to which I
have called them.'[6] What a work that was to prove to be! First
for both of them, and then particularly for Paul, there would
be preaching tours, controversy in synagogues, formation of
infant churches, city riots, cross-country journeys, a major
relief programme, trials before Jewish and Roman courts,
imprisonments, and punishments, letters of practical instruction and soaring vision. The missionary progress was never
predictable but always inspired: first Cyprus, then Asia
Minor, then Greece, then Italy and Rome. In each country
and province Paul heads for the main centres of population.
His converts and delegates like Epaphras are then left to
evangelise the surrounding smaller towns and villages.

Although at times reduced to the very limits of his physical
and emotional reserves, throughout three marathon missionary journeys, and then during his transportation as a prisoner
to Rome, Paul remained at the disposal of God's Spirit.
Wherever the Spirit constrained him he would go; wherever
the Spirit restrained him, he would hold back. Forbidden to
go north, he leapt at the Spirit's prompting to enter
Macedonia and to initiate a decisive westward thrust in the
advance of the gospel. Rome, the capital of the empire, was
the obvious goal, but writing from Corinth to Christians who
had preceded him in Rome, he tells them that his ultimate
objective is to reach Spain, the westward limit of the known
world.

Relentless opposition countered by inspired writings

The Spirit-inspired achievement of that westward surge in
Christian mission fills us with admiration; an impressive
sweep of influence is gained in a short span of years. All the
more remarkable was this progress when we remember the
intensity of the opposition. Paul, the erstwhile persecutor,
was himself relentlessly pursued by fellow Jews who were as
convinced as he had been that the way of Jesus, the Nazarene,

presented a dire threat to true religion. And so Paul was hounded from city to city and finally, having been forced into Roman protection, was brought as a prisoner to the capital of the empire.

Once again the 'Acts' pattern repeats itself; the movement of God's Spirit provokes human opposition, behind which is the hostility of Satan himself. The result is that Paul, a key figure in this westward advance, finds himself on trial for his life in Rome. In this same decade of AD 60–70 Peter was also in Rome and facing arrest and execution. Among the few who closely supported these apostolic leaders were John Mark and Luke, the doctor. The one had listened time and again to Peter's preaching and teaching and the other had already undertaken painstaking research on the life of Jesus. We can readily believe that the threatened removal of Peter and Paul, principal witnesses and teachers in the Christian cause, powerfully stimulated the business of Gospel writing, to which both Mark and Luke were committed.

So what could have been a decisive reversal in missionary progress actually secures a vital step forward: not so much in terms of converts, though Paul's irrepressible witness wins over some of his jailers, but more through an inspired documentation of the good news of Jesus. The Gentile churches are thus equipped with foundation documents, Gospels, the missionary significance of which can scarcely be exaggerated.

To his Gospel Luke adds a companion volume recording for us the post-Pentecost initiatives of the Holy Spirit, which in outline we have been describing. Without Luke's inspired 'Acts of the Apostles' we should not only have been ignorant of key figures and events in the early days of the church, but also it would have been harder for us to discern the key to the whole of mission history: the gracious, powerful, far-reaching moves of the Spirit of God; the obedient and much less than obedient responses of the people of God; and the obliquely or very directly hostile reactions of a world influenced by the Evil One.

In his Book of Acts Luke sees the city of Rome as a major goal in the missionary progress. He does, however, describe the first preaching of the gospel in Ephesus, a lesser but none the less very important centre of communication. There the witness of first Apollos, then Priscilla and Aquila, and then Paul was such that 'the name of the Lord Jesus was held in high honour' by both Jews and Greeks.[7] Even the familiar backlash in the form of a full-scale riot could not weaken the impact of the well reasoned preaching and the impressive demonstrations of the Spirit's power.

What we do not learn from Luke, though, is that Ephesus later became the home of the apostle John. It was in Ephesus that he composed his Gospel. And it was as an exile from Ephesus that John himself, or his namesake nurtured in his apostolic school, wrote the Book of Revelation. So it was that Ephesus, like Rome, gained a vital importance as a source of missionary literature as well as spoken testimony. Under God's guidance the Gospels, the Epistles or letters of the churches, and the Book of Revelation became the permanent undergirding for the Christian mission in the Gentile world.

Eastward advance

Western Christians are inclined to think most about the westward expansion of Christianity. More is actually known about it. Despite scantier documentation, however, we should not be ignorant of a remarkable movement to the East. The biggest leap of all took the gospel to India. The ancient Mar Thoma Church of India takes its name from the apostle Thomas, recognises him as founder, and declares that he was martyred near Madras. Another tradition tells how Thomas was taken by an Indian merchant as a slave to India. There he was instrumental in the conversion of a first-century Indian king. Whether or not this story is factual, the king undoubtedly was; coins bear his inscription in Greek. A Roman commercial settlement discovered near Pondicherry also provides archaeological evidence of contact between India and the Graeco-Roman world, and we can be confident that, together with all the other things that passed between these world regions, the gospel also spread along the trade routes far to the East.

The earliest Indian Christianity had Syrian connections. Syrian Antioch, which had been the springboard for mission to the West, also served as an important base for extension East. From Syria the gospel spread into Mesopotamia. One wonders whether those living in these regions, as they received the gospel, were conscious of Abraham, who in that place had first been made aware of the all-embracing redemptive purpose of God.

Beyond Mesopotamia lay Persia, modern Iran. Jewish pilgrims from Media and Parthia, parts of the old Persian empire, had heard Peter preach in Jerusalem on the Day of Pentecost. Some from their number could well have been included in the first 3,000 converts. If so, they would have brought the gospel home with them. At all events there was an organised church in Persia by the turn of the first century. The names of the apostles Thomas and Simon the Zealot have been associated with its early origins.

It seems that Jewish Christians played a prominent part in the eastward spread of the faith. The Gospel of Matthew, with its emphasis upon the Messiah King, was put together with these Jewish Christian communities especially in mind. This Gospel must have provided an important spiritual and theological foundation for the early Eastern churches, as for others. Their leaders did not, however, produce on such a scale the defences and explanations of faith in Jesus which were so much a feature of the growing churches in the West. In comparison with them the churches of India, Mesopotamia and Persia remained smaller and less influential minorities. There was nothing small, however, about the sacrifice of Eastern Christians. There is evidence that more were martyred in the Persian empire in the fourth century than throughout the Roman empire during the previous three.[8]

Penetration North and South

Jesus had promised that people would come from North and South as well as East and West to feast in the kingdom of God. There are early examples known to us: one involved the creation of the Christian kingdom of Armenia on the north-east frontier. The pagan authorities had tried to compel Gregory, the pioneer missionary, to lay garlands on the altar of the goddess Anahit. He refused, was imprisoned and tortured. Eventually the king himself had a change of heart and worked side by side with Gregory to make his kingdom Christian.[9]

A remarkable extension southwards is connected with the story of two Christian sailors. They were shipwrecked on the Red Sea coast and then carried captive to the court of the King of Axum in modern Ethiopia. They won the favour of the king, were awarded high office and made a number of converts. About AD 340 Frumentius, one of the two, was consecrated bishop by the patriarch of Alexandria, that he might the better serve the newly born Ethiopian Church.[10]

Even in the early years Christianity was spreading far beyond the limits of the Roman empire. The densest concentrations, however, occurred in seven or eight regions governed by Rome. Among these were two parts of North Africa centred on Alexandria and Carthage respectively, Asia Minor, Southern France, Southern Spain, and Italy centred on Rome itself. Judea and Syria we have already mentioned. By the time of the Edict of Milan (AD 313), when Christianity was finally accepted as an official religion within the empire, it is estimated that Christians represented about 10 per cent of the populace.[11]

Here then was the centre of gravity of the Christian movement. This was the great result of that explosion of the Spirit's power at Pentecost, the impetus of which, through many reversals and failures, had carried the church to that point of central influence in the Greek and Roman world.

The first missionary period: penetration, suffering and vindication (AD 33–500)

How can we sum up this first major period in Christian mission? Clearly there were a number of advantages and strategic resources for the young churches: Roman roads, Roman security, a common Greek language and culture, and a prepared people, disillusioned with the traditional religion of the classical gods, and some at least attracted by the one God of Judaism. The missionary church of the first three centuries used the methods and adopted the media that it felt to be consistent with its calling. Its members walked the roads, appealed for legitimate protection, won converts from God fearers, and translated its message into the culture and thought forms of Greek-speaking society.

Where there was a following wind the early missionaries spread their sails to it. All too often though the wind was fierce and contrary. Michael Green, in his book *Evangelism in the Early Church*, describes the task then as 'a very daunting prospect...involving social odium, political danger, the charge of treachery to the gods and the state, the insinuation of horrible crimes and calculated opposition from a combination of sources more powerful perhaps than at any time since.'[12]

In the face of all this, another and necessary missionary 'method' was martyrdom. Men and women both young and old met their deaths with a quality of courage which commanded sympathy and admiration. But there is more to martyrdom than dying; the pure and selfless lives of the early Christians were also a *marturia* or witness of a powerful kind. The persecuting Emperor Julian had to admit that the Christians advanced their cause 'through the loving service rendered to strangers... the godless Galilaeans care not only for their own poor but for ours as well.'[13]

We can call this the classical missionary period, since it has so many instructive features. To effective use of facilities and resources we can add a profound theological undergirding and interpretation of the gospel. Besides the great missionary

strategists such as Luke and Paul there was a host of anonymous missionaries, men and women, scattered by the chances
of life, refugees, traders, soldiers, gossiping the gospel wherever they went. In the more settled life there was the unity,
discipline and pastoral care of local churches also with their
undoubted missionary potential. And in all situations where
Christians gathered (mostly in private houses) there was the
worshipping presence, 'the city set on a hill', the lamp on the
lampstand giving light to the house, the infectious holiness.

No one typifies better than Justin Martyr this witness in the
midst of a sometimes hostile society. His interrogation in a
pagan court is recorded in this way:

> Judge: 'Where do you have your meetings?'
> Justin: 'Wherever we can. Our God fills heaven and
> earth.'
> Judge: 'Tell me where!'
> Justin: 'I live upstairs in the house of Martin... If anyone
> wishes to come in to me there, I pass on to him
> the true doctrine.'[14]

Justin Martyr and many others like him paid for their bold
witness with their lives. Of course the early church was not
wholly holy and courageous! Even so during those early centuries when the church was penetrating society rather than
dominating society there is a particular continuity and consistency with the great Spirit impulse of Pentecost.

During the course of the fourth century this first period of
mission, marked by suffering and vindication, was giving way
to a second. The stability and strength of the Roman empire
was deteriorating and the church itself was beginning to
inherit more temporal responsibilities. Numbers of baptised
members were rising sharply and instead of persecution there
was privilege. For reasons soon to be explained this second
missionary period can be called the period of conquest and
defeat. However, a number of movements on the fringes or
beyond the frontiers of the empire had different qualities; two
are particularly significant.

Goths and Celts

The warlike Goths living to the north of the Danube can scarcely have appeared promising subjects for evangelisation. The child of a mixed marriage—Gothic mother and Cappadocian father—was, however, used by God to establish a church among the Goths. Ulfilas, this remarkable missionary, not only nurtured converts but also reduced the Gothic language to writing and translated nearly the whole Bible into it.

He sustained these prodigious missionary labours for forty arduous and dangerous years (AD 343–83). Their outcome helped the survival of the Western Church, and its subsequent northern advance.[15]

Christians in Egypt began a movement which was to develop into monasticism. Their desire for holiness, coupled with revulsion against pagan excesses, drove them into the desert to struggles against demonic powers. The monastic enthusiasm spread, and churches established in the Roman province of Britannia and neighbouring provinces in those north-westerly islands adopted the tradition. This Celtic Church produced leaders who were not only monks but also saints, not only saints but also missionaries.

Picture the young Patrick, carried away to be a slave in Ireland, up for prayer before daybreak in snow or frost or rain. God answered these prayers in his dramatic escape and then called him back to Ireland to restrain the Druids and to convert its people (AD 431). Whether in his challenge to the King of Tara by lighting the fire on the hill of Slane or through his prayer vigil on the mountain called Croagh Patrick, defying 'every demon, snare and savage force', Patrick won the spiritual battle and laid claim upon an Ireland that should 'keep the faith till the last coming'.[16]

Turn your imagination to Columba at prayer on windswept Iona interceding for his missionary monks in danger at sea in their fragile coracles. In the records there is a glimpse too of him and his monks chanting psalms outside the gate of the pagan Pictish king. It is worth reflecting that Columba began his missionary career as a self-imposed penance for having caused a battle (about AD 563). He went on to found a chain of mission station monasteries. Columba, the leader, is described as showing 'sanctity in the midst of his cares' and being 'open and friendly to everyone'. His secret was that he 'bore the joy of the Holy Spirit in the inmost places of his heart'.[17]

In the sixth and seventh centuries Aidan, Cuthbert, Columban, Gall and Brendan were to follow in this noble tradition of missionary saints, whose beautiful lives matched their compelling message. Aidan and Cuthbert trudged deep into the hills of Northern England carrying the gospel to the poorest homesteads. Columban and Gall won new tribes for Christ in France and Switzerland, and, if the tradition is to be believed, Brendan reached the shores of America in his coracle and was first to preach the gospel there.

The missionary achievement of the Celtic Church was impressive indeed. Here was a spontaneous movement of reverse mission; messengers from the churches on the fringes of the Christian world were travelling back into unevangelised areas nearer the centres. Their method was to establish monasteries as bases for their missionary preaching. Their transport was the fragile coracle made from wooden frame and leather hides. Their apprenticeship was the monastic school. Their skill was the meticulous copying and illuminating of the Gospel manuscripts, and at the heart of their endeavour was a rigorous discipline of prayer and boundless zeal.

New challenge: new leadership

To imagine that this missionary progress was achieved against a background of political calm would be mistaken indeed. To the inter-tribal fighting and warlike migrations which had constantly occurred outside the Roman empire were added the invasion and break-up of the former colonies, leaving even the old centres of power, Rome and Constantinople, vulnerable and exposed. Jerome records the terror of those days,

'Dreadful news from the west: Rome has been sacked! My tongue sticks to the roof of my mouth... If I had a watch tower high enough, I would show you a world in ruins.'[18]

Augustine of Hippo also lived through these catastrophic days, and in his treatise, *City of God*, he described how God's eternal purpose transcends all human reversals and disaster. Was it, though, in the prevailing confusion to be the mission of the Christian church to fill the power vacuum, to be the principal agent of civilisation, and bring cohesion to a world order that was flying apart?

One man at least, the son of a Roman senator, believed that the duty of the church included all these things, and more besides. Gregory inherited a vast property, and sold it to raise money for the poor. He entered a monastery and devoted himself to a life of prayer, but was soon promoted to high office in the church. In the year 590 he was made bishop or pope of Rome. At that time Italy was being devastated by flood, famine and invasion. Gregory, himself, made a peace treaty with the invading Lombards, and in doing so, took the church with him that further step into the sphere of politics and temporal power. Not that he relished such struggle or cherished such ambition. He looked back on the 'unclouded beauty of his former peace' in the monastery, and explained that it was his pastoral responsibilities which compelled him to have dealings with worldly men. In fact, as pope he maintained his monastic discipline, which for him was an 'anchor cable that held him fast to the peaceful shore of prayer'.[19]

Mission to Britain

Gregory's prayer life, his experience of the monastery, and state affairs led him into at least one major missionary enterprise, which was to provide the pattern for a whole new missionary age. A group of bright-faced, fair-haired boys offered for sale as slaves in the market-place caught his eye. On enquiring what race they belonged to, he was told Angles. 'They have angel faces,' he replied, 'and they should become joint heirs with the angels in heaven.' And so, if the historian

Bede's version of the famous story is to be believed, this is how Gregory's mission to Britain began.

What is not in doubt is that in AD 596 he sent off Augustine (not to be confused with Augustine of Hippo) and forty monks to the territory of the Angles in order to convert their king and people. The courage of the brothers seems to have failed halfway across Gaul, and Augustine returned to the determined Gregory to ask to be relieved of this task. The letter with which Gregory sent Augustine back to the waverers is a model of missionary encouragement:

> Gregory, servant of the servants of God, to the servants of our Lord. My very dear sons, it is better never to undertake any high enterprise than to abandon it when once begun. Do not be deterred by the troubles of the journey or by what men say. Be constant and zealous... May Almighty God protect you with his grace, and grant me to see the results of your labours in our heavenly home. And although my office prevents me from working at your side, yet because I long to do so, I hope to share in your joyful reward. God keep you safe, my dearest sons.[20]

Here the spirit of the apostle Paul was surely at work again. Gregory was not speaking idly; before being made pope he had, himself, sought permission to lead a mission to Britain, only to be refused. He lacked neither the tenderness nor the tenacity of the apostle. No doubt many things contributed to the success of Augustine's mission, not least the Christian faith of Bertha, wife of Ethelbert, king of the South Angles. Note here the vital part played by a Christian woman, matching the effective witness of her grandmother, Clotilda, and of her daughter Ethelberga, also crucial in the conversion of their royal husbands. In the kingdom of the Angles the simplicity and holiness of the lives of the missionary monks must have contributed significantly, and the gospel securities would have contrasted vividly with the cruel uncertainties of the times. Equally important, though, must have been the planning and the prayers of Gregory. Hardly had Ethelbert been converted before Gregory was wanting to appoint bishops and create a framework for the evangelisation and pastoral care of the whole people.

The enthusiastic Bede leaves us in no doubt about Gregory's contribution: 'It was through his zeal that our English nation was brought from the bondage of Satan to the Faith of Christ... He transformed our still idolatrous nation into a church of Christ.' Bearing in mind the remarkable pioneering labours of the Celtic missionaries, it may be an exaggeration to describe Gregory, as Bede does, as apostle to the English. Yet in a new way, with Gregory and Augustine's mission, a nation was coming to political and even spiritual birth.

The second missionary period: conquest and defeat (AD 500–1500)

My conviction is that a new and distinctive period of mission begins with Gregory the Great. I do not doubt that the Holy Spirit also initiated this new thrust which, from centres in Rome and Constantinople, carried the gospel throughout Europe and to its northern and eastern edges. Who but the Holy Spirit inspired the devotion and courage of the missionary monks? And surely God's spirit of wisdom directed Gregory's political prudence and missionary strategy as well.

Gregory tried to hold together both political and spiritual power. Impossible! we are quick to say. But many did make credible and even beautiful attempts at such a marriage. Think of Oswald, king of Northumbria, acting as interpreter for Aidan on his missionary journeys. Think of King Alfred, great not only in Christian administration but also in Christian scholarship. Then, too, there was King Stephen who established Christianity in Hungary, preaching to his own subjects.

What does seem to be certain is that, in an age full of violence and chaos, the degree of stability provided by Christian popes, patriarchs and kings was important, if not essential, for the spread of Christianity throughout Europe. The missionary heroes themselves were not, of course, armed to the teeth;

Boniface had only a book with which to defend himself when in old age, on a mission to Frisia, he was cut down by marauders.

All Europe acknowledges Christ

This martyrdom in AD 754 crowned a missionary career begun more than thirty years earlier as an assistant of Willibrord, the English pioneer missionary to what is now Holland. Boniface, whose English name was Wynfrith, had received authority from a second Pope Gregory to undertake new missionary work in unevangelised areas of North and South Germany. In such a task how could he demonstrate that the God he preached was the true and mighty God able to liberate men and women from the power of the gods of the pagans. Boniface decided to fell the sacred oak of Thor at Hesse. As his axe cut into the trunk, a powerful gust of wind toppled the great tree. Thor did not strike back. Boniface emerged from this trial by ordeal unharmed, and gained a reputation which remained throughout his ministry, also extending widely into Frankish territory.[21]

For Boniface support from Rome was vital for conserving new missionary gains. Constantinople served this purpose for Cyril and Methodius (AD 826–69 and 815–85), two missionaries who were the first to preach the gospel to the Slavic peoples and who reduced their language to writing, creating an alphabet which is used to this day.

Rome and Constantinople thus served as church centres enabling to varying degrees the Christianisation of the whole of Europe. The last European country in which churches were permanently established was Lithuania. Her king was baptised in 1386, nearly 800 years after Gregory the Great has been prompted to direct a concerted missionary effort northwards.

Although in these eight centuries it would be impossible to separate missionary advance from military conquest, the sword did not totally compromise the cross. The learned and godly Alcuin (AD 735–804) was a moderating influence upon the warrior king Charlemagne. 'Let peace be made with the Saxons,' he advised him. 'Let threats be relaxed, so that men's hearts be not hardened.'[22] There is even a case of the 'democratic' choice of Christianity; Iceland, with its ancient parliament, accepted the gospel on the advice of its wise men.[23] The Saxon tribes, and the Viking peoples of Scandinavia, however, resisted the Christian advance stoutly and even violently. The monks who followed the 'Christian' armies were for the most part peace-lovers, men of the soil, and unarmed. Theirs was a spiritual victory, often bought dearly following a pagan backlash.

In the first evangelisation of all Europe the gospel won its way not so much through better armies but through better promises. Imagine yourself in a king's hall on a winter's day in the northern lands. The chief men are debating the new teaching about a certain Jesus Christ. While they talk, a sparrow flies in, remains a moment visible in the warm firelight, then disappears back into the wintery world outside. 'That,' says one of the king's advisers, 'is what our lives are like. Man appears on earth for a little while; but of what went before this life or of what follows, we know nothing. Therefore if this new teaching has brought any more certain knowledge, it seems only right that we should follow it.'

This anecdote, preserved in Bede's history, gives a clue as to why Europe promptly and willingly, or grudgingly and eventually, followed Christ.[24] His was a 'more certain knowledge'. However, throughout these centuries from AD 622 onwards there was another religious movement marked by its own confidence and certainties. Islam burst upon the Near Eastern and Mediterranean world like a hot wind from the desert.

The rise of Islam

The story of the prophet Muhammed and the religious and social and military movement he inspired is noble, spectacular, and tragic. This son of a Meccan nobleman was sufficiently influenced by the Christian and Jewish communities living in Arabia to be convinced that there is one God. His mystic experiences, however, led Muhammed to preach what he believed to be a purified monotheism, and seek to unite the Arabian clans into a single community, worshipping Allah. The hostility of his own townspeople to his great purpose provoked him to use arms to defeat those who persisted in 'idolatry'.

In spite of Muhammed's premature death, Islam, the movement he founded, swept through Arabia, Persia, the Eastern Mediterranean lands, North Africa and further into Europe and Asia. Islam spelt submission to the one true God, interpreted through his last and greatest prophet. Its appeal to those who had suffered at the hands of Greek-speaking colonisers was very powerful. Here was a unifying creed which did not appear to be a foreign imposition. The moment was ripe religiously and politically; weak and unpopular empires were vulnerable to attack. Within two years of the prophet's death Damascus had fallen to the Muslim armies, Alexandria was to follow ten years later and within a hundred years the Islamic empire already stretched from the Bay of Biscay to the River Indus. Constantinople and even Rome had been threatened by the Muslim advance.

Christians may be inclined to exaggerate the ruthlessness of these invasions, and the regimes which they established. In fact, once victory was achieved, all subject people were allowed to live in peace, provided they paid their taxes. Christians had to pay tax at a higher rate, were prohibited from trying to make converts, but were not normally otherwise threatened or restricted. Muslim devotion and worship was exemplary, Muslim administration was no worse and perhaps better than many nominally Christian examples, Muslim science, medicine and architecture reached high pinnacles of achievement, and the new Islamic masters were remarkably successful in subduing and even converting those of other faiths.[25]

So how is the rise of Islam to be viewed through Christian eyes? How does it relate to God's missionary purpose in his

Son Jesus Christ? Any estimate of Islam must ungrudgingly recognise the deep devotion of so many who follow this way, and its success in gaining new followers; Islam is the faith of the majority in more than fifty countries of the world today. What then is this massive development in monotheistic religion?

Perhaps the rise of Islam was a strange echo of God's revelation. (One might make a similar connection between what God was doing through the great Old Testament prophets of the seventh and sixth centuries BC and the development of Hinduism and the rise of Buddhism.) Tragically the saving gospel of Jesus was not widely communicated to the Arabian peoples by the Christian communities living in their midst. There was no missionary among them to translate the Bible into their language, as Ulfilas had for the Goths and Cyril and Methodius would for the Slavs. Instead Arabic became the powerful medium for Muhammed's message echoing some parts of the biblical teaching but not its core.

From its effects, there is no doubt that this 'echo' came through very loudly. But echoes produce serious distortions, and in any case we cannot live upon echoes. In his missionary purpose the God and Father of our Lord Jesus Christ had not just sent an echo; he had already sent in person his beloved Son. So here is the tragedy of Islam: although it mirrors some of the biblical teaching and even pays respect to the figure of Jesus Christ, it misses the saving truth that God became man who died for all humankind. The result is that what claims to be the channel of the knowledge of God, and is followed as such by millions, becomes a barrier to the vital knowledge of God, revealed through the Word made flesh.

A barrier made doubly high

Of course the story of Christian mission shows that the Holy Spirit is well able to break through barriers. That is not in doubt. Even barriers erected through the folly and failure of the Christian church can be swept away through the merciful power of the Spirit. That Islam became established at all was a reflection of Christian failure. At that time Christianity was largely restricted to a Greek and Latin mould and Christians who were not at home in this culture were made to feel inferior, and were consequently inward looking and less able to evangelise their neighbours. All this though could have been remedied through a repentant, renewed and Spirit-dependent church. Instead the church of Rome compounded the errors of the church of Constantinople and made the Islamic barrier against the gospel doubly high by launching military crusades against the Muslim empires.

No doubt the Crusades were conceived as Christian mission, and that it was with the intention of honouring Christ that many were involved in the attempt to reconquer the Holy Land and adjacent territories from their Muslim rulers. However, the use of arms, which had partially compromised the northward spread of Christianity through Europe, rendered completely abortive this eastward 'mission' into Muslim lands. So a whole missionary period, which began with Pope Gregory exercising spiritual and political power Christianly and responsibly together, ends with his papal successors moved by a very different spirit and locked into a violent and ultimately disastrous conflict with the Muslim armies.

A return to simplicity and powerlessness

Most saw nothing wrong with fighting the 'infidel', but at least one man held a radically different view: Francis of Assisi. Francis, remembered as a saint, should also be remembered as a missionary. Picture him at the court of the Sultan of Egypt in 1219 during the fifth crusade: a defenceless man in poor clothing, winning his audience with the Muslim lord not through force of arms, nor even diplomatic skill, but through his reputation for holiness. Convinced that the Muslim will be won only through the beauty and simplicity of the gospel, he preaches Christ.[26]

Francis of Assisi, and to a lesser extent Dominic of Calaruega, both of whom founded orders of wandering monks or friars, restored vital qualities to the Christian

missionary movement: poverty, simplicity and mobility.
Francis, himself, attempted missionary work in Morocco and
in the early years five of his friars died there. Ramon Lull,
who was to follow them a generation later, believed that in
missionary work it was more important to learn languages
than to learn war. He founded a school of Arabic studies in his
native Majorca. Though he valued study highly, he had this to
say: 'Missionaries will convert the world by preaching, but
also through the shedding of tears and blood and with great
labour, and through a bitter death.'[27] Lull's own death was at
the hands of a hostile crowd on the shores of North Africa.
With similar courage Dominican missionaries undertook
pioneering work in the Ukraine. Franciscans were also sent to
support an important Christian diplomatic mission to the
Mongol court of the Great Khan.

More defeat than victory?

In this encounter the stakes were high indeed. If the Mongo-
lian empire should become Christian, then the Muslims would
be threatened on both flanks and their power could be broken
once and for all. Were there not Christian princesses at the
Mongols' court? A uniquely important missionary opportunity had presented itself in 1229 with the invitation of Kublai
Khan to the Pope: 'Send me a hundred men skilled in your
religion... And so I shall be baptised, and then all my barons
and great men, and then their subjects.'[28] In the event the
Pope sent just two Dominicans who never reached the Khan's
court in Peking but turned back in Persia. The later Franciscan delegations missed that moment of receptivity and the
greatest gains among the Mongols were made by Islam not
Christianity.

In drawing conclusions about this period of mission history
from AD 500 to 1500 at least this can be said: through the Dark
Ages and subsequent periods of conflict and chaos, the church
survived and extended northwards, preserved holiness, learning and a missionary vision. Its mistake was not in entering the
political arena nor in accepting responsibility in nation build-

ing, nor trying to shape a world order, nor indeed in building up, as Thomas Aquinas did, an impressively comprehensive Christian interpretation of life. The medieval attempt to place the whole of life under the lordship of Christ should call forth our deep respect. Where this intention failed was in its compromise with violence and in its attempt to impose its own domination, seeking greatness without humility. It was this that placed limitations on the church's missionary effectiveness and spoiled it as a vehicle of God's grace. Those who pioneered a new and better way, like Francis' poor preachers, or John Wycliffe's Lollards with their radical protest, were often closer to God's purpose than those who claimed to be his chief representatives. Notable in the omissions of this period were timely approaches to both Arabians and Mongols and an effective communication of the gospel during formative moments in their history. All in all, a missionary period which had promised success and victory ended with lost opportunity and a measure of failure and defeat.

The third missionary period: division and expansion (1500–1900)

As a legacy of the previous period, Christian Europe remained encircled by the Muslim powers to the south and east and all attempts to reach out beyond this constriction largely failed. The first sign of a breakthrough had come from the voyages along the west coast of Africa promoted by Prince Henry the Navigator. We can think of this deeply Christian, even monastic figure peering out to sea from the promontory of Sagres in Southern Portugal, looking for the ships he had sent out for discovery, for 'winning souls for Christ', to test the strength of the Moorish enemy, and to open routes for trade.

In 1492 Isabella of Castille won a military victory over the Moors at Granada, thus destroying the last Muslim power base in Europe. That same year Columbus crossed the Atlantic and reached the shores of the Caribbean Islands. Within six years Vasco da Gama had rounded the Cape of Good Hope and opened up the sea route to India. Within two further decades Martin Luther had nailed his Ninety-Five Theses to the door of the Castle Church in Wittenberg and effectively signalled the beginning of the Protestant Reformation.

Why link exploration and colonial expansion with the reformation and division of the church? The reason is that these two features of expansion and division were the principal characteristics of a third period of missionary history lasting from the sixteenth to the beginning of the twentieth century. It would be a natural thing to assume that a major division in the church would seriously weaken its ability to reach out to the surrounding world, but other factors were at work. Indeed, as a matter of fact, places where two different Christian traditions have been in conflict have also proved to be centres of missionary outreach.

Certainly the British Church with its different Celtic and Roman influences maintained a very significant missionary contribution from the times of Patrick (fourth century) to Boniface or Wynfrith (eighth century) and beyond. There is also a very remarkable vitality in the churches of Moravia and Bohemia founded through an initiative from Constantinople but then governed and developed from Rome. Furthermore the Englishman, John Wycliffe, and the Bohemian, John Huss, were linked together in the first stirrings of the Reformation. Even so this new spiritual life was not yet to bear full fruit in the cause of world mission. It was from among those loyal to Rome that the next generation of missionary leaders came.

Jesuits lead the advance

'Teach us, good Lord, to serve thee as thou deservest, to give and not to count the cost...' This prayer of Ignatius Loyola, accepted as a universal prayer of the Christian church, breathed the spirit of the missionary order of the Jesuits, which Ignatius founded. Through a deep spirituality and a rigorous discipline, the members of this order sought to make themselves totally available for the work of converting those who did not yet believe in Christ, or those whose belief they regarded as in some way defective or mistaken. The fact that some Jesuits were deeply implicated in the cruelties of the Inquisition should not blind us to the missionary heroism and achievement of their colleagues.

First among the Jesuit missionaries, and a founder member of the order, was Francis Xavier. He came to India affected by the early impact of the Portuguese traders. An entire caste of fisher folk on the South Indian coast had sought their protection, and accepted baptism without receiving any instruction in the Christian faith. Francis' task was to teach these thousands of Paravas the faith. With language helpers he prepared rough translations of the Lord's Prayer, the Creed and the Ten Commandments. We can then picture him with the Tamil-speaking boys, teaching them how to teach their own people these essentials of the Christian way. Rapport with these lads, methodical perseverance, strict discipline and gentle holiness clearly brought results; Xavier left behind him an authentic and permanently viable Parava Church.

He was now heading for Japan, still in 1549 an untouched mission field. Here Xavier's language informant served him less well. Even so, intuitively he grasped the local realities and the need to respect the noble features of the Japanese culture. Compensating his limited capacity for communication in words, Francis' Christian character was sufficiently attractive for him to win three groups of converts within three years. Xavier, apostle to Japan, next set his sights upon China, but was overtaken by a fatal illness while on an offshore island, in full view of the continent.[29]

The gospel in a Chinese mould

Unlike Japan, China had already had a long history of Christian contact. Most remarkable of all was the existence of a Syrian Christian Church in the heart of China during the seventh, eighth and ninth centuries.[30] A series of papal delegations during the Middle Ages had led to the establishment of an archbishopric in Peking. Nor was the movement in one direction only; Rabban Sauma, Chinese born and a Christian, had made a journey of exploration and church diplomacy which took him to Rome. Even so, when the Jesuits began their work in China there had been no trace of either a Syrian or a Roman Christian presence for 200 years.

The man to reintroduce the gospel to China was the Italian Jesuit, Matthew Ricci. He followed Francis Xavier's principle of respect for the foreign culture, and when he gained an invitation to the Chinese court he acknowledged the benefit he would receive from the emperor's fine institutions and teachings and expressed the hope that he would be 'of some small use' in return. Consistent with these sentiments, Ricci rendered a useful service by mending clocks and making maps. Thus with the emperor's favour secured, he established himself in the capital and began to draw together those interested in the faith of Jesus Christ. His intention was to make Christianity as Chinese as possible. Well he knew the local dislike of things foreign. And in any case cannot the gospel find a place for the Eastern respect for ancestors? And if ancestors are venerable, is not Confucius also to be respected? Ricci's attempts at accommodating the Christian faith to the customs and values of Chinese culture were sharply criticised by his compatriots. However, at his death in 1610, Matthew Ricci left behind him a Chinese Church numbering 2,000, and an approach to Christian mission which is full of instructive value to those who follow in his steps.[31]

In their missions to the East the Jesuits were confronted by the advanced civilisations and developed cultures of India, China and Japan. Parallel to their work was the trading activity of the Portuguese, but the political power balance in the region was such that European attempts at colonisation were limited to coastal enclaves and offshore islands. Precisely because the missionaries operated in China and Japan from a position of political weakness they were compelled to seek new and creative ways to introduce the gospel in these lands.

No such constraints, however, applied in the newly discovered Americas; the expansion of Catholic Europe into the New World was a very different story.

A stand for justice in the New World

'We have come here to serve God and his majesty, to bring light to the heathen and to get rich.' This confident assertion of one of the conquistadores was echoed in the words and actions of that stream of Iberian adventurers who within a few decades subdued the whole continent. The civilisation and culture of the Aztec and Incas were destroyed, never to be rebuilt. The conquered peoples had to submit to baptism, and in their thousands they accepted this rite. Dominican and Franciscan friars accompanied the colonists and by their presence underlined the Christian intention of the enterprise.

Intention, though, is one thing, execution is another. The Spanish colonists devised a method of forced labour whereby the native people were obliged to work to the point of exhaustion in the fields and the mines belonging to their foreign masters. Could this kind of treatment be reconciled with the good purpose of a Christian empire? To their credit, leaders among the Dominican missionaries declared that such exploitation was indeed contrary to the gospel and a scandalous thing to be suppressed and opposed. 'Tell me, by what right or justice do you keep these Indians in such cruel and horrible servitude?' thundered De Montesinos against the colonising caudillos.[32]

The 'Black Legend' of Spanish oppression upon the native peoples of America was too much of a reality to be countered with rhetoric alone. Bartolome de Las Casas (1474–1566), another Dominican priest, sought to curb the excesses of his countrymen through royal restraint and through legislation. He achieved a large measure of success in getting protective laws included in the statute book. What proved much more difficult in the isolated regions of Latin America was the enforcement of humanising regulations. Whether or not Las Casas' work is to be judged an overall success, it is true that he laboured determinedly for nearly fifty years seeking the welfare of the American Indians. Perhaps his most significant contribution to Christian mission was to demonstrate that those who preach the gospel can never afford to ignore the political and social developments that entangle every opportunity of advance.

An enlightened bureaucracy

The Roman Catholic missions of the sixteenth century were tied all too closely with the overseas interests of two nations: Spain and Portugal. Las Casas had shown that to serve Christ one must serve Christ's just concern for those disadvantaged and exploited. Even so, the political and national patronage of missions remained dangerously strong. How could this stranglehold upon disinterested missionary service be broken? In the event liberation came from a most unlikely source: a church bureaucracy in the heart of Rome. The first secretary of this body, the Propaganda as it came to be called, was Francesco Ingoli. Although he was never a travelling missionary, through statesmanlike discernment he saw that colonising nations must not control the new dioceses in Asia and America. Indigenous ministries must be established there, and the initial foreignness of the churches must not be perpetuated. 'What could be more absurd,' chided the Propaganda, 'than to transport France, Spain, Italy or some other European nation to China? Do not introduce all that to them, but only the faith, which does not despise or destroy the manners and customs of any people, always supposing that they are not evil, but rather wishes them preserved.'[33]

A Brahmin among the Brahmins

Many missionaries no doubt needed that timely advice then; many no doubt still need it today. One man who in this respect was in advance of the Propaganda was another Jesuit, Robert de Nobili (1577–1656). His consuming passion was 'to open the door of India to Christ'. But first access had to be gained to Indians of higher caste. To win the Brahmins, he would become a Brahmin. This goal de Nobili set himself resolutely to achieve. He moved into the Brahmin quarter of Madura, adopted the dress of an Indian holy man, undertook a profound study of the Tamil, Sanskrit and Telugu languages and literature, and engaged with interested visitors in religious disputations. In order to sustain contact with his high caste Indian friends de Nobili minimised his contact with European colleagues, all of whom to the Indians were culturally unacceptable.

When some of the first enquirers accepted baptism, de Nobili received sharp criticism from these colleagues for allowing his converts to retain a number of Hindu customs, some connected with caste. After a prolonged controversy between the expatriates, the Pope's ruling was received and this favoured de Nobili's missionary experiment. He never seems to have enjoyed the sympathetic support of fellow missionaries, but even so during the span of a thirty-eight-year ministry he baptised no less than 600 high caste Indians. Scarcely less remarkable was his unique penetration of the Indian languages, literature and religious thought.

The Jesuit contribution

It would be wrong to exaggerate the overall quality and abiding value of the Roman Catholic missions of the sixteenth and seventeenth centuries. Where, as in India, China and Japan, they were conducted without overriding political advantage, numerical gains were modest and serious losses were always liable to occur. Where, as in the Americas, the Christian colonists held all the power, church growth was artificially inflated and often so coercive to be virtually without meaning. In these circumstances the best missionary contribution was the protection of the exploited from the exploiter. Whether in the East or the West these missions of the Counter Reformation lacked the doctrinal emphasis of the free grace of God.

Wrong though it would be to overlook the weaknesses in these enterprises, the opposite mistake of prejudiced dismissal would fail to grasp the Spirit's initiative. With this new thrust of the Roman Catholic orders, and particularly with the contribution of the Jesuits, something of vital importance was being restored to the missionary church: utter single-mindedness, soldierly discipline, rigorous scholarship, and educational method. When in his prayer Ignatius Loyola had referred to fighting and not heeding the wounds, he had his mind upon spiritual not military battles. As a deliberate act, he had hung up his sword in the chapel at Montserrat when he dedicated his life to fight Christ's battles. The costliness of missionary endeavour in those days should never be forgotten; Stephen Neill quotes the Jesuit casualties from shipwreck and disease on the sea voyage to China as 127 men out of 376 during the period 1581 to 1712.[34]

Another monument to the Jesuits' dedication and discipline were the 'reducciones' or Christian villages for Guarani Indians in what is now Paraguay. While other churchmen had grown lax and given up Bartolome de Las Casas' fight for the rights and dignity of the American Indians, the Jesuits in Paraguay built up these impressive centres for the welfare and protection of these people, complete with church, farm, workshop, schools and well ordered community life. If only the Jesuits in South America had perceived the full value and potential of the native culture, as some of their colleagues had in India and China, then Guarani leadership might have been fostered, thus securing the survival of the Christian communities when the Jesuits were withdrawn.

This expulsion of the Jesuits in 1767 was followed six years later by the suppression by Pope Clement XIV of the Jesuit order, which in turn marked the low point in Roman Catholic missions. Vested interest and political intrigue robbed the Roman Church of its most active missionary body. Already, though, there were signs of a missionary stirring in the Orthodox and, more important still, the Protestant Churches.

Mission from Moscow

Ever since the ninth century when Methodius and his brother Cyril worked for the evangelisation of the Slavonic peoples, missionary initiatives from the Orthodox Churches centred upon Constantinople showed one particular strength and advantage: the acceptance of local languages for the Christian Scriptures and Christian worship. When the northern Slavs, who were to form the nucleus of the Russian nation and empire, began to accept Christianity 100 years later there were already vital tools in the language of the Slavs for the further spread of the gospel.

In fact the vitality of the Russian Church played a crucial part in the survival of the Russian nation. Its people suffered a terrible onslaught from the pagan Tartars but when they were repulsed there arose a new opportunity of both political and missionary expansion. Constantinople had been captured by Muslim armies and so Moscow assumed a new role of leadership in Orthodox Christianity. The lands to be evangelised were as vast as the emerging Russian empire; in the West we may never have heard of such missionary pioneers as Cyril Suchanov and Ioasaf Bolotov but they were spreading the knowledge of Christ into the heart of Siberia and beyond the westward limits of the Russian mainland to islands of the Bering Straits and even on to the American continent before Protestant missions gained any real momentum.[35]

Reformed but not missionary?

Why was it that there was such a long delay before the churches of the Reformation began to play a significant part in world mission? Surely that release of the Holy Spirit through the lives and teaching of the Reformers should have also inspired a new advance of the gospel into the non-Christian world beyond Europe. Was there not a recovery of understanding that the gospel brought free pardon as well as costly commitment to those who received it? Were not the Scriptures, with all their potential for motivating and directing Christian service, newly accessible to believers? And should not release from oppressive priestcraft and a corrupt papacy have liberated new forces for world evangelisation?

All these fruits of the Reformation ought to have brought

gospel blessing to the world beyond Europe, but they did not, not at least for two whole centuries. The Protestants laid themselves open to the serious charge that they lacked this mark of the true church: missionary activity! As we have already seen, the missionary passion was first aroused among those who were seeking the renewal of the church from within the body of those loyal to Rome. In those crucial years there was no Protestant Loyola, nor Xavier, nor Ricci. The Orthodox churches achieved their missionary mobilisation sooner than the Protestants.

However, what came late came strong. When the Protestant nations of Europe were no longer struggling for their political survival, when through their own attempts at colonising they were in direct contact with non-Christian peoples of other races, and above all when spiritual revival came back to the churches of the Reformation, then a new movement in mission began.

This revival in continental Europe took the form of an intense religion of the heart bringing warmth to a correct but cold Lutheranism. Those thus revived were called Pietists. The Protestant monarchs and other authorities were looking for chaplains and missionaries to serve in their new colonies, but who would be adequately motivated and inspired for a task involving so much physical danger and so little material reward? The Pietists were ready for this task. Bartholomew Zeigenbalg (1682–1719) went to India with the Royal Danish Mission and in his ministry in Tranquebar worked out an approach which was to be typical of Protestant missions: early translation of the Scriptures into local languages, education and literacy alongside evangelism, leading to personal conversions, and indigenous leadership for the churches brought to birth.

This was a period of able, devoted and heroic individuals: Christian Schwartz following Zeigenbalg to India, John Eliot and then David Brainerd working and praying and dying among the North American Indians. The influence and inspiration of these men was crucially important, but so far Protes-

tant missions lacked the community dimension found in the
Roman Catholic missionary orders. A man used by God to fill
this lack was remarkable in his vision and achievement, and
yet largely forgotten today.

Christ's man of mission

Nikolaus Ludwig von Zinzendorf was born in 1700 of aristoc-
ratic Austrian parents, influenced by the Pietists and living in
North Germany. Already drawn powerfully to Christ, Count
Zinzendorf gave hospitality on his estate in Saxony to a mixed
group of religious refugees, most of whom were a remnant
from the persecuted Moravian Church of the United Breth-
ren. The refugees named their new home Herrnhut, the
Lord's Watch. Taking their inspiration from the prophecy of
Isaiah chapter 62, they set a prayer watch and claimed from
God a fulfilment of the promise of renewal in the church such
that 'nations would see her righteousness' and that she should
indeed be a source of 'praise in all the earth'.[36]

Such an exalted vision had a more urgent and immediate
application; von Zinzendorf's refugees were quarrelling and
his newly formed Protestant community appeared likely to fly
apart. But the cement of prayer and patience held and in the
'Golden Summer' of 1727 they experienced a little Pentecost.
This outpouring of the Holy Spirit on what was no more than
a village community produced a missionary enterprise with
unique qualities and unparalleled outreach.

At the heart of Herrnhut was the discipline of prayer and
worship, and at the heart of this worship was devotion to the
Lamb of God. When the missionary challenge presented itself
to von Zinzendorf and his community members through the
visit of a freed negro slave, they approached mission as a
'Jesus Christ affair in all the earth'. Their great motive for mission was that Christ's kingdom should be 'peopled'. The
count's advice to George Schmidt, working among the Hot-
tentots, was, 'Tell them about the Lamb of God until you can
tell them no more.'[37] Three of von Zinzendorf's missionaries
working in the most harrowing conditions in Greenland

expressed their commitment in these words: 'We came here resting upon Christ our Saviour, in whom all the nations of the earth will be blessed, not on the principle of sight but of faith.'[38]

It was because Count Zinzendorf and his Moravians were devoted to the Crucified One and because theirs was a 'blood and wounds' theology that they gave themselves without reserve to Christ's missionary cause. Their communities were totally mobilised to this end. During the count's lifetime 226 missionaries were sent out to countries as widely separated as South Africa, Greenland, Surinam, the West Indies, Lithuania, Guinea, Ceylon, Ethiopia, Estonia and Lapland. Behind this endeavour there was not only an abandoned willingness for sacrifice (in the first two years of mission in the West Indies twenty-two missionaries died) but also a relentless sanity of method. Von Zinzendorf's selection and training of missionaries was rigorous in the extreme. He conducted a prodigious correspondence with his far-flung workers and not only supported them in his own profound intercessory prayer but also developed remarkable missionary prayer services in all his communities.

Perhaps it was in the providence of God that refugees should pioneer this worldwide missionary outreach. Even von Zinzendorf was at one stage exiled from Saxony. He welcomed this reversal with brave words which he proceeded to put into effect: 'The time has come to gather the Pilgrim Congregation and to preach the Saviour to the whole world. Our home will be that place where at the moment our Saviour has most for us to do.'[39]

To this readiness for complete mobility in the missionary cause, von Zinzendorf added a distinctive ecumenical vision. His was a Christ-centred desire for unity. He explained his experience of unity with Christians of other denominations in this way: 'We enter into our Saviour in such a manner that we can no longer see or hear anything above or beyond him. Then it is that we remain in indissoluble union together.' Von Zinzendorf bore witness to a 'universal kind of religion' shared by those whose hearts had been transformed because 'He bled to death for our sins upon the cross.'[40]

Christ-centred unity though for von Zinzendorf was necessarily a missionary unity. For Christ's sake he sought to win converts throughout the inhabited world and his concern was that the new believers should be at one with all Christ's people everywhere. During an audience with the Pope the count's envoy assured him, 'Moravian missionaries do not teach the heathen the differences that keep the church at home apart, but only the incarnation of God in Christ, the meritorious life, suffering and death of Jesus the Saviour, till the Holy Spirit enters their hearts with his gracious power. That is the work of our unity in all the earth.' Actions speak even louder than words; of the 700 converts gained in the West Indies by another Moravian missionary, Frederick Martin, he baptised only 30 into the Moravian Church. Membership rolls of other churches benefited correspondingly more from Martin's labours.

With these special qualities, von Zinzendorf's Moravians constituted a missionary church. They had learnt from others: the Pietist pioneers and the oldest missionary societies, the Royal Danish Mission, the Society for the Propagation of the Gospel and the Society for Promoting Christian Knowledge, associated with them. Von Zinzendorf and his co-visionaries had also much to give to others. The most famous missionary of the Society for the Propagation of the Gospel, John Wesley, received assurance of salvation through the influence of one of von Zinzendorf's lieutenants, Peter Bohler. What was happening was that the new life in the Pietist revival in Germany was spilling over into the evangelical revival in England. The fact that this revival gained a world missionary dimension was due in large measure to the Moravian example.

Tenacious William Carey

A crucial step in this same direction was taken in the back

parlour of Widow Wallis' house in Kettering. It was 1792 and the Midland Association of the Particular Baptists was holding its autumn meeting. Fourteen preachers crowded into the small room. One spoke to the others with evident enthusiasm, but overall the atmosphere was sombre. These were hard times for members of a small dissenting church; bereft of her American colonies and with revolution threatening to flow across the Channel from France, Britain was politically and economically at a low ebb. So it was scarcely surprising that an ambitious plan presented by one of the younger ministers was being treated with caution. True, in the spring of that year he had compelled them to face the challenge of world mission with a sermon inviting them to 'expect great things from God' and 'attempt great things for God'. Admittedly he had marshalled powerful arguments for active obedience to the Great Commission through his *Enquiry into the obligations of Christians to use means for the conversion of the heathens*. In one final appeal the young minister waved before their faces another small book, an account of Moravian missions. 'If you knew how these men overcame all obstacles for Christ's sake,' he declared, 'you would go forward in faith.' It was enough. The response was unanimous. A new missionary society was founded. Christian mission from Britain was regaining momentum.[41]

William Carey was so poor that he could contribute no part of the £13 2s 6d pledged at the inception of the society he had been instrumental in founding. Nevertheless he made a priceless contribution to the whole modern missionary movement. He shared von Zinzendorf's combination of zeal and method, but in Carey consecrated method was particularly outstanding. He modestly described himself as a plodder. After receiving his missionary call through reading the journals of Captain Cook, to him a revelation of human need, he methodically, relentlessly and creatively used all his energies towards the fullest possible obedience to the Great Commission. Convinced himself of the missionary obligation, he entered upon an educational campaign to win over doubting colleagues, hence the *Enquiry*.

Everything this self-taught man attempted carried the same marks of tenacity and intelligence: missionary service in India in the face of opposition of the East India Company, study of the Bengali, Sanskrit and Marathi languages and the translation of the Bible into each, the formation of an Indian Baptist Church, the founding of Serampore College for training Indian clergy, campaigning against 'sati', the Hindu custom of burning widows on their husbands' funeral pyre. Carey's 'Pleasing Dream' of a world missionary conference never materialised but even its conception shows how he was already seeking ways of measuring the whole task of world mission and devoting the resources of the whole church to its obedient fulfilment.[42]

A 'Church Missionary Society'

The whole Protestant Church was by no means devoted to this cause but in those closing years of the eighteenth century and early years of the nineteenth a growing number of laymen and some clergy were taking individual and joint action. Voluntary societies, like the London Missionary Society, were being formed in England. The British and Foreign Bible Society, with all its potential for undergirding mission, was about to be established. The Society for Promoting Christian Knowledge and the Society for the Propagation of the Gospel had already been in existence for nearly 100 years, but the less privileged and the dissenters had frequently shown the way; would more privileged members of the established church begin to follow in greater numbers? Would a 'Church' missionary society be formed? The answer was 'Yes.' The Society for Missions to Africa and the East, established in 1799, gained that nickname and became a principal vehicle of missionary endeavour for evangelicals within the Church of England.[43]

Closely associated with the founders of the Church Missionary Society was Henry Martyn. He brought to his missionary service in India a passionate devotion to Christ and brilliant linguistic gifts and training. Complementing the work of William

Carey, he concentrated on the Urdu, Persian and Arabic languages, and produced Bible translations in these of such a high standard that some are still used as the basis of modern revisions. Also of lasting significance from Martyn's intense career, cut short by death from tuberculosis, were his journals. These writings revealed that depth of Christian spirituality needed for the renewed approach to the Muslim world.

The founders and early leaders of CMS, some of whom were politically influential, were seeking to secure in Britain's colonies in India unhindered missionary access to the Hindu and Muslim communities. However, they were also deeply committed to the abolition of slavery and the eradication of the slave trade. This campaign led to an early concentration of missionary endeavour upon West Africa. The CMS Niger Mission was notable in at least three ways: the willingness of the missionaries to expose themselves to fatal disease—fifty died within twenty years; the close association of Christianity with commerce, then seen as a wholly positive alternative to Arab slaving and inter-tribal warfare; and the outstanding leadership shown by Samuel Adjai Crowther, a Yoruba convert and freed slave. The scope given to Crowther was consistent with the vision of Henry Venn, the first secretary of CMS, who believed that the churches born out of mission should be 'self-supporting, self-governing, and self-extending.'[44]

Early nineteenth-century pioneers

In his role as Bishop of the Niger Territories and as 'Apostle of Nigeria', Samuel Crowther was in advance of his time; the nineteenth century was largely marked by European and North American leadership in missions. Outstanding individuals achieved under God crucial advances in different world regions and in different aspects of the evolving missionary enterprise. Alexander Duff (1806–78), the first overseas missionary of the Church of Scotland, pioneered the development of higher education in the service of mission in India. His influence was crucial in establishing the prestigious teaching and medical institutions of Christian foundation, which still retain such importance in the subcontinent.[45]

Adoniram Judson (1788–1850), the North American Congregationalist turned Baptist, began work in India but moved with his wife Ann to Burma where they were the first to introduce the gospel. Judson's work was remarkable for his production of the Burmese Bible, his unwillingness to impose Western ideas of education, and his success in unifying the Baptist churches of North America in the cause of world mission. A period of imprisonment in the Burmese capital nearly broke him, but he retained an optimistic vision for the spread of the gospel even among the Buddhists in Burma, declaring that 'the future is as bright as the promises of God'.[46]

Someone else who gained substantial advances at great personal cost was John Williams, of the London Missionary Society, pioneer and martyr in the South Sea Islands. He trained newly converted native evangelists and thus accelerated the spread of the gospel in the Pacific region. Robert Moffat, commissioned with Williams, was a most versatile pioneer in Southern Africa, and an apostle to the Bechuana and Matabele peoples. Moffat introduced irrigation agriculture, was first to produce a Bible translation from a previously unwritten African language, set up his own printing-press, and resisted the northward advance of the land-hungry Boers.

A second missionary wind

As the first half of the nineteenth century gave way to the second, a number of developments occurred simultaneously: European colonialism began to approach the peak of its influence and Western self-confidence ran high; Roman Catholic missions regained their momentum, re-establishing churches in Japan, consolidating in China and India and pioneering in Africa; Protestant and Roman Catholic missions alike began the penetration of many of the vast unevangelised interior regions of Asia, Africa and South America. Previously most missionary work had been confined to the coastal regions and their more immediate hinterland. Now came the thrust into the interior.

On the English-speaking Protestant side recruits for this new phase of missionary advance came through the evangelistic campaigns and revivals led by Dwight L. Moody. There was not only a new generation of missionaries but also a new generation of missionary societies. The China Inland Mission, the Regions Beyond Missionary Union and the Sudan Interior Mission, all examples of those founded in this period, reflect in their names the vision of pressing on into the 'unexplored' and unevangelised areas of the world. Parallel with the formation of new Protestant missionary organisations came the multiplication of new Roman Catholic missionary orders, notable among which were the White Fathers of Africa.

Behind, and often before, these new organisations was a new generation of pioneers gripped with the desire to penetrate to the heart of the great unevangelised continents. Foremost among these was David Livingstone (1813–73). As a young missionary working with Robert Moffat, Livingstone developed a passionate love for Africa and its peoples and an adventurous desire to open its vast unexplored territories to Christianity and civilisation. Then followed a series of heroic crossings of the continent. The picture of the missionary explorer surrounded by his native bearers, forcing a way across jungles, deserts, swamps and rapids, caught the public imagination. Neither was the significance of this 'opening of Africa' lost upon those with business and political interests. However, what David Livingstone experienced at first hand was the human desolation wrought by the internal slave trafficking. So what he spent himself in trying to introduce was the gospel of Jesus Christ and a way of life based on the fair exchange of goods, not upon the cruel exchange of people. No disillusionment with what colonisation and commerce actually became should be allowed to undervalue the original motive or obscure the earlier misery David Livingstone sought to relieve.

What Livingstone was to Africa, James Hudson Taylor (1832–1905) was to China. A latter-day Matthew Ricci,

Hudson Taylor adopted Chinese dress and sought to establish indigenous churches.

The most precious gift that he exercised in his missionary calling was, however, faith working through prayer. His God-given burden was for the evangelisation of the millions of Chinese living in the inland provinces. None of the existing missionary societies was yet able to contemplate any advance beyond the coastal area. Hudson Taylor had no resources of personnel or money, but resolutely prayed for twenty-four 'willing, skilful labourers'. These, when recruited, formed the nucleus of his new mission, which, without ever making any direct appeal for funds, grew within 30 years to a missionary strength of more than 600. Most importantly, this new impetus secured the gospel penetration of the interior of China. Hudson Taylor's China Inland Mission contributed a major part of this advance, but also encouraged other societies to share in this vast undertaking.[47]

The prayer of the psalmist, 'May he have dominion from sea to sea,' shaped the calling of another pioneer, whose career as a naval officer had taken him around both east and west coasts of South America. Allen Gardiner (1794–1851) had seen the poverty and human degradation in the sea ports and there was aroused in him a deep desire to preach Christ to those throughout the subcontinent who did not know his salvation. The sea captain turned trekker and made extensive journeys through Chile, Bolivia, the Chaco regions and Patagonia. All his many attempts to establish mission centres in South America proved abortive and he died of starvation on the bleak shores of Tierra del Fuego; the supply ship arrived too late to save any member of his party.

Paradoxically, then, Allen Gardiner's special contribution to nineteenth-century missionary advance was suffering and failure. But by a miracle his journal with its final entries was discovered on the beach. 'Great and wonderful are the loving kindnesses of my God unto me. He has preserved me hitherto without feelings of hunger and thirst...' Allen Gardiner had been occupying his dying days with praising God and planning the formation of what was to become the South American Missionary Society, among the first of a growing number to add an evangelical dimension to Christian witness in the sub-continent.[48]

A man who established a very strong Roman Catholic trad-ition in North, Central and East Africa was the Frenchman, Cardinal Charles Lavigerie (1825–92). His White Fathers instructed and baptised converts, practised agriculture, opposed slavery, taught trades and were at the vanguard of Roman Catholic expansion, matching and often competing with the work of the Protestants. Lavigerie also founded the missionary order of the White Sisters at a time when in many denominations women were finding a more active and better recognised role in the missionary enterprise.[49]

Among the Protestants, one such person was Fanny Jane Butler. Newly qualified as a doctor, she responded to the insight that 'women medical missionaries must be the key that would open the door of Indian homes'. As the first European woman to become a missionary doctor, from 1883 until her premature death six years later, she ran dispensaries, worked at preventative medicine, and gave Bible teaching, first in Bhagalpur and then on the Northern Frontier, through which she was looking for an opening for the gospel into Central Asia.[50] Many were inspired by her example, and by the turn of the century for CMS alone the names of 550 women featured on the missionary lists.

A last representative of the nineteenth-century pioneers typifies one vital aspect of their motivation: profound, even anguished, concern for the plight of the lost. To reach out to those who faced the prospect of dying without a saving know-ledge of Christ, Charles Thomas Studd (1861–1931) gave up his fortune, his university career, and incidentally inter-national cricket, and, with other members of the Cambridge Seven, devoted his life to missionary service. Often struggling against ill health, he followed a heroic career first in China, then in India, then in Africa. Exasperating and inspiring by turns, C.T. Studd maintained a stubborn single-minded dedication to the task of spiritual rescue. Among his achievements was the foundation in 1913 of the Worldwide Evangelisation Crusade.[51]

Summing up the advance: range and resources

The career of C.T. Studd carries us into the twentieth century and into a new missionary period. The nineteenth century had seen the acceleration of that process of worldwide expansion of the churches which had begun at the end of the fifteenth century. It is estimated that whereas 19 per cent of the world's population professed Christianity in 1500, 34 per cent professed Christianity in 1900. At the beginning of this period of missionary expansion the church was dominant in Europe, a remnant in parts of the Middle East, and virtually absent elsewhere in the world. These centuries of missionary advance changed all that. In all but a few Central Asian countries, by the latter decades of the nineteenth century the church existed in nucleus or in strength in every nation of the world.

It would be foolish to suggest that all the intense energies behind this remarkable expansion of the churches were derived from the Holy Spirit. The missionary advance ran in tandem with the political advance, evangelisation with colonisation: sometimes ahead and sometimes behind. As we have seen, there was undoubted compromise. Yet there was a profound difference between the values of the missionaries and the colonists, highlighted through the campaigns of those missionary leaders who opposed the exploitation and enslavement of native peoples.

Here then was one way in which the Holy Spirit was regaining the initiative and resisting evil. No doubt calculating colonists were erecting many new barriers against the further spread of the gospel during this period, but the Holy Spirit was beginning to break down others, not least within the established churches of the West. The gospel was breaking out of its European 'prison house'. As our sketch illustrates, there was the awakened desire that men and women of all the newly discovered tribes and races should enjoy Christ's salvation. So, too, there was the willingness to take practical, adventurous, costly steps towards that end.

Practical steps require tangible resources. In this period mission became seaborne; improved navigation opened the coastlands of the world to the missionary pioneer. The printing press multiplied the written word of the gospel to an unparalleled degree. Societies were established to make that most valuable tool of all, the Bible, available to people of an increasing number of different languages. There also was what we would now call an 'intermediate technology' which served the missionary purpose well. Many of the missionaries were artisans and their craftsmanship and skills in agriculture, medicine, and all kinds of pioneering were often necessary, appropriate and beneficial. Another priceless asset was the missionary journal. Through these records that survive we gain an insight into not only the human frailty but also the Spirit power which marked these labours.

The latter years of the nineteenth century were marked by rising prosperity in Europe and North America which in turn made possible the funding by the churches of impressive hospitals and schools in the mission lands. Western medicine and education functioned as allies of Christian mission.

Man and moment of opportunity

The twentieth century dawned with the movement of missionary expansion unchecked. True, some of the competition and chaos of the European colonial powers was reflected by the churches in their missionary enterprises in Asia and Africa, and Oceania. Certainly many millions had yet to hear the gospel in Africa and Asia. But even so, in a new way, the unfinished task of mission appeared 'finishable'. No new and formidable barriers against missionary advance had yet appeared on the horizon. In such a moment of opportunity it seemed right to set before the church a breathtaking challenge: 'the evangelisation of the world in our generation'.[52]

Someone closely associated with this remarkable slogan

was John Raleigh Mott (1865–1955). Equally impressive in appearance, speech and character, this North American had been converted through J.E.K. Studd, challenged to a missionary commitment by D.L. Moody and guided by God's Spirit in a career which was to bring together student evangelism, global mission, and church unity in a combination of crucial importance. The World Alliance of YMCAs, in which Mott was a prominent leader, and the World Student Christian Federation, of which Mott was founder, united a growing membership across the world in a new way: 'Belief in Jesus Christ as God and Saviour, according to the Scriptures'. Most of the members were gifted and young, and so the YMCAs and WSCF provided a unique training-ground for Christian and missionary leadership.

In the middle of this youthful ferment of student discipling, national organisation and international consultation was J.R. Mott, an increasingly influential figure. A five-minute conversation with this man could be enough to alter the whole direction of a person's life. He was both evangelist and diplomat; he believed both in advance and co-operation. Through his international experience and the dynamic thrust of the organisations he represented, he earned his place as chairman of the World Missionary Conference in Edinburgh.[53]

Edinburgh 1910 is rightly seen as a pivotal moment for the church in modern history. Because its first concern was missionary, it had to face questions of church unity. Because it addressed issues of unity, it could not long ignore matters of theology. So out of this conference emerged a framework of consultation and co-operation in mission and unity, faith and order for a growing number of non-Roman Catholic churches. As important, if not more so, new voices were beginning to be heard by the serried ranks of Western delegates. It was not adequate that they should view the missionary enterprise from their own perspective of influence and privilege. Samuel Azariah, an Indian representative, could pay tribute to the professional dedication of his expatriate missionary colleagues, but something more was required: he expressed it simply, 'Give us friends.'

The fourth missionary period: evaluation and testing (1910 to the present)

Four years after the Edinburgh Conference came the outbreak of World War I. Within a further three years the Russian revolution gave another shattering blow to the proud illusions of 'Christian' Europe. The bloodiest, most massive and most destructive war of all time had broken out among socalled Christian nations. A party representing an atheistic ideology had swept to power over a people Orthodox in name and religious by nature. And with its roots in the previous century and now gaining momentum, there was a more subtle, though none the less powerful, force at work: biblical criticism. These three, the bitter European quarrel, the Marxist alternative, and the use of modern methods of historical and scientific analysis to examine the foundation documents of the Christian faith combined to challenge the certainties of a church that had so recently brimmed with confidence. Thus it was that a period of unparalleled expansion in Christian mission gave way to a period marked by critical evaluation and severe testing.

It might be imagined that something as academic, complex and often speculative as biblical criticism would have little bearing on the missionary work of the church. In fact it had a profound effect, and for these reasons. Mission by its very nature involves the faithful transmission of the message of Jesus Christ. This message is attested by both Old and New Testament Scriptures. Study which throws light on the human aspects of the Scriptures should be an aid to mission. The problem arose from the fact that too many of those from within the churches who developed this school of biblical criticism did not consistently or adequately submit to God's authority as it applies to Scripture. In the name of scholarship they questioned authorship, miracles, historical accuracy, indeed almost everything except the presuppositions upon which their modern and Western way of thinking depended. From a missionary perspective, here was a case of cultural assumptions being allowed to remain unchallenged by the gospel which transcends and judges all culture, including the ideas of the 'rational', 'scientific' West.

'All authority,' Jesus had said before Pentecost, 'has been given to me. Go, therefore, and make disciples of all nations.' This powerful critical movement within the mainstream of the Protestant churches, which gave every appearance of weakening Christ's authority, debilitated its missionary role in disciple-making across the world. Furthermore, if Christians are to work together in spreading the gospel they must share a substantial measure of agreement about the nature of that gospel and the way it should be spread. Tragically, just at a time when the experience of world mission was challenging the churches to a new search for unity, controversy over biblical criticism prevented a large number of the most active missionary churches and organisations from identifying with the movement which had found its focus in Edinburgh in 1910. Their evangelical membership rightly clung to convictions of scriptural authority and inspiration, but continued their missionary endeavours without formal participation in the ecumenical movement. In the event, the evangelical convictions and the broad sympathies of leaders such as J.R. Mott could not be held together by the missionary movement as a whole. I believe that the inability of some biblical critics to fully recognise the divine authority of the biblical revelation contributed to strains upon Christian unity such that an outstanding opportunity for its advancement could only in part be grasped.

Parallel with that school of biblical criticism, and shaped by some of the same philosophical influences, was a new kind of political criticism. Karl Marx had dared to question whether the hierarchical (class) ordering of society was for the common good at all, arguing rather that down the ages it had represented a colossal conspiracy protecting the interests of the few at the expense of the many. And because the Christian church, ever since the days of Constantine, had related to the ruling class as well as the ruled, surely its teaching must be part of that conspiracy: an opiate for the people.

If this can be accepted as the crudest summary of the Marxist criticism, what were its effects? No doubt these radical ideas played a part in weakening the general consensus among educated people in the West that Christian teachings were unquestionably true. A decisive confrontation, however, came with the Russian revolution. This event not only brought the downfall of the Czarist regime but also the Russian Orthodox State Church. This church stripped of its political privilege has, along with others, in subsequent years been persecuted and tolerated. What for seventy years the Marxist leadership has not accepted, however, is the open propagation of the Christian faith. The *Soviet Encyclopaedia* equates Christian missions with 'an instrument of aggression' and missionaries as 'secret agents of espionage and sabotage in the service of the imperialistic power'.

Small wonder then that when Mao Tse-tung completed his Long March and established in 1949 the People's Republic the days of the foreign missionaries in mainland China were numbered. From a post-war peak of nearly 10,000 expatriate missionary personnel there was an effective reduction to zero following the expulsions in 1952. The Communist authorities sought to purge the Chinese Church of all 'imperialistic influences' and channel it into a regulated and restricted life on the basis of the Three Self Reform Movement and its Roman Catholic counterpart.

What happened most dramatically and massively in Russia and China has occurred in all countries of Eastern Europe and South East Asia where Marxist governments have gained power. The churches in those lands have lost political privilege, expatriate missionary work has been restricted or prohibited, and the attempt has been made to hinder or prevent the propagation of the faith of the church through its own members. Communist governments taking power in other parts of the world and in more recent years have not all taken these steps but they none the less form the prevailing pattern in the 'Eastern Bloc'. In this half of the world the church has returned to a situation with parallels to that prevailing in the Roman empire before Constantine.

In criticising Christian mission Marxist authorities have repeatedly asserted that consciously or unconsciously it serves the selfish purposes of the capitalistic powers. The undoubted historical connections between missionary work and Western colonisation was bound eventually to provoke a deep and powerful reaction. Many of the colonised regions, like the Indian subcontinent, possessed ancient, profoundly developed religions. These to a degree remained static or quiescent during the period of colonial dominance. However, this state of affairs was bound to pass; the present century has seen both the resurgence of the great world religions and the passionate reassertion of national and racial identity throughout what is now called the Third World.

A sketch of the present period of world mission must take account of the threefold criticism to which mission is being subjected: the intellectual criticism of its foundation documents (biblical criticism); the ideological criticism of its political loyalties (Marxism); the religious and nationalistic criticism of its claims to universal scope and exclusive loyalty (resurgent religions and nationalism).

Now what might appear as a new threefold barrier to the further advance of the gospel the Holy Spirit is in process of breaking down. Charles Spurgeon, who in an earlier generation had engaged in controversy over the authority of the Scriptures, made the comment, 'You don't have to defend the Bible. It is like a lion; you just let it loose!' The power of the biblical revelation cannot be weakened by scepticism. Unslanted examination of the texts, however rigorous, can serve to make their inspired significance better understood.

In a not unsimilar way the Marxist attack upon mission has been powerless to destroy its essential fruits. Admittedly the proportion of professing Christians in Soviet Russia between

1900 and 1970 has fallen from 83 per cent to 25 per cent. However, what was before a partly nominal membership has now changed into a thoroughly active membership, tested by negative discrimination and spasmodic persecution. The church in China has achieved substantial growth in numbers as well as quality under Communist rule.

As significantly, the Marxist analysis of society and its championing of the poor has forced the church to look afresh at its own gospel for the poor and face up to its own degree of failure in challenging social injustice. In this process of rediscovery and repentance there has been the sharpened awareness of materialistic capitalism as a force counter to God's missionary purpose. In any Western country the modest proportion of the population that attends a place of worship on a weekly basis provides evidence that the dominant influence in most people's lives is not religion. Instead, it is materialism. According to David Barrett's statistics, between 1900 and 1970 the percentage of professing Christians in Western Europe decreased from 97 to 83 and in Northern America from 97 to 91.[54] Projected figures for the year 2000 are still relatively high at 76 per cent and 87 per cent respectively. Even so they still hide the very substantial proportion of the people counted in the percentages whose lives were or are governed primarily by materialism, not by the gospel of Jesus Christ.

So the church in the West has been alerted by the Marxist challenge, but needs to be alerted more sharply still to the insidious influence of materialism, not least in its capitalistic framework. All this the Holy Spirit is doing and no doubt will continue to do. His work is a purifying work, and it is a purified church which will be the better able to respond to the criticism and challenge of the other world religions: a dominant issue in the present decade.

Because the missionary enterprise of the church has been confronted during this present period by a number of contrary forces, the missionary spirit has acted not only as a rallying force but also as a purifier. Christians have been forced to see again that the spread of the gospel cannot be measured simply by the numbers of those who call themselves Christian. Very serious questions have to be asked about the extent to which the values of the kingdom of God operate in the lives of these people. Furthermore, how much are these values reflected more widely into the communities of which professing Christians form a part? How far is the light from the lamp radiating? How much flavour is penetrating from the salt?

While the Holy Spirit is prompting such missionary questions as these, he is also in the vanguard of a new advance. In this age of self-criticism and evaluation there has also been a work of God, brimming with vitality and confidence. Massive church growth has occurred. Often uncomprehended and sometimes totally unknown to Christians in the West, there have been huge numerical gains: the Christian population of Africa has jumped from 10 million in 1900 to 143 million in 1970. Between the same years the number of those in Asia who profess faith in Christ has risen from nineteen to ninety-one million. These increases are two, three or even four times in excess of population growth.[55] Neither the population nor the communications explosion account for this expansion; although modern methods of communication are used very effectively in the spread of the gospel, the largest movements of the Spirit have not occurred where the most sophisticated media are readily available. A Pentecostal movement dating from the beginning of this century has flourished among the less privileged people of Latin America and has contributed to the most rapid church growth in other continents.

Even in an age of doubting and questioning the positive, overflowing energy of Pentecost shows no sign of abating. If the Spirit's work of turning people to Christ and producing Christ-pleasing qualities in human society is hindered in one region of the world, it accelerates in another. God's great missionary purpose continues towards its fulfilment, constantly assailed but never defeated by satanic opposition, impeded but never halted by human failure. Because of God's purpose, human history has purpose. It is no exaggeration to say that God's mission through Christ gives meaning to history. God constantly works from the inconspicuous to achieve the far reaching.

Our historical survey can give us a stronger sense of purpose. We gain a heightened awareness of that great crowd of missionary witnesses: apostles consciously acting upon the call and initiative of God's Spirit, used in some surging advance; ordinary people carried about by the circumstances of life, but spreading the knowledge of Christ among their neighbours; pastors, teachers, administrators ordering the life of the church and influencing the life of society; lovers of Christ, bearers of vibrant life and new evangelistic zeal; campaigning organisers devising structures and methods through which that energy may be channelled; prophets exposing the differences between the world as it is and the kingdom that is coming. History tells of the many ways to co-operate in the mission of Jesus Christ. It sets the apostolic standard and warns against any lesser stereotype. Read aright, this story brings perspective and an invitation to take our place alongside those who have gone before us.

We began this missionary journey down the centuries with a bearded activist addressing a volatile crowd in a side street in an occupied city. We end it exactly where we are in the world of today. As we need a missionary perspective on the past, so we need to see the world of the present with missionary eyes. We must undertake a missionary tour and see God's purpose unfolding not only age by age but place by place and day by day.

4

Mission on Six Continents

Carey's map of mission

To the traveller passing through the Northamptonshire village of Moulton the thatched stone cottage of the local Baptist pastor would have been indistinguishable from another five, which formed a row there in the 1780s. This modest home served as manse, school-house, and shoemaker's workshop. Inside the main room hung a home-made world map.

Though the dwelling might have been ordinary, the map was unique. Noted upon it was all the information which William Carey could obtain about the population figures, and the religious, social and physical conditions in the nations of the world. His sources included Captain Cook's journals, the *Northampton Mercury*, and books he would borrow but could not afford to buy. With such strictly limited means he set out to demonstrate in global terms something of what it would mean in his generation to obey the Great Commission. He produced not only a missionary manifesto but a missionary map.

Christians of Carey's time would have had a greater excuse for missionary ignorance. Many Christians of our day have immeasurably superior sources of information but most neglect to inform themselves seriously about the current missionary situation worldwide. Yet there is now an abundance of material relevant to the evangelisation of every part of the world. There is a whole new science of missiology. Sociological methods have been used to identify in every continent 'people groups' within which no church has yet been established. Amazingly detailed information can be found on the growth and composition of the Christian churches in nearly every country. Within the thousand pages of David Barrett's *World Christian Encyclopedia* you can even find a figure for how many Bibles were distributed in 1975 in Equatorial Guinea or the percentage increase that year in the membership of the African indigenous churches of the Ivory Coast.[1] Even allowing for the fact that Barrett's data for more recent years are projections from a 1970 base, his information is prodigious. Statistics on material need are also vitally important in relation to Christian mission. There is no lack of these![2]

So it would be possible to be immersed in a weight of detail: a hazard perhaps for the missionary specialists. But world mission isn't just for specialists; it is for all Christians. Every church member should have some picture of the world Christ came to save and some understanding of that global work of salvation today. All of us need a missionary world-view, and should take serious steps in gaining such insight. I suspect, though, that many whose educational privilege would enable them to draw other kinds of maps would be at a loss to draw a missionary map. If asked to do so the paper would remain largely blank.

I believe, therefore, that together we need to undertake an exercise in missionary mapping: not indeed to reproduce here all the sophisticated information available in the excellent reference books, but rather to gain some missionary perspectives, attempt some rough sketching and see a few glimpses of the missionary scene in different parts of the world. In seeking to be better informed, we will not imagine that we shall have some new capability automatically enabling us to do mission more efficiently. We want to be informed not to be complacent but to be expectant. Missionary exploring should prove an enlarging but humbling experience.

Missionary geography

The way the world should be studied from a missionary point of view is not necessarily the same as from other approaches to geography. Some data will be of interest from any angle. However, mission has its own criteria of measurement, its own primary concerns, its own way of seeing the world. This can be best explained under three headings.

Peoples and boundaries

An ordinary political map of the world shows nation states separated by national boundaries. Such maps have obvious interest from the missionary viewpoint for two specially important reasons: first, within a nation the missionary undertaking will be affected by the attitude of the government towards Christianity and the church; secondly, this attitude and the relationships of governments to one another will affect the opportunities of mission across the national boundaries.

On both these points increasingly comprehensive information is available, though it will need constant updating. David Barrett's *World Christian Encyclopedia* includes among others two colour-coded world maps. One has a key showing for different nations degrees of religious liberty ranging from 'state propagated Christianity' to 'state suppression'. The other features closed, receiving and sending countries, with a key grading countries in these terms according to numbers of foreign missionaries deployed across frontiers per million of national populations.[3]

So ordinary political boundaries are of great missionary interest, but the nation state and its frontiers is not all that matters. When the New Testament is speaking of 'nations' it is referring to groups of people distinguished by language and culture rather than nationality. The nation state, as we know it, is a relatively modern invention. Following the Lausanne Conference in 1974, there has quite rightly been a renewed focus upon evangelising not only all the nation states of the world but also all the different groups of peoples within them. Maps with national boundaries need to be supplemented with more detailed maps showing the distributions of people of different linguistic and racial groups.

Some very remarkable progammes are already in hand to do precisely this kind of mapping. Among them is the Global Mapping Project based at the US Center for World Mission, Pasadena. Here, computorgraphic tools are being used to show the distribution of unevangelised peoples.

Such studies as these have created a missionary sociology which has its own jargon: 'people groups' whose identity and loyalty is based on common language and customs; 'unreached peoples' those who have no indigenous self-propagating church within their number. A missionary world-view relates to all these things, because of its concern that all should share the benefits of the gospel. Evangelisation has to do with hearing the gospel in such a way that it can be understood, but what exactly does that mean? Is it just a formula of words to be heard? Ought not people be able to see signs of the gospel to convince them?

Kingdom relief and binocular vision

Relief maps attempt to portray a three-dimensional landscape. When with both eyes open we see the locality itself, we capture stereoscopically all the depth and perspectives of its contours. A capacity God has given us for our physical eyes we need to use with our missionary eyes. Thanks to the outstanding educational programme of relief and development agencies many Christians now have one eye much wider open: the one that sees the poverty, the injustice, the environmental damage and social concern for the world. Without shutting this eye at all we need to open the other and become fully aware of the increasing millions who live beyond the witness of local churches, the people's lostness and loneliness, the subtle and the blatant forces of evil, the spiritual plight of the human family.

A two-eyed view of the world is equally perceptive to the

beautiful and good where evident in both social and spiritual spheres. What it refuses to accept, however, is that the urgency of the physical needs, or even the scandal of the economic injustices can be fully addressed without confronting the spiritual darkness and inviting people to faith in Christ. The life and death issues of relief, development and liberation cannot be more important than the life and death issues of evangelistic obedience, nor should they be wrongly separated. We do not see the world better by shutting either one eye or the other.

Evidently a one-eyed view of the world must be in some way deficient and 'flat'. It will not pick up all the dimensions of the kingdom which Jesus inaugurated and which his mission seeks to extend. Its growth cannot be measured in terms of church membership alone; the presence of the kingdom requires the qualities of the kingdom reflected in the church and extended into society. Indicators of this kingdom influence—respect for human rights, distribution of wealth, educational opportunity, health care, and the making of disciples—are all essential to the missionary view. Only this way of seeing recognises the troughs of human need in their full depth, and the heights in their God-given potential.

Biblical projection

The overall shape of a world map is determined by the projection, and the choice of the projection may well reflect the values and prejudices of the map-maker. The fact that Mercator's projection, with its exaggeration of the size of the countries of the Northern hemisphere, has long remained popular reflects an assumption held in these countries that they are somehow more important than those of the South. The Peter's projection promoted by the United Nations and the world development agencies corrects this imbalance and gives the different countries their proper relative surface areas.

In this respect the 'Bible projection' is like the Peter's projection. The whole earth belongs to God: the round world and those who dwell in it. People of all races and geographical locations are God's creation and through this fact require equal respect and have equal importance. It is precisely because, through the Fall, this knowledge of the One Universal Creator God has been weakened or lost that the recognition of the equal dignity of all races has been obscured. As sinful human beings we have a fatal bias giving us the illusion that our race is better than other races, our nation more important than other nations and our social group or tribe more deserving than any other section of society.

Against such self-centred, racist, nationalistic, or tribal sentiments the Bible view is totally opposed. God revealed in Scripture did not make some men and women in his image, but all without exception. The political divisions and the differences in language are providentially allowed by him to limit the harm done by sinful wielders of power. However, the Bible still recognises the original unity of the human family. Indeed, the God and Father of our Lord Jesus Christ is the Father 'from whom every family in heaven and on earth is named'. All men and women derive their name, their nature, their identity from God revealed in Jesus Christ.

It is necessary to emphasise this biblical view of the oneness or solidarity of the human family otherwise we shall never draw or interpret our missionary map aright. We share with people everywhere the same essential dignity, the same potential, the same basic failure and guilt. All people, whether they recognise it or not, are solidly together. All are sinners, all are sinned against and to all God addresses his gospel appeal: 'Turn to me and be saved all the ends of the earth.'

The Bible is completely realistic in recognising the way that the nations reject the Christ, the Saviour King. Yet at an even deeper level Scripture shows us that his law, his rule of peace, is the very thing for which all peoples are longing. The destiny of every nation hinges upon the evangelisation of that nation. It is the privilege of every people to bring the riches of its cultural inheritance back to the feet of Christ. All contrary ambitions of national rulers are self-defeating and vain. In following them, they are being misled by satanic powers. However, there is a greater power at work: one which is healing, unifying, redeeming: none other than the Spirit of Jesus, released at Pentecost. So the central focus of the 'Bible projection' is Jesus Christ, and its perspective on all the nations provides a true balance, a profound interpretation, a missionary world-view.

Our global sketch-map

These biblical preliminaries set us an awesome standard. And who in any case would attempt to make a statement about the whole world? We have already noted the vast resources from which a picture of the global missionary scene can be drawn. We will simply reproduce a few statistics from the mountains available. My limitations are such that I will draw upon only a tiny fraction of the literature on contemporary mission in different parts of the world. My geographical and denominational blind spots cannot be hidden.

I do, however, enjoy one important advantage. I live and work in an international centre where at any one time Christians will be present from forty different countries. A significant part of what is gathered here has been gleaned from face to face encounters with people of many nationalities and also from a similarly international group which has responded to letters. It follows that we are sketching, as it were, from a living subject. In this and the following chapters we are seeking to record a living testimony. We begin continent by continent.

Africa

Bare facts

In attempting to sketch a missionary map of this continent the first thing we have to do is to remind ourselves that this relates to the twentieth century, not the nineteenth. Undoubtedly the nineteenth century was of transforming importance for mission in Africa, but Christianity in Africa is not in any way fixed in that period. There were Africans present when the Spirit was poured out on the Day of Pentecost. African Christianity was very influential in the fourth century; African Christians form 15 per cent of the membership of the world church today.

Because Africa has a clearly recognisable and coherent shape it is possible to miss the continental contrasts. Politically it is divided between fifty-nine nation states governed by such diverse regimes as Libya's revolutionary extremism under Colonel Gaddafi and South Africa's white supremacy government, currently under President Botha. Between these poles, more representative leaders pursue better policies. Julius Nyerere, from the recent past, with his African socialism and Kenneth Kaunda, with his nationalism and Christian humanism, come immediately to mind.

The peoples of Africa are as diverse as their governments. North of the Sahara they are predominantly Arabic. Throughout Africa there are perhaps a thousand different tribes. Most of these divide between Bantu and Sudanic language groupings, but few of the tribal languages would be mutually understandable. The African population totals 520 million at present, and is doubling every 24 years. In spite of a rapid flow into new cities the population remains predominantly rural and the average age in Africa is very young indeed.

The latitude ten degrees north of the equator coincides with the religious divide of Africa. North of this parallel the majority population is Muslim; to the south the majority is Christian. But in a broad band spanning the continent from east to west there is the zone of encounter where the peoples of the two religions intermingle and meet. Altogether 44 per cent of Africans profess to be Christians and 41 per cent to be Muslims. Fourteen per cent still practise the traditional tribal religions and have not yet accepted either of these missionary faiths. Of the Christians 41 per cent are Roman Catholic, 29 per cent are Protestant (including Anglican), 13 per cent are

Orthodox and 15 per cent belong to African indigenous denominations.[4] Simplified statistics like these of course hide the immense diversity in Christian traditions and the bewildering fragmentation in the Protestant and indigenous denominations.

Situation for mission

Bare facts about political, racial and religious groupings only begin to describe the context of mission in Africa. An important, indeed essential part of that context remains the traditional tribal society. The limited loyalties and the lurking fears affecting the tribesman and the recurrent danger of inter-tribal conflict may create a negative view of tribal life. In common with other human groupings this established ordering of society has undoubted weaknesses but it also has immense and precious strengths. These deserve full recognition. A traditional African can be closely identified with his forebears, in solidarity with his peers, and rooted in his land. At its best, tribal society is cohesive, accepting, mutual, sociable, free from class divisions, patient, conversational, a logical extension of the nuclear human family. 'Africa's gift to human culture must be in the sphere of human relationships.' So says Kenneth Kaunda.[5] Who would disagree?

Moreover, African tribespeople are profoundly religious. Wherever they go, whatever they do, they carry their religion with them. There is no restriction of religion to one compartment of life; it belongs to the whole. In various ways and degrees they acknowledge a High Creator God. They live in a world dominated by the spirits, some of which are evidently malignant. Evil can be felt, but also the unseen can be seen. If ever a people were ready for the gospel which both affirms and redeems, these people are.

To understand the situation of mission in Africa today it is vital for us to appreciate traditional African society. But of course traditional Africa has suffered the massive impact of the modern world. Full of potential for some benefit and much harm, Western culture has created for Africans a deep dilemma; are they to rebel against the West or imitate the West? The time needed to digest the issues and choose what is best for Africa is scarce indeed. In Kenneth Kaunda's phrase there has been 'a telescoping of time in the African continent'.[6] For the church, too, this telescoping makes it all the harder to discern what is both truly Christian and truly African. Both native and adopted Africans who share in Christ's mission in this continent need from his Spirit in abundance the gift of wisdom and discernment. How else can they discover Christ's way in a situation which is at once so full of paradox, promise and threat?

The threat that hangs over Africa is both spiritual and physical. 'Africa is dying...our ancient continent is lying in ruins!'[7] Such a heart cry from Edem Kodjo, a general secretary of the Organisation of African States, might until the 1984 famine have appeared alarmist. But ever since the 1960s Africa's ability to feed itself has been deteriorating. Growing cities have lived at the expense of poor farmers; impoverished farmers have lived at the expense of eroding soils. The result over vast sweeps of Africa has been severe environmental damage and terrible social dislocation. The number of people fleeing from war and drought and famine has leapt: ten million in 1985, but this is only a small part of the social uprooting. Small wonder that there is an upturn in crime and a breakdown in order. Christian mission which holds out hope for social and environmental harmony must do so against a background not just of periodic famine but of permanent emergency.

Who or what, though, is to blame for the poverty that leaves 100 million Africans hungry, and accounts for the death each year of 5 million of her children? Is it colonial exploitation, or unequal terms of world trade, or corrupt government, or mistaken technical advice? It is all these things, and what is more there is a growing clamour in Africa today to see the wrongs righted, and especially that most notorious of wrongs: apartheid. Black Africa is becoming increasingly politicised; there is a demand for social justice which brooks no refusal. Christian mission, which acknowledges the perfect justice of the kingdom of God, operates among a people hungry for justice. This too is a part of the gospel context no one should dare to ignore.

A false optimism which evades such sharp issues of poverty and injustice is clearly inexcusable. However, any description of the African missionary scene which fails to show the true optimism of the African people and the vigorous growth of the African churches, must be equally foreign and false. Against a population growth rate of 2.7 per cent per year the churches are growing at 3.5 per cent per year. When it is remembered that this figure applies to the whole continent, including the Muslim north, then it is seen to be impressive indeed.

Across the denominations this is a shared growth, but the most rapid expansion of all is found in the African independent churches; these are widespread throughout the continent, flourishing among 500 different tribes, and between a multiplicity of different sects and denominations, involving a total membership of about 30 million. Growth among these churches is such that they are likely to double their overall membership within the space of fourteen years.

Growth among nearly all the churches of Africa must surely be a sign of life. 'If we take numbers and a desire to celebrate in worship as signs of vitality, then African Christianity is vital indeed.'[8] Professor Tite Tienou makes this comment in *Christianity: A World Faith*. Yet he goes on to observe a certain lack of confidence within the African churches preventing them from exerting the influence in the world which the size of their membership might suggest. Such hesitancy is reflected in the fact that these churches still receive many more missionaries than they send. In Nigeria and Kenya churches and agencies are sending out missionaries in increasing numbers (including 650 from one Nigerian organisation alone), but for the continent as a whole there is still only one missionary sent out for every fifteen expatriate missionaries received.

These limitations of mission as yet extended from Africa no

doubt reflect the limitations of mission received. The continent gives the appearance of both stability and flux, peace and turmoil, welling joy and gnawing anxiety. A taxi ride in Eastern Nigeria sums up for me this impression of Christian but also not yet Christian Africa, and of a new Africa balanced precariously on the foundations of the old.

The taxi is hurtling along on the wrong side of the road straining to overtake another speeding vehicle. In my vision is a sticker announcing, 'Be of good cheer. I have overcome the world.' The co-driver is concentrating on reading his book. I glance at the chapter heading, 'Use your witchcraft powers to travel outside your body.' I look up again and a third car is heading straight for us. Our driver swerves violently back into the right-hand lane still intent on making enough runs in a day to cover his extortionate costs.

Rapid change is creating many dangers in Africa. The missionary challenge of the continent must have something to do with the hopes, fears and needs of the thousands like these two young taxi men. At a perilous and crucial time, what may be their future?

The challenge of mission

The gospel of Jesus Christ is good news for the past, for the present, and for the future. For much of traditional Africa, where there was a highly developed sense of the past, only the immediate future had any real meaning. Now the gospel is helping Africans to look forward into God's future, following Christ into the years that stretch ahead. Herein lies an immense challenge.

In meeting the future's massive demands there can be no short cuts. There must be a continued meeting between the gospel and the deeply rooted ways of thinking and living. A mere classroom religion touching only the Westernised parts of African life will be insufficient. Jesus, the New Man, the Second Adam, must be allowed to bring his sympathy and solidarity to relationships beyond the tribe as well as within the tribe. Africans must cling to Christ's cross, the true shelter from the shadow of fear and the heat of anger, the only release from the weight and contamination of evil. Less anaesthetised from the pain of the Fall than the Westerner, who for that reason may be in a worse plight, the African may go straight to that shelter. And he will rightly want to bring his people with him, even, if possible, his ancestors, thus to enjoy all together a full life fully shared.

The missionary inheritance does not always and everywhere stand squarely upon such an African appropriation of Christ and his cross. Much strengthening of the foundations remains to be done. They certainly bear a massive edifice; the number of Christians in Africa has multiplied 200-fold over the past 200 years. Quality and quantity in church life are inseparably bound together. Growing churches do not automatically remain growing churches. There is the challenge to maintain numerical growth. But this depends upon the vitality of church membership which in turn depends on the quality of leadership. And in many areas of Africa, church leadership is alarmingly overstretched.

This problem is accentuated where leadership patterns have been inherited from the Western churches. Inappropriate and irrelevant academic standards have been applied to the training of pastors, thus hindering the preparation of the many needed to care for the large numbers of new converts. The result of this policy of the more conservatively Western churches is that one ordained pastor may have to supervise village congregations scattered throughout an area the size of an English county. News of a funeral the pastor should conduct may arrive days after the deceased has had to be buried. The pastor's response to a request for healing for a sick child may for the same reasons come too late, bringing similarly tragic consequences.

In his book, *The Primal Vision*, John V. Taylor describes the ideal of the traditional African leader: local, accessible, in touch with the unseen world, one with his people, a shepherd who 'cares for the little goats...that they may survive their maladies'.[9] Dr Taylor goes on to point out, 'No peripatetic supervisor can fulfil this role.' Surely today's Christian leaders should reflect the best qualities expected of those who went before them.

So the challenge to identify local leaders and to implement appropriate and agile methods of training them isn't so much a desirable adjustment; rather it is an urgent necessity. The introduction since the early 1970s of significant programmes of Theological Education by Extension has been a promising and positive step towards equipping Christ's African people for ministry. It has taken training out of isolated and costly centres and returned it into the villages and shanty towns where the people are. Those tied by the ordinary circumstances of life—the care of children and elderly relatives, the cultivation of the shamba—study in their own homes and places of work. When they meet together in local tutorial groups they are able to apply the text of Scripture very directly to their own situation. TEE appears to be part of what is needed for African Christianity to be taught in an African way. Even so the process must still have far to go.

There is still the need to discover and equip all the men and women whom God is calling to be the enablers, guides, encouragers of the African churches. At the one end of the spectrum the indigenous (independent) churches have their own way of growing their leaders, while in many cases being open to help from the mission churches. The Roman Catholic churches, often with massive membership, are about to lose through retirement a whole generation of expatriate monks and nuns. An insufficient number of Africans are currently in training to replace them.

Today the African pastor, teacher, community health or agricultural extension worker, serving in the name of Christ, has to confront the crucial issues upon which the future of the continent depends. In our sketch of the African context of mission we identified as key issues the impact of Westernisation and modernisation, actual and potential conflict with Islam, environmental damage and social dislocation, and the gross injustices and distortions of the colonial legacy, most sharply focused in apartheid.

African church leaders are called to a prophetic ministry facing these realities. It may lead them into a costly and dangerous struggle against oppressive governments. Great qualities of wisdom and restraint may be required of them in relating to Muslim power groups. They may be called upon to take a substantial share in nation building or reconstruction where some political tyranny has been overthrown. Perhaps their voice and the dedicated caring of Christian workers at the grass-roots may save great tracts of Africa from becoming a physical and human desert. Unless the churches take a strong and effective initiative in containing the new scourge of AIDS, what other body will do so? Then, too, there is need for a relentless struggle against the subtle pressures of materialism and the dark forces of spiritual evil.

Of all the difficult and exacting challenges facing the African churches and their leaders none is more critically important than their approach to Islam. There are historical precedents for Christians living as tolerated minorities under Islamic powers, and Muslim minorities living peacefully under Christian or Western government. In the zone of encounter in Africa, and most notably in Nigeria, Christians need to seek a way of living with Muslim neighbours in a situation in which numbers of the two communities are roughly comparable.

This combination appears to be the least stable and most explosive. The Muslim desire to dominate and impose their own law upon all citizens is no doubt partly fuelled by previous Western colonial dominance. It creates a situation of the utmost difficulty and delicacy for the African Christian leadership to handle. A young evangelist may find himself in a fierce legal dispute over church property even before he is ordained. The building of a mosque may endlessly complicate the siting of a church. Student evangelism may create a riot. Loving the antagonist, maintaining the missionary motive, neither yielding to unjust pressure, nor provoking the wrong kind of confrontation: these things, only possible through the

Spirit of Christ, are required of the churches and their representatives.

Confronting a challenge of Goliath's proportions the African churches must use the smooth slingstones of their own appropriation of the gospel; cumbered with Saul's armour of imported Western traditions of Christianity they will scarcely survive against the giants. Africans say that their own theology is not yet developed. Yet their knowledge of the living God is profound. They know him in their celebratory worship: an outpouring of joy. They watch the manifestations of his power in miracles of healing and deliverance. They enjoy the warmth of his love in the extended family fellowship of Christ. If they haven't burdened the world with as many opaque and technical books does this mean that they know less of God made approachable in his Son? Besides, martyrdom must teach more than any other discipline, and modern Africa has produced martyrs in a heroic succession.

From what my African brothers and sisters tell me I understand that Christ's church in that continent cannot stand still. It must sustain its missionary expansion and at the same time continue a process of de-Westernisation. What a thought this is for the Western missionary! Cultural sensitivity has always been at a premium; but now perhaps more than ever. But another quality is also vital here. Kenneth Kaunda points to it in referring to post-independence changes in political relationships. He comments, 'To work as a colleague alongside someone who before was the recipient of one's patronage calls for a quality of humility that Europeans have not had much opportunity to develop during their stay in Africa.'[10]

And how much humility have missionaries in Africa developed? How many Western Barnabases are there for the African Pauls? At least this can be said: the East Africa revival grew out of a humbling. Western missionaries discovered forgiveness with and from their African brothers and sisters. Interestingly, this revival provides one of the modern examples of the influence of African Christianity which extends powerfully beyond the borders of Africa. In spite of daunting difficulties within the continent, other parts of the world church can look forward expectantly to the missionary contribution from Africa which, under God, will play such a significant part in the evangelisation of their own regions. Tired Europe may yet experience on a growing scale the infectious energy of African-led worship. Where Asia is resigned to the suffering of poverty, Christ-inspired African optimism may perform a powerful work. For God so loves Africa that he will surely make her sons and daughters fruitful in all the world.

Asia

'Asia must be our care.' So said the ailing Henry Martyn in 1811 to a bemused, expatriate congregation in Calcutta.[11] All Asia! In relation to this giant among continents all Europe is but a small peninsula. The ten million square miles of Asia's land surface is now occupied by three billion people.

In terms of its size alone, Asia, the birthplace of the Christian religion, remains the greatest continental challenge to Christian mission. However, Asia has not only contained the cradle of Christianity but also that of all the other great world religions. Asia matches the spirit sensitivity of African traditional religion with a mysticism, philosophy, poetic literature and social ethic which in her different religions are advanced to a superlative degree. Many of Asia's empires have been much older and much bigger than those of other parts of the world, and have understood themselves as such. In technology the West only caught up with Asia as recently as the seventeenth century.

Small wonder then in the light of such comparisons that some of Asia's spokesmen have declared, 'Asia does not want Christianity.' Jean Herbert, in his book *An Introduction to Asia*, explains: 'The people of Asia are under the impression that they already possess in their own religions all that Christianity can bring them, whether on the plane of ethics or of miracles.' C.S. Venkatachar speaks for many others when he confidently declares, 'The spiritual assault on the traditional Asian societies by the Christian missions must be reckoned a failure.' On a good day the Christian preacher in Asia can expect the response, 'You may be right, but why should we be wrong?'[12]

The dimensions of Asia

How dangerous it would be to underestimate the dimensions of Asia as a field of mission. Our sketch must try to represent the proportions aright. We must attempt to focus our picture of Asia, vast and complex as that continent is. Somehow and in some degree we must grasp the Asian reality in its geographical expanse, its religious and cultural traditions and its political ferment. How the Christian minority already figures in the Asian scene may also surprise us.

Where does Asia begin and where does it end? A rather indefinite boundary with Europe is marked by the Ural mountains and river, the Black Sea and Turkey's frontier with Russia. The Suez canal cuts the narrow neck of land which had joined Africa to Asia. The generally accepted division with Oceania leaves most of Indonesia in Asia but the islands to the east outside it. Geographically Asia contains nearly as much variety as may be found anywhere. Racially, in addition to the dominant Indo-Aryan and Mongoloid types, many peoples of many kinds are found, whether belonging to small tribes or large groupings.

With all this variety does it make sense to talk about Asia at all? Yes, because with the exception of their less accessible parts Asian countries share a long history of people living in crowded communities, elaborately organised, developing among themselves a culture full of beautiful features, yet for the majority yielding only the barest minimum of economic benefits. Typical Asia is populous, frugal, cultured, conformist, and religious. For the mass of the people this means folk culture and religion, for the elite something of great sophistication and depth.

One more clarification is needed. Are we talking about

traditional Asia or modern Asia? Like Africa, Asia has suffered the massive impact of the West. New technology, new power structures, new expectations, new crime and new vices all have come flooding in. Asia it is true has been more critical of Western culture, sometimes devastatingly. 'Where the West goes moral standards deteriorate,' was the considered opinion of Mao Tse-tung. Even so, for better or for worse, many Asian cities have come under the powerful and pervasive influence of Europe and North America. 'Western Asians' are found everywhere. They show every sign of beating the 'Western Westerners' at their own competitive games, but they remain Asian. I would conclude that there are great differences between traditional and modern Asia but also a real continuity and identity linking them.

A clue as to why the winds of change do not completely overturn the established Asian way of life is expressed by Jean Herbert in this way: 'The profane (secular) is absorbed into the sacred...religious, spiritual, mystical preoccupation, with all the ritualism that goes with them, are the main foundations of traditional Asian life...even those who turn towards an atheistic materialism do so in a religious spirit.'[13] We may be sure that religion in Asia is very strong and that it is bound up with every aspect of life in such a way that religion and culture can be almost identical.

This is not to say that the focus of every Asian religion is the same. It may aim to observe a divine law. The goal may be the integration of the self with the Self. Its vision may be the highest truth that can be conceived. A personal God or gods may not feature in the religion at all; it may offer a way of self-realisation independent of any being greater than the self. Personal freedom may come through the progressive abandonment of personal desire. The religion may be concerned almost completely with relationships in society and may amount to an intricate and highly developed community code. The search for perfection and the great harmony may take many forms.

In Hinduism, Jainism, Buddhism, Confucianism, Shintoism

and Islam the religious quest takes widely different forms, but across the spectrum of the major Asian religions levels of devotion and degrees of discipline among adherents run very high indeed. Impressive mastery over the physical body may be gained through severe personal discipline and techniques of meditation. Demands for sacrifice are not trivial; a good Hindu may give away a quarter of income received. A Buddhist lama's training may take up to sixty years!

Nor should we imagine that Asian religion is merely a cold asceticism. As well as reverence there is familiarity, and warmth and generosity. Mahatma Gandhi when urged to take off his necklace of Vaaishnava beads replied to his Quaker friend, 'It is a sacred gift from my mother. I cannot without sufficient reason give up the necklace she put around my neck with love.' Gandhi's biographer comments further on the mother of that remarkable son: 'Her abounding love, her endless austerities and her iron will left a permanent impression upon him.'[14]

It would not be a service of the gospel to be grudging in admiration for the beautiful, the human, the loving and indeed the lofty mystical experiences which manifest themselves in religious Asia. That this continent has a special loveliness there can be no doubt. In common with others, it also has a special ugliness: a special cruelty as well as a special kindness. And perhaps not so surprising this cruelty manifests itself in the political as much or more than in the personal sphere.

Asia has the longest experience of poverty. Privilege has been deeply entrenched there, and so has misery. For many their place in society has been secured with the double lock of caste. The search for freedom and dignity through religion has so often been made against the background of immense political disadvantages. The oppressive and enslaving powers operate in the political and spiritual spheres. The forces from which both Abraham and Moses broke free still stalk Asia.

Should not Asia then have gained some hope of political freedom from the 'Christian' West. Tragically, through Western merchants and colonisers, there was added in Asia a new brand of exploitation. Admittedly they offered a prospect of freedom, but it was too distant. They developed a pattern of administration, but it was too proud. They provided a share for local people in the newly generated wealth, but it was too small.

One of Gandhi's struggles was to gain recompense from the European indigo planters on behalf of the poor tenant farmers of Bihar. He conducted an exhaustive investigation of the abuses of the system under which the tenants worked. When the world price of indigo dropped, the planters forced up the tenants' rents, taxed them for water from non-existent canals, and charged a death duty for the right of succession in the scheme. A commission of enquiry was forced to accept the overwhelming evidence of illegal exactions Gandhi had gleaned from 8,000 witnesses. Reluctantly the colonial administration requested a 25 per cent refund from the planters and reluctantly they repaid the tenants this fourth part of what they owed them.

There were no signs here of the Christ-inspired, repentant generosity of Zacchaeus, who willingly restored his debts fourfold. Over the recent past and until now, Christ's values have been sadly lacking in so many instances of Western involvement in Asia. As we have already seen, there has been a profound difference between the actually Christian missionaries in Asia and many of their nominally Christian compatriots in commerce and colonial administration. It has not been enough, though, that the missionaries were better. Many people in Asia have judged, and do judge, Christianity by the lives of its least appropriate representatives: those who make the cross appear to be a symbol of self-interest, not self-sacrifice.

This being so we cannot be surprised that Asia has reacted against the 'Christian West'. In the political sphere the movements on the grand scale have been Marxism (China, North Korea, Vietnam) and nationalism (India, Burma, Indonesia). In the programmes of Islamisation taking place in Pakistan and Iran the attempt is being made to build or rebuild the state upon the foundation of a religion which is seen as belonging to the place and the people.

For all the reasons stated so far it would be a bad mistake to underestimate the degree to which Christianity is unaccepted in Asia. It would be equally wrong, though, to remain unaware of the extent to which Christ's religion is being embraced. The proportion of professing Christians out of the total Asian population may seem small at 5.3 per cent, but when the overall numbers are considered it can be appreciated that Christian populations can be very significant in size. How many English people know that there are now more practising Christians in India than in their own country? Are we alert to the fact that throughout the Asian continent the membership of the churches is increasing more rapidly than the population? Did we know that the number of Asian nationals registered as full-time Christian workers is now a quarter of a million? Christian Asia is undoubtedly dwarfed by non-Christian Asia, but is itself already substantial in size and growing by 4 per cent every year.[15]

It might be tempting to focus exclusively upon the new and dynamic in the Asian Christian scene, but to appreciate its richness and depth tribute must be paid to its ancient and surviving churches. Predating Islam in Iraq and Iran and tracing their origin back to New Testament times (Lebanon and India) the ancient churches have maintained a Christian presence through the centuries and down to the present day. At best theirs has been a sustained and recognised holiness. Their mission has been to persist in face of unrelieved disadvantage and occasional persecution. In such circumstances their very survival is an eloquent sermon for those with ears to hear.

This not to say though that survival of churches can ever be taken for granted. In the Middle East the ancient churches are endangered by their divisions and more immediately threatened in some places by conditions of insecurity and violence. Nearest to where Christianity was born it still struggles to survive.

The experience of minority status for the ancient churches of Asia goes back for nearly two millenia. The churches born out of Roman Catholic and Protestant missions also begin to have a substantial history. They may be heirs to some movement of deprived peoples who saw in the gospel or the bearers of the gospel some hope of security and betterment. The leadership of these 'missionary' churches may now be in the hands of the descendants of individual converts: more privileged people who risked losing everything in standing out against the strongest social and religious pressures to gain Christ. Some of the missionary churches have become united churches. Particularly in the Indian subcontinent a divided Christian minority has been gravely disadvantaged in witnessing to vast Hindu and Muslim majorities. The formation of the Churches of North and South India and the Church of Pakistan has been a very positive step towards Asian Christian unity.

But now in Asia there are not only ancient surviving churches, the older missionary churches, but also the new dominant churches. The Roman Catholic Church in the Philippines cannot be called new; it has a similar past to that of Roman Catholic churches in Latin America. What is new is the influence of that church together with its Protestant sisters in securing the peaceful revolution of February 1986 which deposed the Marcos dictatorship. South Korea, following the Philippines towards a Christian majority, also has not only witnessed the largest evangelistic rally in history but also taken a decisive stand against abuses of human rights. In a similar way the Presbyterian Church in Taiwan has become champion of the political hopes of many people on that island. Churches in Indonesia have been outstanding in evangelistic vigour and the demonstration of miraculous signs. There are other remarkable instances of where Christian presence is most concentrated, and where Christian influence is most striking. Some of the tribal peoples of Asia are among the most deeply and completely evangelised of any in the world; the Mizos and the Nagas spring immediately to mind.

The challenge of mission

The missionary challenge of Asia is also inescapably a theological challenge. Quality and authenticity in Christian witness are surely at a premium in Asia. Anything foreign or secondhand will prove increasingly inadequate for Asian evangelism. 'If you bring us Christ, do not show him as a civilised European but as an ascetic Asian whose fortune is communion and whose wealth is prayer.' So said Keshub Chandra Sen.[16] His sharp challenge must be accepted. Mission in Asia must spring from, and nourish, *theology rooted in Asian soil and clothed in Asian dress*.

Like their brothers and sisters of other continents Asians have both hidden themselves from God and searched for him. There is a sense though in which the people of Asia have searched longer and harder for the Divine than those of any other continent. But if their search for God is to be truly related to his greater and sufficient search for them, then there need to be some very important connections. We have already thought about the rigorous disciplines in Asian religion and the mystical insights. A most remarkable climax of this religious quest is expressed by a Shintoist priest, Saigyo, before the altars of Ise: 'Who lives here?' he cries. 'I do not know, and yet I shed tears of gratitude.'[17]

However we are to understand such words as these, one thing is clear: the evangelist in Asia must present Christ in such a way that he is fully recognised. Sundar Singh, a convert from Hinduism, a Christian mystic and missionary to Tibet, describes a vision of the glorified Christ in this way: 'I felt when I first saw Him as if there were some old and forgotten connection between us, as though He had said, but not in words, "I am He, through whom you were created."'[18] The Sadhu Sundar Singh knew the living Christ as he is: not a figure in foreign dress but one who makes intimate communion with the Asian. In Christ, the Redeemer, he also recognised the Christ, through whom he, Sundar Singh, had been made, together with all creation. Thus the Sadhu grasped the 'old and forgotten connection' between the estranged creature and the loving Creator.

Such discovery and recognition must be the goal of both Christian theology and mission in Asia. Here is an essential part of its challenge. But this objective will not be reached without another essential: *sacrificial service, responding to the sufferings of Asia's Christ.* Asia knows a lot about religion; only the revelation of the authentic Christ can satisfy its quest. Asia knows a lot about suffering: only the suffering of Christ can heal its wounds. Those who preach the cross in Asia have also to carry the cross.

What easy words these are to write, but they are impressed upon me by the costly experience of Asian Christians I am privileged to meet: a Sri Lankan pastor risking the fury of Singhalese neighbours by protecting local Tamils; an Indian agriculturalist menaced time and again by powerful land-owners on account of his work alongside peasant farmers. Examples of cross-bearing like these also suggest how a third missionary challenge in Asia must be approached. Christian mission has to create *community which transcends Asia's divisions*. Churches in Asia formed perhaps from groups from one deprived and disadvantaged class now, through the power of Christ, need to build real relationships with people who are socially or racially different. How hard this is any-where in the world, but also how rewarding and fruitful if the price is paid.

A fourth and vital aspect of the missionary challenge in the continent is the gaining and the acting upon a *focused vision of evangelistic outreach among Asia's peoples*. We have reminded ourselves already of the vast and overwhelming dimensions of non-Christian Asia. Those outside the mem-bership of the Asian churches number more than two and a half billion. Each country in Asia has tens, hundreds or even thousands of parts of its population mosaic within which, as yet, no church exists. These contain people, the vast majority of whom have never heard the gospel and have none of their own kind to share it with them.

This challenge which faces our Christian brothers and sisters in Asia clearly exceeds all human resources. Only the direction and energy of the Holy Spirit is sufficient for this missionary task. Further, a non-Asian would rightly hesitate to bring any more detailed focus to the vision. Prompted by the Holy Spirit, however, the Asian churches are seeing clear objectives in the spread of the gospel. Among the emerging missions of India, the Friends' Missionary Prayer Band has set itself the goal of establishing evangelists in every state of the country. Comparable organisations, such as the Indonesian Missionary Fellowship and the Philippines Missionary Fellowship, are developing in other countries. The Gulf States are becoming the mission field of the Pakistani Church. Under the impulse of a charismatic revival the churches of Singapore are seeing the countries of Eastern Asia as their missionary responsibility. Libya, firmly closed to Western missionaries, affords access to some from Korea.

An evangelising church can also be a prophetic church. Yet another aspect of what the ascended Christ is requiring of his Asian people is that they should increasingly *declare his will to society at large*. Evidence of a response to this demand is found in the increased interest in political issues on the part of Indian Christians. More than before there is a Christian voice on matters of political importance. And there is every reason to be; unique among the Asian religions, Christianity looks to a purposeful future rather than an idealised past. In the face of otherwise intractable political problems the Christian can point towards hopeful political options, and all because the coming kingdom of Christ provides the key to such resourcefulness and hope.

'Islamisation is a friend of gospel advance. Its ultimate failure to satisfy becomes progressively more apparent.' 'Pakistan is looking for a viable alternative to Islam.' 'India is waiting for the full emergence of that costly expression of Christianity, which bears its own stamp of authenticity. Then there will be a massive turning to Christ.' What fanciful words these may appear! Yet they are the considered opinion of experienced missionaries, derived from what Asian colleagues have themselves discerned. The further the other great religious quests are pursued the more relevant God's sacrificial quest in the Person of Jesus Christ may be seen to be. Perhaps Asia does want Christianity. Certainly so, if it reveals, and not conceals Jesus, her Saviour.

Europe

Birmingham, in the English Midlands, together with Dusseldorf and Milan, mark out Europe's golden triangle, its wealthy heartland. I sit there on this northern apex doing my missionary sketching. Birmingham is my vantage point. I am a European looking out upon Europe. How far can I see from this perspective, limited as it must be? The highest hills outside Birmingham are the modest Lickeys, only just high enough to see across the city with its tower blocks jutting through the haze. What chance, I wonder again, is there of seeing across a continent?

Last summer a crowd of Christians met on the ridge of the Lickey hills to pray over the city of Birmingham. They prayed for local government, the police, schools, medical and social services, homes, and of course churches. Since then more have joined them in subsequent acts of prayer and witness. To pray over a city is to see it in a new light. Here, surely, is the way to see across the whole continent of Europe: to pray over it. That must be our task as we try to see in clear outline the missionary situation and the missionary challenge in Europe today.

Facts about Europe

But what is Europe? Vast as it is in our estimation, with its thirty sovereign states, it occupies a relatively small peninsula and offshore islands at the western end of the Asian landmass. Asia's ten million square miles of surface area makes Europe's two million appear quite modest. Equally, in terms of population Europe is no match for Asia: half a billion as against nearly three. Complicating the picture, Russia sits astride both, massive in area (eight and a half million square miles) but rather less dominant in population (a quarter of a billion).

History, more than geography, explains the significance of Europe in the world as whole. In the providence of God, Europe has been over many centuries the principal steward of his revelation in Christ. Her culture more than that of any other continent has been enlivened and enriched by the sustained influence of Christian revelation. Though members of her churches have so often underestimated or even been ignorant of fellow Christians in other parts of the world, it is still true that European Christians have outnumbered all others for most of the centuries since Pentecost. As late as 1900 there were as many or more professing Christians in Europe than in all other continents put together. As late as the 1970s Europe was sending out the largest number of Christian missionaries.

We shall not come to grips with Europe as a mission field if we ignore the Christian vision and achievement of the past. In order though to understand the present we have to recognise that even when Christian influence was at its strongest many challenges within the continent remained unmet, many danger signals ignored, and many peoples unevangelised. The nineteenth century was the great century of European expansion. Yet even when Europeans were busy altering the political and religious map of the world, another ideology, mindset, pervasive influence was gaining ground at home. In their optimism our Victorian forebears built their imposing Gothic churches. A subtle enemy of the gospel has now left so many of these buildings half deserted or derelict and empty. Their physical decay bears witness to spiritual retrenchment.

The missionary situation

In describing mission-field Europe, we must start with the dominant religion: secularism. This is now the principal factor shaping the lives of the majority of all Europeans. Eastern

Europe claims to be socialist, but isn't. Western Europe claims to be Christian, but isn't. Neither the gospel of Christ nor of Marx has gripped the minds and hearts of the mass of people in either half of this continent. Instead, incredible as it may seem, their hopes are fixed and their energies devoted to a strange mixture of materialism and humanism, never explained or justified, always assumed to be all there is, always pretending to be fulfilling and liberating, always in the end disappointing and enslaving.

Let us, though, put in a few good words for this monster. At least it has stripped away some false pretensions of the churches. In a secular state the church no longer operates from a position of power and privilege. It no longer controls welfare and education; instead the church is free to serve in these areas of life in which it no longer has monopoly. Secularism even releases people from some gods of superstition, sweeping aside some irrational fears and some crude beliefs.

We should be grateful for these gains and even see the hand of God in them. But then there are the grievous losses: the shrinkage of people's awareness to the narrow confines of the here and now, of the seen and the material world; the illusion of human self-sufficiency. Equally damaging is the way the secular mentality anaesthetises human consciousness so that for many the great issues of life and death pass apparently unnoticed. In this climate of thought good and evil become a matter of convenience. Small wonder then that Europe is a mission field again and that mission in secular Europe is an extremely difficult task.

Europe is not only depressingly secular but alarmingly divided. There is no suggestion that the continent was ever a political unity but now the divisions in Europe are more serious than ever before. The ideological divide between East and West Europe remains as a legacy from the Communist revolution and World War II. Ideological fervour in the East may be burning low, but a harder-line capitalism seems to dominate in the West. Perhaps more serious than the ideological disagreement itself are the methods by which the populations of East and Western Europe are held within their respective political systems. Coercion in the East is greater and more obvious; coercion in the West is less but more subtle.

Totally out of proportion with these differences, deep as they are, is a build-up of weaponry and military power either side of Europe's east-west boundary, which is immeasurably more dangerous than anything that has ever been experienced in her deeply troubled history. There is nowhere in the world where the menace of nuclear war has been more keenly felt than in Europe. For most people on the surface of their lives the threat is not acknowledged. Little is said, but it is felt none the less. Returning to Europe from Latin America in the late '70s I felt this threat in a new way even though no one put it into words. One must hope that this climate of fear is substantially improved if the East-West treaty on intermediate range nuclear weapons is ratified, and that other kinds of armaments do not replace the weaponry scrapped.

The wickedly devastating power and the absurd overkill of the weapons still facing one another either side of Europe's ideological curtain give expression to her most obvious division. But there are others. In spite of common markets in both East and West, narrow national interests and rivalries prevent the degree of mutual benefit and enrichment which would otherwise be possible. Europe has never been racially homogenous, but now the minorities of people of Asian and African origin are substantially greater than before. As a result there is a new degree of both ethnic and religious plurality in society. Although there are examples of harmonious integration between races there is also the constant threat of racial tension and the occasional explosion of racial violence in Europe's cities. And, as if ideological, national and racial divisions were not enough, there is a gap between the generations. The nuclear family in Europe is pared down to an unstable minimum leaving many individuals alone in an impersonal and unsupportive world.

But is the European scene really as bad as this? Not as I

look out of a window and a wintry sunset lights up a tree-lined suburb. Surely, though, this view is not typical; what do I see from a high-rise flat in the inner city? The outlook from the one I know is not bad either: the spectacular curves of a motorway junction, a boating lake, a hypermarket and more high-rise blocks. In both cases the pleasant appearance reflects Europe's material prosperity, for which we may be grateful indeed. However, behind the appearance lies yet another division: the growing separation between the affluent European and his poorer neighbour who suffers a special kind of pain from having so much less. It is not the locals who go in for windsurfing on that lake near Spaghetti Junction; dole money hardly stretches that far!

We must emphasise Europe's material prosperity, as well as her complex divisions. Equally, we must keep in view not only her secularity but her Christianity. And here we come up against a difficulty that has been in the background all the time. European Christianity is almost as diversely different in its local expressions as Europe itself. How can any generalisation have any value? Will a sketch bear any relation to reality?

In answer, let's start with the rather prosaic statistics. According to the *World Christian Encyclopedia* the percentage of nominal Christians in Europe as a whole is estimated at 84.2 for 1984. The figure for individual countries varies between 99.5 for the Republic of Ireland and 5.4 for Albania where the state is so hostile to all religion that none can be professed openly. Though the highest figure that can be categorised as 'Christian' varies as widely as this there are other almost universal trends.[19] Weekly church attendance is consistently much lower throughout Europe. Of the 96 per cent of the population of Norway which belongs to the Lutheran church there, only 3 per cent will be in attendance on Sunday. Of the 99 per cent in Italy who adhere to the Roman Catholic Church, only 6 per cent will receive Communion each week. In England, where 87 per cent of all people claim some Christian allegiance, weekly church attendance varies between 8 and 11 per cent in different regions. In East

Germany, where there can be few prizes from the state for professing to be a Christian, nominal church membership remains surprisingly high at 63 per cent. Actual attendance is much lower.[20]

If we turn our attention to the other end of the religious spectrum we find the percentages of people who have deliberately opted out of any Christian identity correspondingly small. Throughout Europe (excluding the USSR) about 10 per cent of the population is classified as non-religious. The proportion of declared atheists peaks at 19 per cent in Albania, where presumably incentives to deny belief in God are strongest. Without any such compulsion nearly 12 per cent of Sweden's citizens describe themselves as atheists. In Russia, though, there are still fewer professing atheists than professing Christians

It would be tempting to imagine that the main religious differences in Europe are between East and West. There is, of course, a major North-South, Protestant-Catholic divide, and it is easy for a Northern Protestant to give an unbalanced perspective. The South naturally has its own characteristics. Modern Spain, with all its changes, still struggles to come to terms with its religious past. It is as if the ashes of an old fire of piety and zeal are choking new spiritual life. The Roman Catholic Church suffers from the political power and social influence it wielded in the past. A younger generation of Spaniards are determined that it should not control life to that extent again.

In Spain there are uncertainties not only for the Roman Catholic majority but also for the evangelical minority. No longer suffering discrimination or even persecution, as they did under Franco, they need an even clearer self-understanding and identity. Meanwhile Spain lives in a spiritual vacuum. Evangelicals able to demonstrate the authentically Christian, national and international quality of their life and message have a true solution to Spain's religious dilemma. The charismatic movement in the Roman Catholic Church is also a means of meeting an unsatisfied spiritual thirst. Some very creative work among young people is being done by both Catholics and evangelicals.

The major non-Christian religion in Europe is Islam; this faith is held by nearly 2 per cent of people in Europe. Immigration and higher birth rates as well as missionary fervour is producing considerable growth of Muslim communities in some countries. This is generally, however, from a relatively low base. Vision and ambition is not lacking: 'We are few but we can change this country,' a Muslim spokesman in Northern England asserts with immense confidence. Even so the future progress of Islam may be as threatened by secularism as other religious persuasions are. Percentage of Jews, drastically reduced as a result of the crimes against them during World War II, now remains steady at 0.3. European Muslims and Jews are numbered in millions, Hindus, Sikhs and Buddhists in hundreds of thousands, Chinese Folk Religionists, Baha'is and Spiritists include tens of thousands.

Profoundly important as they are in themselves and as a focus of evangelistic concern, the peoples in Europe who profess some other religion or who confess atheism are much less numerous than those who retain a nominal allegiance to Christianity. The Christian church in Europe evidently has a small core but a massive fringe. Secular values largely control the lives of this majority, but some residual belief, some partly Christian folk religion remains operative among these hundreds of millions of people.

God forgive us if we forget Europe's Christian fringe. But what are we to think of the core? In all its varied forms, how are we to picture it? A densely packed congregation standing shoulder to shoulder at an Easter service in Moscow... Young people praying outside the perimeter fence of a missile site... A relaxed and colourful crowd at a family service in Western suburbia... An old priest, defying Albanian law and baptising a baby... A football stadium filled for an evangelistic crusade, its stands echoing and alive with gospel music... A great Gothic shell of an inner-city church with a little group huddled around a blow heater... Christian leaders drafting a plea for international reconciliation... Little children excitedly showing mum and dad their Sunday school paintings.

From one point of view Europe's Christian core is very weak. Between, and even within, denominations its churches are divided. The lives of its members conform too closely to the materialistic ways of non-churchgoing neighbours. What is perceived as a 'scientific' outlook is allowed to inhibit belief in the saving acts and intervention of the living God. Parochialism is the number one disease among European Christians. Those in the UK were ill-prepared to receive and welcome their brothers and sisters immigrating from the Caribbean. All too often they still look neither beyond their own nation, their own district, nor their own social group. In comparison with the joy of the Africans, the energy of the Americans and the quiet depth of the Asians, European Christians may appear blinkered, uncertain and lacking in vision.

In overall terms the figures for church growth in Europe reflect this negative picture. In nearly all countries numbers of affiliated church members are either increasing at a slower rate than the population or else decreasing. A notable exception, however, is provided by the Soviet Union; here church growth is now higher than population growth, and the Russian churches are said to be gaining a million new members per year.

Across Europe very substantial increases are occurring among renewal groups drawn from the reservoir of membership of the majority churches. Typical of these is the 'Lord's Army' in Romania and 'Oasis' in Poland.[21] Both in East and West, Pentecostal churches also show substantial and widespread growth.

Such trends as these point to that other side of church life in Europe today. Think of the resilient stubbornness which keeps the Christian flame burning in Eastern Europe long after official propaganda predicted its extinction. Even the affluence and indifference of Western Europe has failed to quench the fires of the Spirit there. The best qualities of European Christianity are reflected in vigorous movements of evangelism among students, a serious grappling with political issues that leaders of government are failing to address, the provision of meeting-places where people can find acceptance, warmth and reality, commitment to painstaking social caring in areas where other agencies of concern are hopelessly overstretched.

Overall the church in Europe may not be evangelistically dynamic but it is not impotent. There may be many inconsistencies in its own social relationships and attitudes, but what it aspires to in these terms is not easy for even one-party governments to ignore. After all, the Christian churches remain by far the largest voluntary grouping throughout the continent. 'Their small army of full-time professional workers and big army of unpaid voluntary ones would be the envy of any political party.'[22] This comment by David Winter on the British churches would find an echo in many other nations. He continues: 'The army of Christ may be a motley horde, with regimental rivalry, bickering generals, and a stubbornly independent yeomanry, but it exists...and it is on the move.' The missionary situation in Europe today is determined not so much by the frustrating failures of her churches, but, in the hands of God, by their surprising potential.

The missionary challenge

If Jesus Christ with his first handful of followers could propose the evangelisation of the world, then the fifty million or so of his European disciples active today could surely contemplate the re-evangelisation of their continent. Should such an evangelistic idea appear to us naive or extravagant then we Europeans must have relinquished the missionary confidence, which, with our other Christian brothers and sisters, is our birthright from the Day of Pentecost.

Recovering the missionary confidence Mission is all about moving out with the love of Christ to the other person or community. Paradoxically, for Europe, there needs to be a powerful process of 'moving in'. Europe's Christians themselves need to hear the gospel afresh, digest it deeply, appropriate it personally, wonder at it intensely, and glory in it exultantly. There are special reasons why European Christians have given a muted response to the gospel, but now there are special reasons why that response should be wholehearted and complete.

It is no excuse that we should be trapped by our history. What if 500 years ago Europe was Christendom and all her citizens were theoretically 'under the gospel'? Haven't we had long enough to wake up to the urgency of the missionary situation we are in? And suppose some of our nineteenth-century forebears exhibited in some respects the wrong kind of confidence in the gospel, confusing their cultural assumptions with the ways of Christ? Does this mean that we should spend yet another century bewailing their missionary mistakes? Are we to allow a fear of wrongly imposing our culture upon others to inhibit a proper contribution in Christ's mission today, while we remain unaware of the extent to which our cultural assumptions weaken our own grasp upon Christ's saving truth? Christ's truth is the reliable truth of the faithful Father God. This truth, which gives the Old and New Testament Scriptures their unique quality, judges all other truth. Our Western scientific truth cannot proudly arbitrate over revelation. Scientific truth becomes less predicable the further it is pursued. Western technology cannot determine what we should and should not do; the nuclear and other accidents of 1986 are reminder enough of its fallibility and dubious benefit. Our European culture both traditional and modern needs to be corrected and reshaped by the gospel of Christ, thus setting our people free.

The recovery in Europe of missionary confidence depends upon her churches putting confidence in the right place. Christ, the Sin Bearer; Christ, the Saviour-Healer; Christ, the Humble Servant; Christ, God who reveals God: this Christ, to whom the Spirit bears witness, is the unique and sufficient foundation upon which confidence and hope can be rebuilt. In the pluralistic and pessimistic society of Europe, Christ-

centred confidence stands out in a special way. Because Christ
is the Person for all people, no one belonging to any social or
racial group need be excluded. He welcomes all. Because
Christ's own approach has a quality of hiddeness and humility, the radiant resurrection hope that he brings shines with
the purest light. A more confident European Christianity will
not be brittle and brash; not if it is true to the Christ whose
name it bears.

Assuming the missionary responsibility 'None of us is inno-
cent any more. We all share the sinfulness of our situations
and we are all in need and we all have something to offer.'
Barney Milligan, quoting Philip Potter, in his book, *The New
Nomads*,[23] is arguing that the end of European dominance in
mission creates the opportunity for Europe's re-entry upon
the world scene on a basis of 'equality and mutuality'. European churches need not be leaders but they can be partners;
they do not have to call the tune, but they can contribute to
the harmony. With the balancing discernment of Christ's
Spirit they can look back; with the humble hopefulness of
Christ's Spirit they can look ahead.

Through the generous grace of God, Europe's Christians
are being invited again to assume their full share of responsibility in Christ's mission. To do so they must combine in an
obedience that has many different but complementary
expressions. First they must confront the powers of evil still
entrenched in their own society. The body of believers must
attack the invisible spirits of materialism: all that trivialises
life, depresses, manipulates and puts to sleep. Worship of the
living God provides the truest liberation from the deadening
influences of a secular and materialistic world. Out of this
worship must spring a theology which is biblical, contemporary, lived out in ordinary lives.

A knowledge of the living God discovered in the context of
modern secular Europe must challenge the devils of hatred
and division which still walk at large. Across the East-West
divide in Europe the churches must be increasingly engaged in
'detente from below'. At a cost on the capitalist as well as the

Communist side, Christians must continue to find ways of affirming their membership of the one international family of Christ and of opposing government policies which threaten those beyond their borders. Following a notable French example in 1978,[24] other European churches must do all they can to ensure that immigrants from Africa, Asia and the Caribbean are treated with equal rights and opportunities as citizens.

Economic interests are often entangled with racial discrimination. Christian influence needs to be mobilised on the side of every plan aimed at a genuine sharing of economic benefit. In challenging Common Market or national governments to fight poverty Christian people need to ensure that their own actions and generosity truly reflect Christ's priorities. With the re-encroachment of poverty in the deprived areas of an increasing number of European cities, the churches will need to take responsibility for the kind of social engagement previously thought only to be necessary in the Third World.

In Europe, as in all other continents, the mission of Jesus Christ confronts evil, serves good, converts sinners and trains saints. Perhaps more than any others, European Christians have been guilty of trying to divide the indivisible. However, Christian missionary responsibility is such that neither its evangelistic nor its social dimensions can be separated or evaded. Without weakening social commitments or even political interventions, now is the time in Europe for the making of disciples. Our missionary responsibility in this continent is to further the missionary vision of the first apostles to Europe. They looked forward to transformed societies composed of converted people. Why should their successors commit themselves to anything less?

Grasping the missionary opportunity If only to watch and pray and wait, every moment is a moment of missionary opportunity. The question is: what kind of opportunity for mission presents itself in Europe now? The responsibility laid upon the churches is a great and inclusive one. There is a basis for the recovery of a confidence with which to face up to such responsibility. How receptive though is Europe in this decade for the gospel of Christ?

We have already seen that Europe contains a very large Christian fringe: a body of people who do not identify with the churches in active membership yet who hold back from any formal repudiation of Christianity and retain some of its belief and values in the background of their lives. This fringe group is massive indeed; perhaps 300 million people throughout Europe. The presence of such an element, unparalleled in either Africa or Asia, must have some bearing upon Europe's missionary opportunity.

It may be safest to say that this 'Christian fringe' makes Europe potentially rather than actually receptive to the gospel. Stanley Davies of the Evangelical Missionary Alliance has commented to me that, 'an incipient Christianity has inoculated people in Europe from the real thing'. Certainly the continent does not beckon the Christian missionary with easy pickings. Life in its cities is fragmented and impersonal, in its rural areas warily conservative. It is difficult to gather people for any purpose wider than some specialist interest. Secular materialism has bitten deep into Europe's soul and leaves an aching pain.

But herein lies the opportunity: it is an invitation to enter into sorrow! Christian mission in Europe must be a compassionate self-identifying approach to those whose secular world is disintegrating and full of sorrow: the agonising sorrow of the drug addict in withdrawal; the unrelieved sorrow of the lonely flat-dweller; the uncomforted sorrow of the divorcee. The harvest of such sorrows is abundant; the European way of life produces them with ruthless efficiency.

This being so, authentic Christian mission in Europe must involve weeping with those who weep. Christ asks such sympathy for its own sake. Many of those who are reaching the end of their secular road, whether or not they can articulate their need, are crying out for something better. 'Isn't there a better song?' is the plaintive question posed in the film, *Educating Rita*. To which there is the typically secular reply:

'No! Only a different one.' But the truth is that there is not only a better song but a new song. It tells of a Man who entered into our sorrows that we might enter into his joy.

Christians in Europe cannot complain of a small missionary opportunity, only a difficult one: too difficult in fact for them to grasp unaided. Particularly in Western Europe, where the felt need may be less, the actual need is greatest for significant missionary reinforcement from other parts of the world church. In the East the churches are modelling a way of life which is clearly and attractively different from that presented by the secular state. In the West we need other Christian brothers and sisters to share with us in discovering and demonstrating a more compassionate, less compromised, life pattern here. With the contribution of missionaries from Africa, Asia, the Pacific and the Americas, the effect of this international inter-cultural ministry should not be under-estimated. Authentic cross-bearing, barrier-eroding witness could yet win back the whole continent.

Oceania

As its name suggests, this continent is given its special quality by the ocean which surrounds and separates its widely scattered islands. Apart from the great landmass of Australia (nearly three million square miles) and the moderate sized Papua New Guinea and New Zealand, Oceania consists of thousands of small islands set in the vastness of the Pacific Ocean. From the Polynesian Islands in the far east, through Micronesia to Melanesia it is 6,000 miles: more than the distance from Britain to Bolivia.

With this huge stretch of water within its compass, Oceania matches any of the other six continents in geographical extent. In terms of population it is much smaller: 26 million as against 2,700 million in Asia. The majority of these people are of European immigrant stock; in Australia the Aborigines represent only 1 per cent of the population. However, though small, the Pacific Islands are densely populated and in these the indigenous peoples vastly outnumber Anglo-Australians or other immigrants. Fiji is unique in having a substantial population of Indian descent.

Again the question presents itself: where is the unity in such a diverse and scattered region of the world? What connection, if any, is there between Sydney and Samoa or between Tasmania and Tonga? Obviously there was a wealth of traditions, customs, laws and beliefs shared by the Pacific peoples before the arrival of Captain Cook and the adventurers, colonisers and missionaries who were to follow him. With all the massive changes of the past 200 years, what now? Where is the orderly design that makes sense out of the mixture of haunting beauty and brooding tragedy characteristic of Oceania?

The missionary situation

The missionary situation in this region today is the result of a short but remarkable history. It is true that Australia and New Zealand were made at least nominally Christian largely by immigration. The Pacific Islands, however, have a missionary story which far outstrips in interest the popular stereotypes. Not only were there the European heroes and martyrs such as John Williams. Names such as Vahapata, Ruatoka and Joeli Bulu deserve equal respect. They represent the hundreds of South Pacific missionaries who travelled with unwearied cheerfulness in open canoes, along unfamiliar shores, working in new languages, building houses, leading village after village into Christianity by conversations round cooking-fires and kava bowls.

This, with the attendant setbacks and failures, is the theme of John Garett's *To Live among the Stars*. He explains, 'Pacific Islander Christians have a special way of comprehending the world. Most human beings look outward on solid earth. Islanders live on small pieces of earth surrounded by the wealth and menace of the sea... Travel and arrival, life and death, the Good News and the prospect of "life among the stars" have distinct meanings... Christ is the Pacific Prince, Chief of Chiefs, come from afar... An ocean of suffering is illuminated by the cross... There is hope for island ancesters who awaited a covenant of grace.'[25]

South Pacific missionaries and South Pacific understandings played a vital part in the evangelisation of this region. They did their work well; today in the islands professing Christians represent more than 90 per cent of the population. Churches which grew out of Presbyterian, Methodist and Roman Catholic missions co-operate in a Pacific Council of Churches. When natural disaster has struck one island, Christian influence has been strong in mobilising support from other islands. Christian leaders are prominent in the struggle to rid the region of nuclear tests and other threats to the environment. Now they face the challenge of working out together a just solution to the conflict of interests between indigenous Fijians and the Indian community on that island.

But why the emphasis on the Pacific Islands when the larger part of the population of the region is concentrated in Australia and New Zealand? It is easier to comment on the islands because the churches there have the stronger distinctives. The European settlers in Australasia brought their Christianity with them. Their Christian descendants are now saying that they are seeking a way of following Christ which is not prepackaged and imported from the West. Currently 84 per cent of the people of Australia profess a Christian allegiance and approximately 20 per cent attend church regularly on Sundays. This last figure is high, by British standards at least, and so too is the number of missionaries sent out by the Australian and New Zealand churches. (One missionary sent overseas as against eight full-time Christian workers in total, as compared with one in ten in the UK.) Who knows what benefit might follow some further outworking of renewal both watered by the Spirit and rooted in Australian and New Zealand soil?[26]

The missionary challenge

'We are all here: men, women, children and dogs before you.' Thus begins a village prayer in the islands. Tahitian chorus music sounds like 'an ocean wave coming in with growing strength as the voices grow in intensity, breaking and rolling and bounding, and then dying down and gradually disappearing in a long sustained note'.[27] 'We want to see Christ born in our local places... We must recognise him as one of us.' Such is the vision of Leslie Boseto who served as moderator of the United Church of Papua New Guinea.[28]

The prayer, the music and the leader's challenge reflect the way the Pacific peoples have accepted the gospel and allowed it to transform the traditional life of the islands. But already a powerful secular way is breaking in and there is a new generation to teach and to win: young people deeply influenced by the values of the sophisticated modern media, contrasting so sharply with the simple preaching of the village pastors. In the nineteenth century Christianity was advancing at the double. The danger now is that it should be marking time.

A clear priority for the churches in the islands is that they should evangelise the new generation and enlist young people in every kind of Christian service, tackling the social as well as the spiritual needs of the communities. Where this is happening a new missionary thrust can be seen; Pacific Island missionaries are serving in the Aboriginal communities in Australia and contributing to the movement of renewal which many of these peoples are now enjoying.

Looking though at the region as a whole, including its centre of gravity population-wise in the cities of Australia and New Zealand, then the missionary challenge is greater still: to bring the hope, the healing and the vitality of Christ to so many people affected by the dead hand of materialism and all the injustices and slaveries associated with it. In these urban areas there are also young people, many at present unemployed, who need to hear the gospel and see it demonstrated.

In this situation of rapid change, spectacular development, and incipient decay the Australians, New Zealanders and Pacific Islanders need each other. Might not a newly strengthened missionary partnership between Christians

from Austral-Asia on the one hand and the islands on the
other pave the way for a substantial advance of the kingdom
of Christ? Perhaps the Pacific missionaries should not only
serve among the Aborigines. Might they not give added
impetus to evangelistic work more widely in Australia and
New Zealand? Might there not be an experience of race relations among the churches in those countries which could contribute to Fiji's special problems? Perhaps Anglo-Australians
and islanders will discover entirely new spheres of mission in
partnership. Certainly it will be with the diversities of people
together that an Oceanic Christianity will come to full flower.
That will bring a fruitful purpose not only to a surf-lined continent but also to a searching world.

Northern America

When I worked in South America people would sometimes
ask me, 'Are you from the United States?' 'No,' I would
reply, 'I'm British.' Then they would say, 'Isn't that part of the
United States?' 'Not exactly!' Clearly Canada is no more a
part of the United States than Britain is. Even so, for the purpose of this missionary sketch we will group the two nations
together. Between them they occupy a massive seven and a
half million square miles. Canada has the edge on the United
States for land surface, but the US, with a population of 224
million, has nearly 10 times more inhabitants.

Marks of history

Like other regions of the world, Northern America is indelibly
marked by its history. For both the United States and Canada
there is the hard-won survival of the pioneer settlers, the cultural dislocation, 'trail of tears' and material loss of the native
Indians, the progressive exploitation by the transplanted
people of Europe of the vast resource of land with its rich minerals, timber and agriculture. Both nations have received and
assimilated an avalanche of immigrants. Both have succeeded
in forging a degree of unity out of much diversity.

The founding fathers of the United States invented not only a constitution but a nation. It was their optimism and ingenuity in counterbalancing interests that gave lasting validity to the clause: 'Governments are instituted among men, deriving their just powers from the consent of the governed.' They expressed the vision that 'all men are created equal... endowed with unalienable rights... to life, liberty and the pursuit of happiness.' And, it was soon added, 'the acquisition and protection of property'.

The capacity to do just that was characteristic of the very first colonies on the Atlantic seaboard. These were commercial companies as well as settler communities. Capitalistic enterprise and entrepreneurial drive have been typical American traits from the beginning. In time mechanisation greatly increased the business man's capacity to make money; Eli Whitney's cotton gin was just the first of a series of different machines and innovations culminating in the factory assembly line, mass production, and most recently the microchip and the communications revolution. Each time there has been a new commercial need there has been a new invention to meet it.

Unfortunately technical inventiveness does not meet all human need so readily. The black slaves still worked sixteen hours a day in the plantations. Under the robber barons the newly arrived immigrants still worked seventy hours a week in the factories. As Alistair Cooke observed, 'The lowly status of the Negro has relentlessly mocked...the American declaration that all men are created equal.'[29] On a Thanksgiving Day even in the 1980s there are poor whites as well as poor blacks who go homeless and hungry in the wealthiest country in the world.

Marks of the gospel

Commerce was there undoubtedly at the founding of both the United States and Canada, and so was Christianity. William Crawshaw, preaching to those embarking for Virginia in 1607, reminded them that religion was the 'maine and cheefe purpose' of the colony. 'Take nothing from a heathen against his will, but in fair and lawful bargain. Cast aside all cogitations of profit; the enlarging of the Kingdom of Jesus Christ is inducement strong enough.'[30]

The New World would have been a thousand times new if this advice had been followed consistently. The conflicts, injustices and tragedies of the last 400 years are sufficient witness to the failure, but these must not obscure the fruits of 'collective faithfulness'. The truth is that in part, though not in whole, the gospel did guide and inform the development of the colonies and the emerging nations. There was William Penn's 'Holy Experiment' in setting up in 1682 a colony featuring religious toleration and just treatment of the Indians. It was during the period of evangelical revival between 1725 and 1760, called The Great Awakening, that Jonathan Edwards first glimpsed a world role in Christian mission for his country, thus permanently influencing US history. Meanwhile the churches effectively followed the westward movement of population on the expanding frontier. The saddle-bag parson was 'courier of news, teacher of children, bringer of comfort' even 'catalyst for change'.[31] In Canada particularly the missionaries were there first. It followed that 'the Canadian west was never to be the "Wild West" experienced south of the border. There were no Indian massacres, no Cavalry charges.'[32]

Rodney Booth, in *Winds of God*, pays tribute to the missionary contribution among the Indians in this way. But clearly both north and south of the border there were many whites in need of conversion. In this situation 'revivalism' developed as a new and distinctive approach to evangelism. With the religious freedom which was so much a characteristic of the newly independent United States, people belonged to a variety of Christian denominations, or none. Vigorous preaching aimed at winning back the unchurched. Over the years millions came to adopt a significant and personal faith, having walked forward down the 'sawdust trail' in the evangelists' tents.

As the twentieth century dawned the Protestant denominations were coming close to making the United States a Christian nation. They could begin to see in religious terms a decisive world role for their country, first anticipated by Jonathan Edwards. A high point came with the intervention of the US in World War I and the resultant victory for the Allies. President Woodrow Wilson declared, 'Everything for which America fought has been accomplished...We are to be an instrument in the hands of God to see that liberty is made secure for all mankind.'[33]

The mainline churches enthusiastically supported the president's vision, related it to the task of world mission and had high hopes for the League of Nations. What they discovered, though, in the post-war years was that they could not carry the public with them: a public that was becoming more secular than Christian. There also emerged a deep rift between liberals and fundamentalists, and evangelicals began to identify as a distinguishable group, within and outside the mainline denominations. After the euphoria of 1918, Christians in the United States faced divisions within their ranks and indifference without.

The missionary challenge today

If the churches in Europe need to reappropriate the gospel of confident hope the churches of the United States need to discover again the gospel of authentic unity. At one level it is a matter of generosity of spirit and affirmation of each other's vocations. As a non-American I am always impressed by the generosity of American Christians. Generosity is one of God's gifts to his American people. These generous Christians of different traditions now need to be generous to each other.

I am not so much thinking of generosity across the Catholic-Protestant divide, but rather across the evangelical-ecumenical or evangelical-radical divide. It has been a vital concern of American evangelicals to declare the authority of Scripture, the givenness of revelation, the uniqueness of Christ, the sufficiency of his cross, the imminence of his return, and the imperative of making disciples. For Christians this is an authentic and essential calling and should be unhesitatingly and warmly affirmed. Ecumenical and radical Christians are deeply committed to God's requirement of justice and peace in society, to solidarity with the victims of political and economic oppression, to the rooting of the gospel in the rich diversity of human cultures. These concerns are also unquestionably and essentially Christian, and should be approved as such.

And herein lies the missionary challenge. Both these vital areas of concern must be held together for a full missionary obedience. If the first is weakened or denied, the gospel is robbed of its substance. If the second is not attempted then the gospel is not adequately applied. So the evangelicals must affirm the radicals and the radicals must affirm the evangelicals in their truest intentions.

Difficult as that may be in North America with its Christian polarisations, it is still not enough. I dare to say that appreciation of the other needs to be combined with criticism of the self. Both evangelicals and radicals are liable to distort the very gospel they are so zealous to obey. Ironically both may make the identical mistake: identifying the gospel too closely with the political ideology they most favour. In the wake of the Irangate scandal it is easy for the watching world to see the mistake of Jerry Falwell and his Moral Majority in their support for Ronald Reagan. For the Christian left a heavy Marxist filter can obscure the glory and the love of God. And how wise is it to assume that each new radical cause is righteous? There are no short cuts to Christian discernment and obedience. The search for an authentic Christian unity between dissimilar disciples is an essential step. Its urgency in the United States is great because divisions there are so readily exported around the world.

A Holy Spirit-prompted unity between Christians equips them for mission. Such unity brings together people of different cultures. The USA currently has 57,000 Christian workers serving beyond her borders and Canada 10,000. The two countries together receive nearly 22,000 workers. The sending and receiving of missionaries on this substantial scale creates a great opportunity for mutual learning. This process will be beneficial for all, not least for evangelical churches which God has blessed in the sending and the teaching. God will bless them again as they are corrected and taught by the converts grown into leaders coming back to them from the Third World.

Humanly very difficult, but full of potential good, will be the further reconciliation between white and black and Amerindian Christians and churches. Both the depths of the wounds and the extent of the healing possible through Christ need to be discovered. Rodney Booth tells the story of Thomas Crosby sitting in council with a tribe on Vancouver Island. 'A young brave, under the influence of alcohol, had shot his own father. "Oh missionary," one old brave said, "You bring us good words, the Book tells us of good things, but look at that dead chief. Are you not ashamed of your white brother? Why don't you convert him? He had the Book. Why doesn't he stop making and selling whisky?" As the old orator poured forth his eloquent address in his own language, I felt, for the first time, ashamed that I was a white man.'[34]

The white world, and not only in Northern America, is shamed by the dawning realisation of the destructive effects of its way of life upon that of others. The question is what do we do with this shame? Suppress it? Remain submerged in it? Bring it to Christ and to the offended brother and sister for repentance and forgiveness and reconciliation? If the white radicals and evangelicals come together so much the better. The first may help the second to repent and the second may help the first to believe.

It may seem strange to give such a strong emphasis upon unity and reconciliation in trying to identify a Northern American missionary challenge. What about the outreach, the discipling, the confronting, the breaking of new ground?

Well, authentic unity and costly reconciliation do break new ground, and, moreover, they represent a vital preparation for the next steps.

Like Europe, Northern America has a large body of people on the fringe of its churches, some of whom are predisposed to accept membership if the Christian message is presented to them and Christian caring demonstrated. Indeed the North American energy and genius for organisation is bringing them into the churches. Even with such vigorous life, however, the overall number of Christians shows only a marginal increase, less than population growth. Furthermore numbers who specifically deny Christian belief are increasing steadily in both Canada and the United States.

It follows that within the region there are more and more people who are either intellectually or socially alienated from the churches. Effective evangelism among these 'outsiders' will demand new qualities from the Christians: new degrees of reconciliation between churches of different ethnic groups and different traditions. When it comes to penetrating the 'gaiety and grief' of the pleasure cities like Las Vegas, the frustration and fear of Chicago's east side, or even the anonymity and foul air of Los Angeles then an authentic, in person, and costly witness is required. The full vertical dimension to which the evangelicals point and the wide horizontal about which the radicals are concerned will both be needed. Thus equipped, the American churches so long divided could discover a unified quest in reaching out to the neediest and most alienated in their midst.

And then there is something which overshadows the needy and the affluent, the integrated and the alienated American. Dwight Eisenhower in his farewell address as president spoke of it in these terms:

> Until the latest of our world conflicts the United States had no (permanent) arms industry...the conjunction of an immense military establishment and a large arms industry is new in the American experience. The total influence—economic, political,

even spiritual—is felt in every city... We recognise the imperative need for this development. Yet we must not fail to comprehend its grave implications... We must guard against the acquisition of unwarranted influence, whether sought or unsought, by the military-industrial complex... The potential for the disastrous rise of misplaced power exists and will persist. Only an alert and knowledgeable citizenry can compel the proper meshing of the huge industrial and military machinery of defence with our peaceful methods and goals.[35]

Alistair Cooke departs from the usual urbane style of his American commentary in making a similar and very sharp point: 'The greatest danger is that the technology of the unthinkable war will enchant its practitioners, growing so subtle and mighty as to acquire a momentum all of its own, which mere men will be powerless to subdue.'[36] Now neither Eisenhower nor Cooke talk about these misplaced powers and enchantments in the language of the New Testament. What is indisputable is that since these warnings were given, both in the United States and among all the nuclear powers, they have grown more threatening still.

So with sister churches across the political divides, the North American churches have to confront the runaway powers. This is an inescapable part of their mission. Forces of chaos must be banished from the centres of military power. Like Boniface of old, Christians must fell the sacred oak of Thor, the war god. A trial by ordeal, a great exorcism, is needed to hold in check and then put into reverse the arms race. The dimensions of the missionary conflict are of this kind. Nowhere is it more critical than in the United States of America.

Conclusion

The short history of the two northernmost nations of America leaves its deeply graven pattern. Its heritage is to leave one of them in advance of all other nations in material resources, technological development, military power, communication capacity, indeed every manifestation of modernity, including the negatives: drug taking, street violence, and social disintegration. This position out in front is an exposed and lonely one. A nation which after World War II set out to 'restore the fabric of Europe' cannot escape a world role.

The nation cannot escape a world role and neither can the churches. Much is demanded of them: pioneering a Christian way in society reshaped by 'third wave' computer technology; combining the opportunities of material wealth with the attitudes of spiritual humility; redirecting the nation itself so that it becomes unambiguously a force for world peace; continuing unabated and indeed intensifying their commitment to global mission while willingly taking second place to Third World churches in new initiatives. All these only 'Spirit possible' things will require of our Northern American brothers and sisters new degrees of unity and reconciliation among themselves.

In America the race is on between decadence and vitality. For the sake of God's missionary purpose, God's whole people there must influence the result.

Latin America

The region

In many British atlases the South American continent and the Latin American countries appear on the last pages and in small scale. In a missionary atlas the scales should be consistent. Now for us Latin America is top page. We discover at once there is much more to America than the United States and Canada, great as these countries undoubtedly are. To be precise, Latin America means 8,187,000 square miles and 419 million people: a greater surface area and nearly double the population.

The most natural place to divide the Americas is through the Isthmus of Panama. Latin America, however, includes Mexico in North America, six Central American republics, three of the biggest islands in the Caribbean, and thirteen republics which occupy the southern subcontinent. Brazil was colonised from Portugal and retains Portuguese as its national language. With the exception of Haiti with its French influence, the rest of this vast region shares a Spanish colonial history and has Spanish as a common language.

Although shared languages aid communication in Latin America, there are massive natural barriers. The Andes wall, traversing the subcontinent, is more than 4 miles high at its highest and 500 miles wide at its widest. The Amazon Basin is three times as big as any other river basin anywhere in the world. In the Pampas, Argentina has an agricultural area comparable with the North American prairies. Buenos Aires, a southern counterpart of Chicago, developed as a great city of the plain. In size it has already been outstripped by the mega-cities: Mexico City and Sao Paulo.

In spite of such vast and sophisticated developments within the region, Latin America remains Third World America. Northern America contains 6 per cent of the world's population and enjoys 30 per cent of the world's wealth; Latin America contains 8 per cent of the world's population but enjoys only 5 per cent of the world's wealth. The history of this region is a Third World history: more centuries of colonial domination, leaving the task of nation-building that much harder. The colonial legacy in Latin America has left a racially mixed, socially divided population, distorted economies disadvantaged in world trade, crippled with debt burdens, too dependent on single agricultural products and the export of minerals. Whereas Northern America has been capitalistic in its growth, Latin America had feudal beginnings which are still felt in the grossly unequal distribution of land. Even characteristically Third World hazards of earthquakes, droughts and floods are endemic in the region. In the wake of these, and the ravages of guerrilla and security forces, major refugee problems now show up as another heartbreaking feature of this Third World America.

The people

Latin America, rich in problems, is rich in people. Optimistic, ebullient, patient, stoical, heroic, devious, tender, tyrannical, blinkered and devastatingly perceptive: this kaleidoscope of contrasting qualities is represented even in the same individuals. Think about these perceptions: 'The rich get richer, and the poor have children.' 'Universal misery has divided the world into two groups of human beings: those who do not eat and those who do not sleep...those who do not sleep live in the richest areas of the world, but they do not sleep for fear of the revolt of those who do not eat.'[37]

Who are these people who look out on the world with such pessimism, and yet contrive to celebrate today and believe in tomorrow? Racially they are yet more of a mixture than the North Americans. Many more of the indigenous peoples survived than in the North and there was much more intermingling of races. Especially in the Andean countries, and in Central America and Mexico, large proportions of the population are Amerindian or Mestizo. White Latin Americans are by no means all of Spanish or Portuguese descent; through massive immigrations Italian surnames figure prominently among the River Plate people; Germans and other Central Europeans contribute very significantly to populations in Southern Brazil. The descendants of the black slaves who worked the plantations of Northern Brazil and Columbia have intermarried extensively. There are now more mulattos than blacks in these two countries.

The personal hopes and political preferences of these people are as various as their ethnic backgrounds. The Amerindians retain a great longing for the restoration to them of their land. The Mestizos crave identity and if they are newcomers in the shanty towns they may be totally absorbed in the struggle for survival. In recent years the election of a Communist mayor in Lima was said not to be a vote for Marxism but a vote against hunger. Afroamericans may seek their route to identity and even power through spiritist cults brought in by their forebears. Privileged, modern-sector Latins want to achieve and maintain living standards equal with their North American and European counterparts. Their personal energies and political allegiances tend towards that goal.

The religion

'I was shocked. They are very religious!' A young Western anthropologist gives away his own prejudices in a true description of the Mataco Indians of the Argentina Chaco. But the point is more universal: all the Amerindian peoples are religious, the blacks are religious, the European conquistadores and immigrants were religious. Even the statistics are religious! Throughout the region 94 per cent of the people profess Christian allegiance and only 3 per cent claim to be non-religious. Of the professing Christians 88 per cent relate to the Roman Catholic Church.[38]

The dominant position of a powerful and authoritarian church established among a religious people might suggest a picture of strict ecclesiastical conformity. Nothing could be further from the truth; there is more chaos than conformity. From the beginning attitudes towards Roman Catholicism have been very mixed. It has been the church many have neither been able to join nor leave. Attendance at mass in Roman Catholic Argentina, a nation dedicated to the Virgin Mary, is reckoned at 12 per cent. A prosperous and sophisticated suburb of Santiago, Chile, is full of people with no effective links with the Roman Catholic Church and who resort to 'curanderos', spirit therapists, in their moments of distress. Negative attitudes towards the Catholic priests are widespread in many republics. The Roman Catholic estimate of the situation in the region is that it constitutes a mission field. They describe it as 'a continent of people who have been baptised but not evangelised'.[39]

Yet even in the darkest days of the eighteenth century when the Jesuits were expelled from Latin America, there have never lacked examples of Catholic zeal, sacrifice and devotion. Today there is certainly Roman Catholic retrenchment, but there is also Roman Catholic renewal. There are even vigorous manifestations of the old Catholic folk religion: for the Feast of the Miracle, commemorating the abatement of an earthquake, the quarter of a million population of Salta doubles in size with pilgrims who come to see the images paraded through the streets. Such events are witnessed in all the traditional cities.

Much more recognisably Christian to Protestant eyes is the charismatic renewal growing apace among Roman Catholic congregations. David Barratt's figures for growth among Catholic Pentecostals or charismatics are high throughout the region and almost doubling every year in Brazil. Catholic charismatics relate readily and warmly with evangelicals and Pentecostals, and because the Roman Catholic leadership has been uncertain where these relationships may lead, there has been a move to discourage such mixing. The recent formation of Catholic Independent Churches in Latin America gives similar evidence of Spirit ferment not being channelled adequately by traditional disciplines.

Another, and more widely reported, aspect of Catholic renewal has to do with protest against injustice. Nearly five centuries ago Bishop Antonio de Valdivieso was stabbed to death in a lonely farmhouse on the Yucatan peninsula. He had just dispatched letters to the King of Spain protesting at the cruel treatment of the native peoples by the Spanish settlers. Seven years ago Archbishop Oscar Romero was gunned down while celebrating mass in his cathedral in San Salvador. He had just spoken of the risks he faced through his defence of human rights, and said that he was willing for his blood to be a 'seed for freedom'.

Roman Catholic engagement in the struggle for social justice has roots that go back to the Spanish conquest. The episcopal conference at Medellin in 1968 proved, however, a powerful stimulus for the church to identify with the poor, to denounce 'institutional violence', of which so many governments with their security forces were guilty, and to promote popular education and social action through grass-roots communities.

Such pronouncements, the new style ministry in the shanty towns, and the programmes that accompanied them produced a savage backlash in a number of countries under military rule. It is estimated that in Argentina alone, between the Medellin conference in '68 and the Puebla conference in '79 no less than 1,500 priests, nuns and lay workers were arrested, interrogated, tortured, exiled or assassinated. The sacrificial witness of such people is one legacy of this movement. Another is the proliferation of grass-roots communities: groups meeting under lay leadership for worship and Bible study and to engage in corporate action to bring about changes in society round about. Figures of 150,000 such basic ecclesial communities are estimated to have been formed over the past two decades in Brazil.

Fifty years before these rapid developments in parts of the Roman Catholic Church began, a movement of revival, healings, and ecstatic speech came to birth in the evangelical churches and has continued as something of great significance and hope for the whole region. A night watchman had a dream and encouraged a missionary pastor, an Italian American had a vision and made an improbable journey to Brazil, a few small congregations experienced God's power in new ways. From such beginnings the Pentecostal movement has grown over the past eighty years to number fourteen million out of twenty million evangelical Christians in Latin America.

Other evangelical or Protestant churches in Latin America have a less spectacular but none the less significant story. They took their beginnings from ministry among North European and North American expatriates in the early post-independence years. Colportage and evangelism among Spanish and Portuguese-speaking settlers followed. The new governments saw Protestantism as linked with the educational and material progress of the North Atlantic countries and in some places missionaries were allowed entry for that reason. The missionaries for their part sought personal conversions and taught believers the evangelical faith. Their work was not always carried out against a background of toleration; persecutions and the martyrdom of some evangelicals has taken place, especially in Columbia.

These beginnings gave an emphasis upon personal religion in the evangelical churches. Although numerically small, the Anglican Church is among those that have combined evangelism with social development and change, having a commitment to both tribal peoples and urban-dwellers. A feature within the region has been the active participation of expatriate personnel whose contribution has been specially strong in leadership training. The Pentecostal churches by contrast have developed with relatively little expatriate assistance in personnel and still less in money.

The missionary challenge

Latin America is the world region with the highest percentage of people professing to be Christian, and these Latin Americans now constitute more than one quarter of all those throughout the world who have some allegiance to Christ's church. It is indeed true that 'the future of the Universal Church is bound up with the future of the Church in Latin America'.[40]

The missionary challenge in Latin America certainly has important global implications, but within the continent itself it struggles with the gap between the fragile Christian veneer of the majority and the deep and authentic Christian faith required for personal holiness and the transformation of society. Like Europe, Latin America needs to be re-evangelised. The Christian foundations in Latin America are in some ways weaker: the legacy of a gospel imposed through conquest; a denial for three centuries of the liberating influence of the Reformation; nations with less inner cohesion and weaker traditions of public morality. But though the original foundation may be weaker the rebuilding is yet more vigorous. If evangelism in Europe is at a jog, then in Latin America it is at a sprint. Where in Europe Christians are worrying about social justice, Christians in Latin America are paying for it with their lives.

There are, of course, many parts to the missionary task in the region: evangelism ongoing and unchecked; the work of healing both scientific and miraculous; exorcism of the evil spirits which bind the individual; confrontation of the evil powers which pevert justice in society; the compassionate care of the victims of a harsh world; the equipping of leaders and pastors and guides. Progress on these fronts would be greatly enhanced by a growing co-operation and mutual respect between churches. This, together with a further flowering of Latin American spirituality and theology, could herald the vital contribution to world mission from this continent which in its beginnings is already there to see.

But how are the parts going to come together? Will there be some miracle of ecclesiastical rationalisation? In Latin America that kind of miracle is least likely of all. Rather, I would expect to see a continuing and spontaneous process of friendships and mutual inspiration. My own reflection focuses upon ten words: inclusive freedom, sufficient peace, blended flames, sighted guides and global rejoicing.

In Latin America the search for freedom has been long and agonising. 'Libertad!', the cry that went up at independence, proved a hollow one for so many in the new republics. A different word, 'Liberacion', rallies those who seek a Marxist or socialist revolution to overthrow tyrants. Into this world of longing for freedom comes Jesus, the True Liberator. His freedom is the 'freedom of the sons of God'. An exultant sense of identity and self-worth for the rural people newly arrived in the shanty town and otherwise at the bottom of the social pile; freedom to shout God's praise in a babble of sound in a Pentecostal service, freedom to face a government official with a request for piped water.

This freedom of Christ is for the poor whose lack of freedom is otherwise obvious and overwhelming. It is also for the rich who are oppressed in more private ways: family breakdown, financial instability, the weariness of the secular scramble for wealth. Christ's freedom is inclusive because it is offered to every kind of person in every situation. It is a freedom which does not bypass politic choices (most of which are very hard ones in Latin America) but it does go far beyond them. This freedom is of personal sins forgiven as well as the freedom to be a whole person even when society bears cruelly and unjustly down. It is freedom for time and for eternity.

Mission in Latin America involves the sharing of Christ's inclusive freedom. It also means entering into his sufficient peace. At first this phrase might not seem appropriate; mission in conflict is the description given to a book on *The Church and Change in Latin America*.[41] Conflict in Latin America is unavoidable, but if Christians allow it to become the controlling factor in their lives then they lose their way. After all, the very last thing needed by a society barely holding together is unnecessary conflict.

'My peace is with me.' This expression of a tribal people, now evangelised, is deeply instructive for a whole continent and indeed for the world. This is not a greedy peace: satisfaction from a surfeit of things. Instead it is a simple peace. Like Christ's freedom this peace is offered to all. It is peace with God, peace with the neighbour, a forgiving peace even with an enemy, a peace which endures.

What it is not is cosmetic peace. And this is where the radicals do well to insist that social evils should be withstood and exposed. They bravely serve peace if they take their stand in the power and through the Spirit of Jesus.

Latin Americans are passionate people. Latin Christians pour passion into evangelism. Where else in the world would you find an evangelist jumping on to a bus, courteously asking the driver's permission and then preaching earnestly and eloquently to the passengers? Every opportunity is there to be taken for telling the good news of Christ's love. Anglo-Chilean, Alfredo Cooper, tells of how he found himself in a menacing situation between demonstrators and security guards in Santiago. Both fell silent as this street preacher told the story of the cross.

Enough has been said to show that the passion for evangelism in Latin America is matched with a passion for social justice. In each case there are the errors and mistakes of passion, but each represents parts of the mission of Jesus Christ; each burns with a bright light. The point to observe though is that each burns separately. Indeed, in Latin America the evangelists and the social activists may look askance at each other. But just suppose those two flames could be blended together and purified by the Holy Spirit of God. What sort of a Pentecost might there be then in Latin America?

Meanwhile a fluid and dynamic situation in the region makes heavy demands upon leadership in the churches. Rapidly growing churches have a need for a rapidly growing number of leaders. Traditional methods of training prove hopelessly unsuitable and inadequate. Latin American Pentecostals developed an apprenticeship approach to ministerial training. What begins with testimony on a street corner ends with the effective establishing of a new and self-supporting congregation. Then ordination is the seal of a proven evangelistic and pastoral gift. Theological Education by Extension was pioneered in Guatamala and provides a culturally more relevant alternative to the academic residential approach to training.

The methods of training are varied and versatile. The challenge to raise up leaders is immense. On the evangelical side of the church there are half a million leaders of congregations needing appropriate training. Among Pentecostals half have only primary education and four out of five are first generation believers. What surely is needed for all churches is farsighted leaders able to discern Christ's way. They need to be guides and enablers for the things of both time and eternity.

It is here that the evangelical-radical issue raises itself again. The need is not for every Pentecostal pastor to become politicised, nor for every leader of the Basic Ecclesial Communities to become quietist. What is required is breadth of understanding and sympathy so that each can make a relationship with the other, and gain some true appreciation of each other's work.

Inclusive freedom, sufficient peace, blended flames, sighted guides, all lead to global rejoicing. When the Latin churches bring their full contribution and genius to the worldwide missionary task, then it will be time for a celebration. Latins adore a party. In Brazil a more effective kind of evangelism is 'fiesta (event) evangelism'. Latin American missionaries who have learnt their Christianity against a background of heavy sorrow will help the world church to lightheartedly rejoice. So may freedom flow, peace rule, and the flame burn brightly in Latin America. Then our brothers and sisters from that neglected but brilliant region of the world will make us more joyful in the missionary service of the Saviour.

The continents together

The world, as an arena of mission, includes all six continents: each vast, complex and different. In four, Europe, Northern and Latin America, and Oceania the overriding priority is re-evangelisation. With the gospel Europe needs a humble confidence, Northern America a healing unity, Latin America an integral freedom and Oceania a reaffirmed identity. Africa, to a lesser extent now, but Asia still on a massive scale contain communities that have never been evangelised even superficially. Mission in Africa confronts almost every challenge simultaneously. In some nations the church is a bulwark against disintegration. Except in its war zones Asia appears more secure. Ancient religions flourish and so does secular materialism. Yet Asia's search will find its satisfaction only in Christ, born of an Asian woman and Saviour of all her people.

In putting the continents together now in conclusion the aim is to draw attention to two features which may not have been apparent in the separate accounts. The first concerns the world religions. Four people out of five in the world today adhere to one religion or another. Apart from the total of 1.5

billion that identify themselves as Christian, 800 million follow Islam, 650 million are Hindu and 300 million are Buddhist. Chinese folk religionists number nearly 200 million and
traditional tribal religionists retain 100 million adherents, a
number now exceeded by new religions. Judaism involves a
membership of fifteen million, but has a proportionally greater influence in the world. There are similar numbers of Sikhs
and also Shamanists. Particular attention should be given to
the fact that Muslim numbers are growing faster than general
population growth. Christianity at present is not quite keeping pace with overall expansion.[42]

In the number of their followers, and their renewed vigour,
the world religions present a very sharp challenge to Christian
mission. Moreover, people with different religious loyalties
are living in closer proximity than ever before. How can the
churches approach the other faith communities with respect,
with friendship and above all with the good news of Jesus
Christ? In some places Christians need to work to lessen risks
of violent confrontation. Some might see evangelism as
jeopardising this task of strengthening fragile inter-commun-
ity relations. In fact evangelism of the right quality and caring
is uniquely beneficial. In strife-torn areas, no less than others,
only the gospel peace is strong enough to hold.

A second feature needing mention concerns the political,
linguistic and social boundaries and barriers which intersect
the world and turn it into such a complicated mosaic of inter-
relating yet separated peoples. Crossing national boundaries
for the officially identified Christian missionary is becoming
more difficult. For either nationalistic, ideological or religious
reasons more governments are restricting or preventing
movement of missionary personnel. Tetsumsao Yamamori in
God's New Envoys estimates on present indications that by
the turn of the century 83 per cent of the non-Christian population of the world will live in countries to which traditionally
sponsored expatriate missionaries will not have access.[43]

Spread within and often across these national boundaries
are groups of people identifiably one in language or dialect,

and culture. Various estimates are made of the number of these so-called people groups: MARC through its research has identified 6,000 such groups yet to have self-propagating congregations established within them. No claim is made that this list is complete. Some 'unreached' people groups are small, others are numbered in millions. Here is another area of missionary concern that an outline of the global situation highlights. It calls not only for a new way of deploying witnesses, and a multiplication of their numbers, but also, in the quality of that witness, a close reflection of the character of Christ.

5

Mission in Six Localities

The global and the local

The book, *Come out the Wilderness*[1] begins with the story of Don Benedict, a seminary student, who discovered a 'neglected continent' only a few blocks from his college chapel: an area situated between Fifth Avenue and the East River in East Harlem, New York City, and virtually abandoned by the church. We have just been trying to find our way around the global continents and discover some missionary bearings worldwide. This is good. We need some idea of our missionary way globally. What is just as important, and more immediate, is that we should know our way in mission locally.

There is in fact an essential unity between global and local mission. It has to do with God, himself, who 'so loved the *world* that he gave his Son', but in so doing localised himself in a few Galilean villages and a Judean city. God's own way of working brings together the global and the local. We do well to follow this pattern and this principle.

Having, therefore, completed a bare outline survey of six continents—a global missionary sketch-map—we now turn our attention to six localities. From a small-scale map we now switch to a large-scale map. We have seen that all six continents are mission fields. We shall discover that all six localities are equally mission fields. All the continents have features in common, yet distinctive qualities. All the localities have similarities, yet important differences.

In a world of such complexity and diversity, what do I mean by just six localities? Can these be typical? Yes, even with the infinite variety, I believe six main types characterise most localities throughout the world. If we take two of the most obvious divisions of the modern world—urban/rural, and First World/Third World—this gives a beginning to a classification. But then the cities both in the North and the South are divided within themselves into privileged and deprived areas.

With these differences in mind the list of localities is as follows:

Shanty towns	(deprived urban areas in the Third World)
Modern sector	(privileged city centres or suburbs in the Third World)
Inner cities	(deprived areas of First World cities, usually situated in an inner ring)
Suburbia	(privileged areas of First World cities)
Third World village	(rural communities in the Third World, often tribal)
First World village	(rural communities in the First World)

Since we are simply sketching some typical localities of mission, this list will serve. We will bear in mind though another division: areas marked by government hostility towards Christian mission as opposed to areas of toleration or support. Another kind of locality, tragically more and more in evidence, is the refugee camp. This has some characteristics in common with the shanty town. If excuse is needed for having four urban localities to only two rural ones, then it should be borne in mind that the urban population in the world is rapidly outnumbering the rural, and the urban mentality is spreading far beyond city boundaries. Local spheres of mission might of course include anything from an oil platform to a space station. Appropriate mission on such islands of modernity gives food for thought. Meanwhile we return to the missionary 'mainland' and the principal localities.

The shanty town

As the tropical daylight rapidly fades the rhythmic music of the Young Ambassadors gains in intensity. A youth stands at the back of the listening crowd with his thoughts in a turmoil. With the acrid smell still lingering, how could he forget last night's fire that had swept his part of the township. 'It was that pig of a landlord; it must have been his men who started the fire; he wanted space to build bigger and charge more rent... Why ever did we come to this valley outside Nairobi. Mama said that when Grandfather took the Mau Mau oath and the British put him in prison, the family followed him here. But it's been no good. We've never had enough to live on.'

The boy's smouldering anger flares hot. Then just as suddenly the music bursts into his consciousness, and it makes him think how the pastor comforted his mother and offered her bricks and roofing-sheets on easy credit. Perhaps there is some hope after all...

...The sky is grey, the stony hillside above Lima is grey. Even the flimsy woven panels that form the walls of the shack take on the same grey colour. In this particular shack a woman is nursing a two-year-old, no longer crying but with her tiny body still shaking. The mother had to leave her locked in and alone while she went out to a job washing clothes in a big house in the city. Her eleven-year-old is just finishing a plate of beans. He has been out selling matches and come back with money in his pocket. He deserves to eat first, and in any case there only is one plate and one knife, spoon and fork. Could one of the sisters look after my Teresita? Certainly tonight it will not be all hard and grey. In the little chapel there will be bodies healed, and demons sent away, and hands reaching high, and voices shouting, 'Glory to God!'...

...The slim form of the cathedral volunteer crouches on the pavement among the regulars. This is 'operation twilight', an

encounter with some few of the two million people who make
their home on the streets of Calcutta. One old man is a relative newcomer. He is wanting to tell his story: how the death
of his wife, mounting debts, pressure from the landowner,
have finally driven him from his small plot of land. 'What
about your children?' asks the volunteer. 'Only one son survives. He joined the army and was drafted to the frontier. He
sent us money, but it wasn't enough.'

The conversation subsides. The pavement noises intervene. Then the old man rouses himself again. 'There's a holy
woman who takes in the dying. Her religion is of the Jesus
God. Could you tell me a little more?'...

...' "We toiled all night, and took nothing." That's our situation exactly.' The dockyard worker from Hong Kong
wouldn't describe himself as a religious man and certainly is
not accustomed to Bible study. This verse from Luke's Gospel, though, has struck him forcibly. 'I agree,' says the industrial missioner, also Hong Kong Chinese. 'That's why we keep
encouraging you to organise. If the labour force can only act
together, then it can gain its rightful share in the prosperity.'

The men glance up as a bird flits across their view through
an open window and disappears into the trees on the hillside.
'It's all right to talk in these surroundings. In the docks the
pressures can break us. If you begin to take responsibility,
then people come at you from every side.' 'But look what happened in the Gospel,' is the reply. 'Jesus was in the boat when
he said, "Put out into the deep water and let down the nets." '
The docker is staring out now past the wooded hill to the
crowded city that lies beyond. Quietly he repeats, 'We toiled
all night, but, because you say so, I will.'...

Pictures such as these can be pieced together from the testimony of those engaged in the deprived areas of Third World
cities. They are typical, and yet they are not typical. In each
there is a Christian presence and a deliberate witness to the
gospel. In our search for the typical shanty town we have to
face the hard fact that in the majority of such localities there
is at present no Christian witness at all. Even in nominally

Christian Latin America a priest will take a missionary on to the flat roof-top of his house, wave an arm across an area of poor housing, stretching as far as the eye can see, and say, 'You choose your place!'

Worldwide the people are moving into the shanty towns faster than the churches are moving in. The decade of the 80s is seeing a massive one billion migration from the rural areas of the world into the cities. Most of these cities are Third World cities and the areas of the cities which receive the immigrants are the shanty towns. The speed of this process is breathtaking. On one day a stony hillside on the edge of Peru's capital city is bare and featureless. By the next day it is already marked out in plots and covered with wickerwork shacks. They are called 'young towns' in Peru, 'mushroom cities' in Chile, and, most graphic of all, in Turkey they are named 'Secekindu', meaning built after dusk and before dawn.

The economic base upon which these rapid developments are resting is precarious in the extreme. In fact the visitor to a shanty town will be very hard pressed to discover how it is that so many people manage to survive at all. Battered buses bumping down dusty roads take some to workplaces miles away in other parts of the city. People sell bits and pieces from trays and barrows and little kiosks. Others tackle the honourable business of making a living by resorting to the dehumanising business of crime or prostitution or drug trafficking. Frightening though it may appear, these last three may be the main 'industries' of a shanty town locality. Urban growth in the Third World lacks almost totally any comensurate growth in secure employment opportunities.

Shanty towns are built on precarious economic foundations, and physical foundations. A tropical downpour in Rio de Janeiro can bring a whole section of a favela crashing down a hillside in a catastrophic landslip. Shanty towns spread out along dry river beds, on flood plains, on planks and poles over tidal estuaries. And if by chance the development should take place on land with appreciating value, then the bulldozers may arrive and other more powerful interests may lay a claim. 'There's no room for people,' complains a Brazilian woman. 'When the farm owner switched to mechanisation, we had to move out on to the highway. The highway department moved us and we went outside the city. When the city grows out towards us, then the developers take the land to build a motel.'

Shanty town-dwellers need security and they need infrastructure for their neighbourhoods. Most urgently, they need clean and adequate supplies of water. All too often the limited quantities brought by tankers to the shanty towns have to be paid for at prices people can ill afford. But they need other amenities. To keep pace with the growth of her shanty towns Lima would have to build, equip and staff a new school every day. Even where there is political will to respond, the volume of need is overwhelming.

So what is left on the positive side of the balance when all the social deprivations have been weighed? Quite simply, people. In each locality there are thousands of people, many of whom are children, many of whom are young. Against a background of the most appalling dangers and neglect there is this dynamic potential, this overflowing treasure: the turbulent, confused, contrary, resourceful, adaptable people themselves.

The missionary challenge

The first challenge of the shanty town locality from a missionary perspective is to see its unique importance in today's world. We might almost say that we live in a 'shanty world', with the greatest increases in people living in such new makeshift situations. These are the growth areas. More and more this is where the poor live, and it is here that we find the mass of the unevangelised.

Raymond Fung argues that just as in the first century the church ceased to be the church of the Jews only but became the church of the Gentiles, so in our time it will no longer be the church of the privileged, but most typically the church of the poor. Certainly Jesus saw the poor as the special, and most characteristic, recipients of his message. And certainly the shanty towns are full of poor people. There is every reason for these Third World urban outgrowths to be given the very highest missionary priority by the world church.

Priority recognition and prompt action: both are urgently required. Visualise a woman with bewildered fear in her eyes, a child clinging to her skirts and a bundle on her back, standing in a crowded bus station. She has come from the village to the city, looking for a grown-up son. But where is he staying? And when she finds him how will she live?

There are even literal cases of the missionary church meeting the new urban-dweller at the bus terminus. Certainly the gospel of God's welcome, through Christ, meets a ready response from people who are otherwise made anonymous, deskilled, despised and disorientated in the sprawling conurbations. The new arrivals have an urgent need for physical, psychological and spiritual support. They attempt to reproduce in the unfamiliar city a more familiar world by grouping with members of their own kith and kin. But one uprooting leads to many more and individuals are left alone, exposed, and at the bottom of the social pile.

To people who have lost one identity and lack another the gospel announces that they are sons and daughters of the living God. Some might say that shanty town-dwellers must be constantly occupied with the struggle for survival. How can a spiritual gospel be relevant to their condition? It can only be an escape. It is in fact fruitless to argue whether these people want a spiritual and supernatural gospel or a politically radical gospel. The truth is that like everyone else they need the gospel with all its powerful dimensions unimpaired. And yes, they take a special delight in the unseen glory.

The new urban-dweller does not forget his rural past, and retains from it a religious bent and a spirit sensitivity which the evangelist must understand. For those with little access to modern health care, miraculous cures are more than a nine-day wonder; they are an everyday necessity. Shanty town churches witness healings and exorcisms and even raisings from the dead. They also suffer from many imperfections, but are mercifully spared some of the deadening effects of secularism suffered by their brothers and sisters in more privileged situations in the world.

In these terms the missionary challenge is to express the gospel to the full in a situation which threatens to deny the gospel in every way. In the shanty towns there is a conflict at every level, including the political level. Political factors have brought the people there in the first place; and political factors will influence their future, making it more or less tolerable. The mission of the church in the shanty towns is to encourage its members to grasp hold of their whole situation and struggle for improvements that approximate more to the qualities of the kingdom of God. For someone I know, defending these values of the kingdom literally meant standing in front of a bulldozer as the driver prepared to demolish an old man's house on a strip of wanted land. Wisely a friend had asked the press to come and take some photographs, so both protester and house were left standing.

But where will the leaders come from who will be the evangelists, and the teachers, and the exorcists, and the pastors, and the healers, and the social workers and the political activists who will carry these emerging churches forward on so many fronts? Isn't there an obvious and acute shortage of educated leaders in these localities? People like this are scarce enough in the most privileged areas.

The answer is that the shanty towns of the world are rich beyond many people's imaginings in an undiscovered leadership strata. Lack of opportunity leaves much potential unrealised. Gifted people use amazing effort and ingenuity equipping workshops with home-made tools. Qualities, skills and supernatural gifts there undoubtedly are. What is needed is a quality of church life and an appropriate kind of training to discover them. This also represents a vital missionary challenge.

Conclusion

Local mission in a shanty town area may appear to be played out on a small stage. The buildings are small, the headlines are few, the people may appear forgotten. The stage may be small but the back-cloth is panoramic. Over the past year nearly a million people have arrived in Mexico city. The task of welcoming and evangelising this vast number must stretch all known resources of the churches. Of the nearly half a million people during the same time entering the city of Bombay far fewer will have any prior connections with the Christian church. The evangelistic task in that city must be even more herculean.

With the dramatic influx into the shanty towns surrounding the cities of the Third World the whole pattern of urban mission is changing. At the turn of the century more than two thirds of the urban population of the world professed the Christian faith. Now less than half does. A principal factor in the difference is the entrance into the cities of large numbers of non-Christian peoples. Yet as we have seen, some of these, for a time at least, are particularly responsive to the gospel of Christ.

Religious zeal may of course turn another way; David Barrett in *World Class Cities and World Evangelisation* speculates on the role of anti-Christian cities dominated by a militant and militarised Islam.[2] So whoever wins the cities wins the world. True, but may we Christians never forget that our King rode into a hostile city unarmed and in peace. It is his special design to extend that peace in today's shanty towns. Each locality, each small stage, is crowded with players, the backdrop spans the world, the audience of angels strain forward. The world church has one final opportunity to serve the urban poor Christ loves, and do so in Christ's authentic way.

Modern sector

What are we talking about?

To refer to a vastly significant feature of the world today as 'shanty towns' may not be polite, but at least it is understandable. What on earth though are 'modern sectors'? With apologies for the ugly jargon, these are the parts of Third World cities with strong international connections. In these suburbs and city centres there are people with the very highest educational standards: sophisticated, privileged bearers not only of their countries' most cherished traditions, but also deeply influenced by the all-pervasive secular world. Men and women in this modern sector of Third World society have many things to enjoy, and many things to lose. Theirs is a special luxury and a special anxiety.

What though is mission in the 'modern sector'? Can we catch a few glimpses of its reality?

... 'After they prayed, the place where they were meeting was shaken.' A group of elegantly but casually dressed Chileans are laughing and laughing. Flecks of white ceiling plaster are floating down on to their heads. Their all-night prayer meeting in a house in their Barrio Alto of Santiago has ended with an earth tremor strong enough to open up some cracks in the fabric. This, surely, is the strong hand of God: a sign to them that, like the first disciples, 'They will all be filled with the Holy Spirit, and speak the word of God boldly.' ...

... The meeting of the leaders of the Chung Hyeon Church in a prosperous market area of Seoul, South Korea, is being conducted with the accustomed deliberation and solemnity. Their pastor, a veteran of past struggles, suffering and witnessing under the Japanese, is making a proposition. 'I ask you to commit yourselves with me in the formation of the Overseas Missions Association.' Gravely, but willingly, all present give their assent.

Fifteen years pass and from this one congregation seventeen missionaries are sent to twelve different countries of the world. Their Overseas Missions Association takes its place alongside vigorous outreach through their Young People's Mission, and their Policeman's Mission, and their Prison Mission, and their Mission Foundation for North Korea...

... Regaining her breath, a fifteen-year-old girl is sitting in the cool patio of a beautiful house in the city of Khartoum. She is hot and flustered and still wearing her school uniform. Eager to go on to study medicine, she had stayed at school after hours for extra maths lessons. Hurrying home, she cannot fail to see two little boys in a dusty corner of the market clasping each other, crying silently. She pauses, hesitates, and slips two coins into their battered cup. They do not notice. But others do: 'Where have you been? Playing around, no doubt.' The sneering innuendo in the harsh male voice is unmistakeable. The girl speeds home, never even looking round.

Now she has different thoughts. 'Will my father let me train to be a doctor? That can't be against our religion. He even sent me to a Christian school. I wonder, does the Christian religion make a woman free?' ...

... A sixteen-year-old boy is sitting in the garden of an architect's showpiece house in a riverside city. The young maid brings him out an iced drink. His eyes are irresistably drawn to the curves of her slim body beautifully shaping her thin dress. Then the thought: 'There is nobody else in the house. She won't dare say no to me. This is my chance to do what my friends boast of. Even if he found out, father wouldn't care.' But in another moment he can hear in his mind freshly spoken words of a young teacher who has been telling him and his classmates about another way. 'I wonder,' he asks himself, 'Is this gospel for men?' ...

... The view from the tallest building in Sao Paulo is spectacular indeed; all around tower blocks reach upwards from the streets and traffic far below. A pastor stands on the observation platform scanning the vista of man-made mountains. Suddenly he is weeping. 'How can the churches reach the millions in this city? How can we penetrate the concrete jungle?' ...

Pictures can be multiplied and so can questions. In all the variety, what are the common factors in these wealth areas of the poor world? To begin with, all are subject to unpredictable change and retain relatively fragile security. All these modern sector economies are vulnerable to fluctuations in world markets and overshadowed by international debts. The young man's father struggles hard to maintain an impressive lifestyle amidst the corruption of the workplace, and hardly notices what may be happening at home. Besides, there may be rumours of an impending coup. There are calculations to be made, and investments to be transferred to safer places.

As in the shanty towns, so in many modern sector areas, people live by their wits. The only difference for the privileged is that the physical environment is softer and the financial stakes are higher. Levels of psychological stress may even be worse. Families may be divided, not violently as in the slums, but through relentless pressures of a more subtle kind. What goes on behind the security gates and the watered lawns may be zestfully enjoyable or squalidly brutal. The tight-rope between the good time and the bad time is as tight as that.

One thing many of those living in these areas contrive to be is both very religious and very secular at the same time. This introduces yet another paradox. It makes a difference from the secularism of the First World in which people's religious sensitivities may be severely deadened. Here is something to which the missionary should be specially alert. And there is another thing as well. The poor world spills into the modern sectors. Raise your eye a fraction above the luxury hotels of Rio and you will see the favelas on the hillside. Look into the corner of the plot containing that half-finished Miami-style villa in La Paz and you will see a tiny shack, home of the night watchman. At least the poor are in sight even if temporarily out of mind.

The missionary challenge

The first step in mission to the unchurched in the sophisticated city centres and suburbs in the Third World is to get an invitation to a party! Amidst the tensions there are always the celebrations. Jesus went to parties with rich people. There are occasions when his modern followers should do the same. Here perhaps is the special opportunity of the expatriate missionaries. Less tightly locked into the complicated class distinctions which tend to limit access of nationals to people outside their social group, they may find themselves at the party. Then what they have to do is to make friends and enjoy themselves.

But isn't that a bit too glib and simple? Well, it is just one first step, but the point is that in many of these situations of the world there is a remarkable openness in face to face encounters, even where the public proclamation of the gospel is strictly prohibited. Where no such prohibition at present exists, as in many parts of Latin America, the party can flow out into the parks and the plazas. The missionary challenge then for our Christian brothers and sisters there, who do these open-air celebrations and proclamations with special grace and gusto, is to adequately follow up and befriend the many who respond to the preaching.

By the time this stage is reached the party is likely to be over and Christian mission is no longer simply responding to people's joy but grappling with their sorrows. Out of a significant urban experience in South America, Alan Hargrave writes, 'Amongst the upper middle classes marriage breakdown, nervous disorders, alcoholism, drug abuse and problems with adolescents are the order of the day. Here is a group of people needing the healing love of Jesus Christ.'

To counter marriage breakdown, marriage encounter weekends, first developed by Roman Catholic churches in the United States, have met a very positive response in Latin America. The discovery is made that Christ who can make marriages new can 'make all things new'. He can save privileged people from, and in, the accidents and tragedies of life, from which money and power do not exempt them. The missionary church needs not only to weep with those who weep in shanty town shacks, but also in the modern sector mansions.

Once members of this privileged sector of Third World society have experienced the healing love of Christ, then they have many special gifts to offer in his service, and much they can do for others. But first some connections must be made.

There needs to be some shaking, like there was in that house in Santiago after the prayer meeting.

As they have developed, these monthly nights of prayer have brought together members of Anglican churches from both wealthy and poverty-stricken districts of the city. People who would never meet socially in the normal course of their lives were spending whole nights together praying. Even in class-conscious Santiago class distinctions do not stand up too well to that kind of exposure and treatment!

Where in this way the Holy Spirit breaks down the inner barriers immense scope is created for the spread of the gospel. The more educationally and economically privileged members of the churches have their vital contribution which extends outwards from their own districts to other parts of the city and beyond. Doctors, teachers, lawyers, business people in the Third World all have dramatically new opportunities and options if they apply Christ's criteria in their working lives.

With a wide social spectrum represented among congregations, these professionals have many people they can help even within their own churches. That Christians should help Christians is good and right, but the opportunity includes a more insistent demand for social justice. In a letter to me Alan Hargrave again comments, 'The salt and light of the gospel are sadly lacking in the courts, in business, in government and in the armed forces. The church has attempted to raise a prophetic voice from without, but who will raise the prophetic voice from within?'

This comment, and much of what is written above, reflects a Latin American experience of a Christ-given relationship between people of very different social groups. I have belonged myself to a small city-centre congregation in Salta, Argentina, in which eight tribal and European languages have been represented among the worshippers. Generally speaking, the situation in Latin American cities may be different from that elsewhere in the world in so far as there is no dominant non-Christian religion focusing resistance to the spread of the gospel and prompting governments to restrict evangelism. Even so, in the contrasting situation of conservative Islamic countries there are remarkable evangelistic opportunities in face to face encounters between people, and not least among the socially privileged.

Where in Latin America, or any other continent, the widest freedoms remain, the modern sector churches have another and not unrelated opportunity. A prophetic voice can also become an evangelistic voice and the typically city methods of communication—radio and television—can be employed in its diffusion. Some members of city-centre churches often have a degree of access to the media, expertise in the communication skills, and money to buy time, which their brothers and sisters in the shanty towns may lack. A communications alliance between them has much to offer and can in its own way penetrate the concrete labyrinth, beaming gospel words into many homes. The pastor who wept over Sao Paulo's sky-scrapers now has a daily radio programme sent out from stations throughout the province. These broadcasts not only awaken a response from the unchurched, but also link church members from the interior of the province and the outskirts of the city with the centre. This network of acceptance is also a fruit of the gospel. The challenge is to extend the net and keep it whole.

'For reaching large cities or urbanised areas the possibility of placing programmes on local stations should always be explored first.' This is the advice of Francis Gray of the Far Eastern Broadcasting Company. Where this is possible the kind of co-operative link between the city centre and 'peripheral' churches, to which we have been referring, can be very fruitful. It is estimated though that there are nearly one and a half billion people in the world for whom this freedom to receive local Christian radio is withheld: part, of course, of many other political and religious constraints. In this case international broadcasting provides an alternative. How, for instance, can that city-centre church in Seoul spread the gospel back into North Korea? By radio, is how it can, and how it does.

Our move from the shanty town to the modern sector of the Third World city and a confrontation of the missionary challenge there leads us beyond the face to face communication of the gospel to the modern media, particularly radio. This has powerful possibilities: the large multiplication effect, the ability to cross closed frontiers and enter closed doors, the intimacy and the versatility of the medium itself. But the communication technology is nothing until it leads us back to the people themselves: people like the boy tempted to misuse the maid, and the young Muslim girl with her longings for personal fulfilment. Behind the ugly jargon word, modern sector, are millions of people whose lives can be made truly beautiful through the Spirit of Jesus. Herein lies the challenge of mission and its good purpose.

The inner city

We turn now from the rich part of the Third World to the poor part of the First World. Just as Third World cities are sharply divided between areas of wealth and poverty, so are First World cities so divided. A difference is that typically the shanty towns are improvised new developments sprawled around the outside of prosperous city centres and suburbs, whereas the inner cities are decaying areas of old housing trapped between the centres and suburbia.

The phenomenon of the inner city shows up with almost mathematical precision in the city of Birmingham. The West Midlands Districts Joint Data team has produced a series of maps plotting the areas where high levels of unemployment, single-parent households, overcrowding, and child accidents are most heavily concentrated.[3] Each of these indicators of poverty shows up in a closely corresponding inner ring. Less dramatically but none the less significantly these features are evident in scattered outer estates; these also are part of the overall pattern of urban poverty, at least in Britain.

Brixton, Toxteth, Moss Side, Handsworth: the otherwise

forgotten inner-city areas of Britain have gained their public exposure through the tragic consequence of riots. In name at least these and others like them are 'urban priority areas'. For Britain's UPAs and for equivalent areas in other First World cities how are we to visualise the priority and the reality of Christian mission?

... An old white resident living alone in inner-city Birmingham is lying in bed, his breathing becoming increasingly painful and difficult. Over the past few years he has been receiving regular visits and practical help from a West Indian woman belonging to a local church. 'I must see her,' he tells a neighbour who comes by. He struggles for breath until she arrives, and then supported by the black woman he dies in her arms...

... The roof-tops of the tenement buildings are the coolest places during a New York summer evening. A fourteen-year-old climbing out through the top door hasn't come though to take the air. He sits by the parapet, fixes a borrowed hypodermic needle into the end of an eye-dropper, rolls up his sleeve, and using this improvised apparatus, injects heroin into a vein.

In the stifling atmosphere of the street below his mother approaches a small store-front office. Over the door is a sign showing a cross falling and breaking a glass syringe. She enters and is welcomed by the woman inside. 'Got trouble in your family? Don't feel ashamed. We will try and help.' ...

... The play area behind the terrace houses is alive with children. Mothers in saris look on from a distance. The children are engrossed in the games and the singing. With equal enthusiasm they act out the fall of Jericho and the Good Samaritan. Their holy book also tells about Jesus, and the Christian helpers at this event commend him as the one who can bring peace and hope in their neighbourhood and in people's hearts...

... The twelve-by-ten-foot room contains three men, three beds, and an unpleasant-smelling bucket. One of the men is lying reading a small book with double column print. Another is looking at him with cynical amusement. 'You've been going to too many chapel services. I can tell that!' 'Why shouldn't I?' comes the embarrassed reply. The second man persists, 'It's all right just to get a break from the cells on a Sunday morning, but reading the Bible is going a bit too far.' Then a more thoughtful answer: 'Far or not. Maybe it's where I want to go.' ...

In attempting to describe the situation of people living in inner-city areas it would be a mistake to rush into an exercise in hand-wringing and unrelieved pessimism. 'We have found grounds for encouragement and hope. We have observed an amazing variety of human responses to conditions of adversity; we have seen courage, resilience and dedicated service; we have encountered local pride and profound human loyalties.' This testimony of the Archbishop's Commission is based upon extensive visits and hours of interviews in Britain's urban priority areas.[4]

Their reference to 'amazing variety' picks up another feature of inner-city areas which is universally characteristic. David Barrett makes the general point that 'the world's cities have entered a whole new era of multi-racial, multi-ethnic, multi-lingual and multi-religious pluralism, unprecedented in the entire history of urbanisation.'[5] Over recent decades the populations of the less privileged areas of First World cities have ceased to be monochrome and become very diverse. Forty different ethnic groups can be found in the one London district of Plaistow. One street in Winson Green, Birmingham, will contain equal numbers of Afro-Caribbean, Asian, and white residents.

These plural communities in the inner cities, subject to rapid changes in composition, struggle with an environment of disadvantages. Their areas contain the features which other more favoured districts mostly avoid. Many inner cities are scarred with dumps and abandoned factories, divided by railway lines and motorways, and dominated by massive institutions such as prisons or psychiatric hospitals which serve a wide catchment area and don't 'fit' in the locality. All too often, the picture otherwise is of elegant houses no longer elegant and newer utilitarian units never as practical as the planners intended. This housing stock may be holding up fairly well, falling into dereliction, or already bulldozed to the ground leaving abrupt patches of emptiness.

A bleak and blighted visual outlook in these poverty pockets of the First World is matched with depressing economic prospects. Local industries are in decline; new industries are starting elsewhere. Youth unemployment is perhaps one of the most tragic and destructive results of this failure of the economic base. The total situation produces in people 'smouldering anger and quiet despair'. The Archbishop's Commission explains, 'Poor people in Urban Priority Areas are at the mercy of fragmented and apparently unresponsive public authorities. They are trapped in housing and environments over which they have little control.'[6] To poverty is added powerlessness.

This analysis relates to Britain in the eighties. Bruce Kenrick, in *Come out the Wilderness*, talks about the residents of East Harlem in the sixties thus: 'A few lived self-respecting lives, others took to violence and crime, the great majority simply drifted...the main escapes were either dope or sex or drink.'[7] Disparaging words? No, a stark reality then and now. And where would you or I be, if we had grown up in conditions such as these? Would we have become prostitutes, pushers or pimps?

It seems as if First World urban poverty has a special intensity of deprivation. The poverty of the shanty towns is of course absolute and extreme. Welfare provision may be totally lacking and the physical results devastating. By comparison, welfare support in the inner-city area is much greater. Instead of absolute poverty there is comparative poverty. But the consequence of this, and the dependency which goes with it, is specially destructive socially and psychologically. In the shanty towns things may be at rock bottom but can only go up. At least there is a vigorous struggle for survival and improvement. In the inner cities it may be hard to believe that things will ever stop going down. And then suddenly resignation turns into revenge. This can be said very clinically: 'Youth unemployment allied to black alienation and a feeling of being discriminated against can lead to communal breakdown.' 'If despair is not displaced by hope, overt violence or more self-destructive activities may surge again.'[8] When it happens, though, there is all the horror and fear of the petrol bombs and the bullets and the burning houses and the maimed bodies. Inner cities thus become occasional, or at worst semi-regular, battle grounds.

'An "irrelevant" church amidst the riots.' Is this newspaper headline following the Tottenham riots in London fair? From the point of view of size and political clout then most churches in most inner-city areas are irrelevant. But they are there, and so are their ministers with 'no ulterior purposes whatever, no profits to make, nor careers to advance'. The inner-city church is a paradox: 'Often threatened, often struggling to survive, often alienated from the community it seeks to serve, it is often also intensely alive, proclaiming and witnessing to the Gospel.'[9]

The missionary challenge

All too easily the missionary challenge of the inner cities is evaded altogether. Protestant churches especially have tended to follow the migration of their members into more prosperous suburbs. Roger Greenway, in *Christianity a World Faith*, makes the further point: 'The spiritual, social and emotional needs of the masses in the cities are so enormous that Christian workers tend to turn away in search of smaller, less bewildering places of ministry...they tend to interpret the urban environment as being inherently inhospitable to Christianity.'[10]

People tempted to think like that will never be short of evidence to confirm their fears. However, the challenge requires that such negative attitudes should be turned into double positives. Out of his experience in Chicago, Ray Bakke insists that it is no good saying, 'I hate the place, but I love the people.'

Instead it must be: 'I really like it here. This is where I belong.'
Here is the Christian voice in the inner city. Heavy-hearted
heroics just will not do!

A superficial optimism will of course not suffice either; it
will be swept away like chaff in a gale. In their mission the
inner-city churches certainly have to bring hope to their
localities, but cannot do so without plumbing the depth of the
local despair.

One horrifying expression of such despair is drug abuse.
Bruce Kenrick describes the struggles of the East Harlem Protestant parish against the devastating effects of narcotics, and
entitles his chapter 'Crucifixion'.[11] A devoted and sacrificial
team effort by lay people, sustained prayer, successful political lobbying, improved treatment, endless counselling,
yielded a few precious deliverances from addiction, and some
partial control of the habit in other instances. For so many
young people contacted and cared for no way was found to
check them from this physically destructive, criminalising,
brutalising process.

Most agonising of all were the relapses; one addict, won-
derfully converted in prison, worked zealously in the parish
medical unit on release, only to relapse fatally and finally
eighteen months later. His parting from his friends was
expressed in a dark parody of the twenty-third psalm: 'Heroin
is my shepherd. I shall always want... I will dwell in the house
of misery and disgrace for ever.'

Christian hope in the inner city has to look despair in the
face: this dramatic despair of 'self-crucifixion'. But also there
is the nagging, perverse and apparently trivial despair of van-
dalism, petty crime, truancy and the rest. Christian mission
has to take infinite pains in reversing a tide of hopelessness
into a current of hope.

But there is also a parallel transformation: Gabi Habib, secretary of the Middle East Council of Churches, made this
appeal on a visit to Belfast: 'Let us replace the logic of hate
with the logic of love.' The experience of one strife-torn city
has much to teach another. In *A Tale of Three Cities* David

Bleakley draws upon the lessons of Beirut for Belfast and of both for Birmingham.[12] The miracle of reconciliation has to take place within the deprived or even devastated inner cities. Very different groups of people brought together by economic and political forces can, against all human odds, live together in harmony. This is the gospel of Christ, who can break down every wall of partition.

From another angle, Ray Bakke, in his book *The Urban Christian*, has a very perceptive interpretation of what distances people psychologically and socially in the inner city. He argues that people there really hunger for first-class relationships. They are, however, badly hurt by 'rip off' relationships and consequently wary of an approach that may prove superficial, insincere or injurious. The point is well made, however, that the more impersonal the city becomes, the more personal must be the ministry of the churches.

Now unless the church has more people in the inner city it is hard for it to be more personal there. How then are new local church members and church leaders to be raised up? Making disciples in the inner city can never be made a secondary concern to social and political action. If the churches are not committed to all the urgent local concerns of life, there are likely to be few conversions. But if conversions are not sought and nourished then there will be few Christians to bear their social and political witness, which, like the evangelism, also depends upon the making of warmly human, 'high quality' relationships. It is perverse to separate personal transformation and collective responsibility. In the inner city it is particularly obvious that they belong together.

It still has to be recognised that in Britain at least conversions in the inner cities are very hard won. David Hewitt describes twelve years of ministry in Tower Hamlets, East London. He explains the relationship built up with local people in this way: 'We are strongly identified and involved with Lefevre Walk estate, its life and concerns. Through visiting homes we know almost everyone on the estate. We are respected and many people turn to us for help, but at present

they are still afraid of making a commitment to Christ...
When people here do respond, I believe they will respond in a
mass.'[13]

A breakthrough for the churches in the inner cities is not
simply the hope of one individual but the growing conviction
of a growing number. It is based on the realism of experience
as well as the optimism of faith and the discernment of prayer.
There will be people turning to Christ even in situations which
are religiously deadening. There will be local Christian
leadership built up even where natural leaders have for generations been moving away. The missionary challenge of the
inner-city locality is undoubtedly the most daunting. Massive
disadvantages there are, but so too there is the abundant com-
pensation of Christ's redeeming love.

Suburbia

Again we are in difficulties over a name. This section is about
more privileged urban localities in the First World. Often
these are situated some distance from city centres but with
easy access to these business areas and at the same time close
to parks or forest or other natural amenity. The more prosperous city-dweller doesn't necessarily live in suburbia, but this
word may be sufficiently representative to serve our purpose
in sketching in another typical locality of mission.

From my perspective suburbia is too close for comfort. It is
where I was brought up. How can I focus on something that is
still a part of me? For fear of appearing complacent, shall I
launch headlong into an attack on its values. No, that would
be just as false as blindly defending them right or wrong. Life
in suburbia has false foundations and true foundations. The
church in suburbia has some counterfeit manifestations and
also possesses the priceless asset of Christ's indwelling life.

... An elderly invalid lady sits in her straight-backed chair.
A small white cloth is placed on the table beside her. Everything is ready. In comes the young minister to celebrate Communion with her. As he reads the service and breaks the bread

he suddenly and vividly becomes aware of God's presence. The celebration complete, the young man tells how he had this intensely personal experience of meeting with God. The old lady betrays no surprise, simply smiles and says, 'I prayed you would.' ...

... A young courting-couple are sitting on a bench in a Moscow park. A foreign visitor comes and sits down next to them and introduces himself. He tells them that he is a Christian and a pastor. The girl turns to the boy and says, 'I've never told you, but I am a believer. It is my grandmother. She prays, and I learnt from her.' The boy looks at her wide-eyed. 'I never told you, but I'm also a believer! I passed a church where they were singing. Somehow the worship enveloped me, and after that...' Words are no longer needed. Their bond of love, indescribably deeper, embraces the foreigner too...

... The avenue of almond blossom, symbol of suburbia, is in full view from the bedroom window. A youth is staring out and away down the road... He has been reading John's Gospel for himself for the very first time. The living Christ has, as it were, stepped out of the pages. He assures the fifteen-year-old that he died for him and loves him. Then as the conscious sensation of this encounter fades, a magnetic attraction remains to deepen as the youth becomes a man...

The rich world of the North, either side of the ideological divide, has centuries of Christian influence in its history. This heritage leaves its mark in the local scene. Even the prosperity itself will be partly connected with the biblical peace and well-being promised to God's people. Partly it will be a denial of that peace, because some of the affluence will have been won at the expense of others.

This suburban locality, partly shaped by the gospel, partly formed by very different influences, has some built-in contradictions. There is certainly a gracious veneer: beautiful houses, well kept gardens, abundantly stocked shops, successful, articulate people. On the surface their lives appear fulfilled or at least self-sufficient. It may be hard though to get to know the residents of suburbia; they may live very private lives. Even in conversation with them you may not penetrate the carefully moulded mask. There is a lot of human isolation in these much sought after, prestigious localities of the world.

No impression should be given though that suburban lives are lacking in activity. These people may not run the world but they certainly run their regions. Business is in their hands, they staff the schools, man the medical services, organise local government, oversee security. They engage in a web of activity which not only affects the community where they live, but also the lives of those who live in neighbouring areas, not least the inner cities.

These positions of influence are linked with educational attainment. Just as those who live in the privileged modern sector areas of Third World cities are the principal bearers of their nation's traditional culture, so the suburbanites are among the principal bearers of theirs. Every kind of expertise and insight in art and science and technology will be represented, but one thing may be lacking. Typical suburban communities are not nearly as mixed as inner city communities; all but a narrow social band are priced out. In all the sophistication there may therefore be blind spots and blinkers.

With all the immense privileges of suburbia there are also undoubted deprivations. The need to succeed is the great imperative but the human supports for the struggler may be fragile. Family life may not be so badly eroded as in the inner city with its many single-parent homes, but suburban divorce is common indeed. Tension at home may mirror the acute and unrelieved stresses of the workplace. Suburban people who reap many material benefits from the capitalist societies of the First World have to bear a heavy load in keeping them intact. They have to brace themselves in the commercial competition, give whatever first aid the state may spare to the casualties of the system, and hold in check the malcontents. More privileged people living in the Communist 'North' don't seem to live very stress-free lives either.

As the suburban areas of the First World have grown so

have the churches within them. Their buildings and grounds, like the houses and gardens around them, are beautiful. Interiors may be similarly carpeted. Activities may be similarly intense. Suburban churches, not surprisingly, reflect the neighbourhoods in which they are situated. The way they correspond and yet are different is the key to the effectiveness of their mission. That is what we must explore next.

The missionary challenge

Thank God for the fruits of the gospel in suburbia. Let us joyfully affirm the authentic Christian lives of so many ordinary church members. This suburban laity with their ministers are those who are engaged in the local mission of Christ and who face its continuing challenge. Through their witness to friends and neighbours, a steady stream of people from these privileged yet stressful areas are being brought to a vital faith in Christ. As a result, even in England, a recent survey shows that nearly one church in five is growing in membership.

What is authentically and dynamically Christian in suburbia, as anywhere else, is our precious inheritance and our only starting-point for missionary advance. It is no part of our missionary calling to undervalue what the Holy Spirit has already achieved in his people. Yet there is a need to ask what is a complete gospel obedience in these localities. Very properly, the editors of *Ten Growing Churches* asked their contributors what impact their churches had on their local communities.[14] In other respects the accounts given of the more suburban churches are deeply impressive. They are relatively silent, however, on engagement in social concern and the defence of the values of the kingdom in the locality and beyond.

A report in 1977 on St Michael's, York, a church which has achieved remarkable growth both in membership and quality of its fellowship, raised a similar question about its lack of emphasis upon social concern and political action. Commenting on this, the vicar, Graham Cray, says, 'Since that time there has been far greater emphasis on the need for social righteousness.' He continues, 'One of the key future needs is to work through the social and political connotations of being Christians today in York and to face the conflicts and difficulties that such a process would involve.'[15]

The point at issue is this: responding to the whole range of scriptural demand, how can the suburban church embrace the gospel obedience in its wholeness? Churches in inner-city areas may be forced to address social issues because they are so pressing, urgent and immediate. It may be that local people will quickly write them off as irrelevant if they do not tackle these matters as they should. There is, however, a different dynamic at work in the suburbs. Locally, social needs, though never absent, are less apparent. There is the temptation for church people, wearied by social or political strife in their working lives, to seek refreshment in a church life functioning on an entirely different and separate plane.

As part of his missionary challenge, I believe Jesus is asking us to make the connections. He is asking congregations to combine an unflagging zeal for making disciples, and a compassionate service of those in need, with a courageous political stance on issues of justice in society. Now this is asking a very great deal, but who would imagine that the Lord would ask only a little of those to whom he has given so much.

But you say, 'There are no crying social needs in the suburbs.' But have you made all the connections? How, for instance, the inner cities have declined while suburbs have thrived. Isn't it time the suburbs contributed more to the renewal of the inner cities? The members of suburban churches have working connections way beyond the places where they live; shouldn't these regional and even international involvements be opportunities for gospel righteousness to be upheld? And which Christians have the kind of gifts which will enable them to sift through the complexities of such things as trade agreements, and apply to them a biblical concern for justice? Should not suburban Christians number prominently among them?

If the strong wing of evangelism beats in harmony with the

strong wing of social concern then the church can rise to new levels of effectiveness. Possibilities of gospel communication are thus enhanced. Communication possibilities are bound up with communication methods. A church which is doing the right things carries conviction when it is saying the right things. And those things need the right media for them to be rightly heard.

Commenting on the radio ministry of an Alliance Church in a Jewish suburb of New York, Waldron Scott declares, 'Any congregation wishing to expand into a large diverse urban area needs to reach out to the entire area, something made possible by utilising the mass media.'[16] This particular church uses its radio programme to publicise the idea of a Bible study group on every block of the city, an appeal which fits the New Yorkers' need for 'intimacy in relationships'. Here is one church showing the potential of so many others in the suburbs: having an authentic message to share and suitable means through which to share it.

'Authentic' and 'suitable', though, are key words. And here we may be at a crossroads. As I write a record attendance is expected at a Christian resources exhibition in suburban London, and in the European religious broadcasters' convention which follows closely on its heels. Pat Robertson, the American television evangelist, is billed as the special guest. The second convention hopes to formulate a policy for Christian broadcasting in the future in Europe. The relevance of these events to the challenge of mission in suburbia is this: the church there has the responsibility of communicating the gospel throughout and beyond its own locality. Ever more technically powerful means of communication are available to the church; now is a time surely to take the most careful measures to avoid distorting the gospel in the spreading of it. The honour of Christ is at stake.

In the providence of God airwaves may be secondary channels for the gospel, but people are the primary channels. Suburban churches are full of mobile people: mobile for study, mobile for careers, even mobile for leisure. Now surely is the time for them to become fully mobile in the missionary service of Christ. Privilege needs to be translated into mobility: not a restless purposeless shifting from one place to another, but a deliberate willingness not only to serve the Lord and his church where he chooses to place one, but also the readiness to acquire new skills and understandings needed for that next step in service.

The missionary challenge to the church of the suburbs is to deploy its people at the prompting of God's Spirit within their localities, and in less privileged neighbouring areas, and throughout the world. To complete in this way its pilgrim adventure the church must make its connections. It will need to receive helpers as well as send them out. The exercise will be in partnership. Christ's suburban servants may be required to contribute all kinds of skills—some traditional, some innovative and sophisticated. Whatever happens though, God will always find a place in suburbia's missionary offering for such as the old lady in the upright chair whose prayers he delights to answer.

Third World village

In their missionary thinking over recent years the churches have been adjusting to the rapid process of urbanisation and the critical importance of the cities. Even if belatedly, this adjustment has been made. However, a concentration upon the cities at the expense of the rural areas that sustain them makes no sense in missionary terms or in any others. All too easily a growing rural crisis can catch the church ill-prepared just as the urban crisis has done. We must never forget that countryside and city are mutually dependent. In our very proper concern for what is happening in the swollen cities we dare not ignore the neglected fields. Half the human family still lives in rural areas of the world. Even if their proportion should drop to one third, as seems possible on current trends, their importance in God's creative and redemptive purpose must remain of the highest order.

Not all rural peoples live in villages. My mind turns to the isolated 'puestos' of the Chaqueno cowboys of Northern Argentina; others would think of scattered homesteads of trappers, or ranchers in different parts of the world. It remains true, though, that the village is the typical human grouping of rural life, and is therefore a vital focus for rural mission. Third World villages may be partly urbanised and very sophisticated. Many, however, have a very simple structure on the surface of things: served by a dirt road, a cluster of mud-brick dwellings, bare earth and some surviving trees, a well, stream or spring, wandering livestock, a circle of gardens, a small store, and a church or shrine.

Such a village inventory can tell you something and nothing. And of course it is the village people who make the village. So we must try again to glimpse the reality of Third World rural life and of the mission of Jesus Christ within it.

... 'The earth is the Lord's, and the fullness thereof... Seek the Lord while he may be found... Draw close to him...' The silence of the early morning is broken by a voice echoing among the green hills of Southern Chile. The old Mapuche pastor standing on a grassy ridge, hands cupped to his mouth, is announcing God's good news to the lonely dwellings on the slopes and in the valleys below him...

... Nupe villagers in Western Kenya have harvested their crop of millet and the grain is spread out on the ground to dry. The afternoon sky has darkened, spots of rain are beginning to fall and so everybody, including the visiting development expert, scoops up the millet in sacks which are quickly collected in a house with an exceptionally weather-proof roof. Sitting on the sacks, most of the village gathers and there follows a rich and flowing conversation all about agriculture and all about God. A girl passes round a bowl of cornmeal porridge and then through an interpreter they ask the expert, also a Christian, to talk about development.

For a moment he hesitates. Then he says, 'In my country the people live inside their own homes. Often they work alone. Neighbours don't need each other so much and don't know each other so well. Would you like to live like that?' A rapid interchange in the tribal language, and the interpreter gives the verdict: No! 'Well, I am here for you to teach me development. My people need to learn to work together, to relax together and to share. Could you help us?' ...

... 'Now we know that Jesus speaks in our own language.' The Aboriginal preacher, the firelight reflecting in his face, has ended his discourse. The crowd gathered under the night sky is subdued and still absorbed in the message. 'God chose the weak things of the world to shame the strong.' Among the people a deep conviction is growing that, weak as their communities are, they have a place, even a key place, in the powerful modern Australia. Soon they will be singing again their new songs of praise to Jesus. But in this brief moment of silence they are affirming their regained identity: Aborigines in Christ...

... It is a festival day in Andhra Pradesh and the village shrine has attracted many pilgrims. A group of women are talking together excitedly. 'It was after I made my prayer to him for her healing.' The speaker, for a moment oblivious of her little daughter running to and fro between her neighbours, was eager to complete her story. 'After she was better, I had the dream. He stood in front of me, and called me by my name. I believe that Lord Jesus has blessed me. I believe that Yesuswami is most powerful Lord.' ...

Perhaps as much or more than any other locality today, the Third World village is a place of community: a community in fact as well as in name. The people not only know each other's faces but also each other's life stories. A topic in the village does not have to be introduced with elaborate explanations; simple allusions will do because everybody knows what you are talking about anyway. The bonds of the wider family are strong. Each person in the village knows his or her place in the web of relationships.

So there is still a cohesive unity, but there are also sharpening divides. All sorts of new pressures may bring different kinds of people into closer proximity with each other: population increase, guerrilla activity, drought, government policy, colonial legacy. The result may be that members of different tribes may be competing for the same land, immigrant and indigenous races may occupy neighbouring sites, or cattle herders may be too close to small farmers for their comfort or the safety of their crops.

Some divides are sharpened by closeness; others are widened by distance. Take Zaire for example. A recent Church Missionary Society newsletter tells of a Kenyan pastor serving in Zaire and walking through sixty miles of swamp and bush to reach an outlying village. The physical distance and the difficulty of access from the Third World village to the Third World city may be very great indeed. The one relatively easy link is radio. People in even the poorest village have transistors. The trouble is that the village people can neither be free from the city nor can they gain the city's benefits. The city calls the tune, but they can't join the dance.

And all the while Third World village life disturbed in its traditional rhythms is subject to new external threats. At worst it may become part of a battle area between guerrilla and security forces. Or perhaps the land used by the small farmers has a high development potential and is wanted by powerful people for large-scale cash-cropping development. Another threat may come from the deteriorating environment: a combination of more people, more cooking-fires and so fewer trees leads to dramatically less soil and ugly gashes in the hillside and flooding in the valley below.

The things that affect village life in the Third World are serious in themselves, and many pose a grave threat to their stability and welfare. Realism forces us to face the fact that these disturbing changes are accelerating. So where the church of Jesus Christ has taken root in Third World villages then this is the situation it confronts: surviving community, sharpening divisions, growing threats and accelerating change. In parts of Africa and in most of Asia it is also surrounded by thousands of unevangelised neighbours.

The missionary challenge

If this scenario corresponds to the reality of rural life in significant sectors of the the Third World, then some urgent prescription might be pressed upon the church to take emergency measures. Those from whom I learn would, I believe, commend four things instead.

In the Third World villages *let the church be true to itself*. This has to do with what John V. Taylor calls the 'thread of sanctity'. Twenty years ago he was commenting on the funeral service of the last survivor of the first generation of Ugandan clergy. Kezekiya Kaggwa he described as a man who 'carried through into these more complex times the essential simplicity and ardour of a faith that had been born in the tumultuous early days of the Church of that land'. Now all who have been privileged to work with the church in Africa, Asia, Latin America or the Pacific will know men and women like Kezekiya. We will recognise in people we have known John Taylor's 'thread of sanctity'. 'Its marks are a supreme love for Jesus, an absolute simplicity of life, and a will, at whatever cost, to live at peace with all.'[17]

Hold these qualities together with the situation so many churches are facing, and their value is priceless. These are the foundational things. The old leaders who embody them bear a vital witness. The new generation is called to a similar obedience. But reflecting on this, John Taylor quotes Adrian Hastings: 'We must not falter in our old faith, nor in the painful effort to maintain its relevance to a new world.'[18] For many in the rural areas of the Third World this 'new world' shows signs of being a disintegrating world. New qualities in the church's leaders and members are demanded, but the 'thread of sanctity' will never be dispensable. Against all that tears apart it is the only binding strong enough.

In the villages of the Third World *let the gospel be the whole gospel*. The starting-point for this is in fact the holiness or wholeness of the older generation of believers. For them all things come within the loving concern of the Father God.

Both the temporal and eternal future are in his hands. To grasp the missionary challenge is to grasp both these aspects of God's providence.

This confidence has nothing of complacency; it will have been tested by extreme hardships in the past and faces even greater difficulties ahead. On existing trends of food production and population growth the map of Africa is a map of famine. Vast centrally organised schemes have failed to produce food for the people. The African small farmer remains the only one to whom to turn for food now and in the future as well as in the past.

What then is the whole gospel for a community of small farmers? Peter Bachelor, through his involvement in 'Faith and Farm' in Nigeria and his subsequent consultancy work throughout Africa, is able to show convincingly that cultivators are good evangelists. Those who use responsible appropriate methods in their cultivations and do so in praise of Jesus gain the attention of less satisfied neighbours. 'Why are you taking time with us? We are not Christians and you are not making a profit.' Peter Bachelor's *People in Rural Development* contains stories of Christian 'motivators' whose practical help has evoked such responses as this.[19] The whole gospel, demonstrated in Christ's own way in selfless and practical actions, embraces people's welfare in the indivisible spirit and material world. Logically, it bears both spiritual and material fruit.

Let the fellowship be an unbroken fellowship. The gospel has much to offer the small farmer in his struggle to produce food and make a livelihood. The gospel does not demand, however, that he should struggle alone. The gospel must first repair some divides in the church. Again drawing upon Adrian Hastings, Simon Barrington Ward in a more recent CMS newsletter points to 'a great gulf fixed between the centres of power in the church... and the ever growing mass of congregations in the countryside'.[20] The church 'superstructure' is in some danger of failing the local congregations just as the governmental 'superstructure' is failing the people.

The missionary challenge is to reverse this trend and to strengthen the bonds in Christ between the central leaders and the rural members. Who will plead for a better deal for the small farmers in the places of power? Might not the church leaders do so, especially, though of course not only, in Africa? But when the political or other problems are stubborn and that kind of help is not forthcoming, the bonds of Christian fellowship have even more value.

This recognition, born of experience, shapes Peter Bachelor's view of rural development: 'Living among people, sitting down humbly and listening to them, until with the passing of time conversation becomes less reserved and trust comes. It means forbearance of a kind which is prized and recognized in cultures where impatience is much more of a sin than it is in the western world.'[21] Bonds of fellowship can still embrace the Western expatriate missionaries in these situations, but they must learn the lessons of patience, of which Peter Bachelor speaks.

Let the vision be a broad vision. In places uncluttered by office blocks visual horizons have a wider sweep. My contact with Chaco Indian communities, among the poorest in Argentina, teaches me that through the influence of the gospel such rural people can have a wide view of the world. Their readiness to go out and evangelise in other villages in the region would shame many First World congregations. Not enough money is there to pay for the settled pastoral ministry (that is fulfilled without financial reward). Collection money is used instead to feed families left behind when their bread-winners set off on evangelistic journeys.

More privileged Christians might applaud the way Third World villagers spread the gospel among their own kind. The vision though is wider than this. 'At university I met theology; among the Matacos I met the living Christ.' This response of an Argentine teacher of sociology to the impact upon her of the tribal people of a Chaco village led to a very beautiful and effective vocation among them. It also demonstrates the scope of witness of those without economic advantage. So too did the effects of the friendship of Philippino villagers towards students visiting from Tokyo. Initial suspicions, born of war memories, were broken down. The affection of the farewells had a converting power for the sophisticated students.

Glimpses such as these may help us to begin to recognise the rich treasures of the gospel of which God's people in the Third World villages are the bearers. Their mission focuses upon the immediate and pressing spiritual and social concerns of their locality. Outside threats may bear upon them hard, but their witness also shines out beyond their local world. Few, if any, ride in jet planes to international conferences. But we all so urgently need their wisdom. Their call to mission is inextricably bound to our own. Like us, the Mapuches on their green hills and Aborigines under their southern stars must live by seeing, ever more clearly, the Saviour of the world.

The First World village

We come to the First World village as the last but not least of our localities of mission. Missionary thinking may not be applied so widely to this local field of mission. Fewer people may think of it in missionary terms at all. Rural areas of the First World do not compare with the areas characterised by the five other kinds of localities in terms of the overall numbers of people living in them. Even so, First World villages and their surrounding countryside constitute areas of missionary activity and concern which not only have their own acute needs but also their far-reaching potential.

… With a fine rain and a high wind blowing off the Atlantic a little group stand huddled on the grassy cliff-top. Bracing themselves, they look out over Bardsey Island, ringed with white surf and swirling currents, a grey mass under a grey sky. 'That was their base,' shouted the Welsh pastor. 'The Celtic missionaries evangelised this part of Wales from there.'

'Then we should pray that the gospel will triumph again.' The visitor speaking is a Ugandan bishop. So the group unites in prayer: Welsh and Ugandans, Indians, a Nigerian and an Englishman. A little fragment of history is made on a peninsula whose missionary story is not yet done.

... As she pushes open the heavy wooden door she isn't sure what to expect on the other side. She is a newcomer and from the notice-board it is not clear what time the service is due to start. After the brilliant April sunshine the interior looks impenetratably dark. 'Oh they're already receiving Communion!' The newcomer can now see all eleven members of the congregation kneeling at the communion rail. And at the end there is a gap. 'That must be for the missing twelfth. Could that be me?' ...

... 'This is my work station.' The Bible study was over and the host was showing a farmer member round the cottage.

'What's this then?' said the farmer.

'This is my computer console and teleconferencing equipment.'

The farmer looked at the screens and keyboard. 'Unlimited information at your fingertips, eh? What about grain prices? Could you get those out of that machine?'

'I'll try if you like.'

'No, don't bother now. There will be time in the morning. Do you know I have to admit that I resented you buying up old Ben's cottage and turning it into a kind of office home, but now we've all come into this new experience through the church, other new things don't seem so bad any more. What was it we were reading tonight? "Behold, I make all things new".'

The man with the hardware smiled. 'More than computers, I think.' ...

In the First World the drift into the cities is over. After 200 years of decline in numbers, population in many rural areas is beginning to show a modest increase. In Britain, while those living in inner-city areas have decreased by 10 per cent, the rural population has increased from 22 per cent to 24 per cent. In some of the remotest areas of the country the population is increasing twenty times the rate elsewhere.

For people generally the rural areas do not conjure up an image of expansion, nor indeed of modernity. It is assumed that tradition is the order of the day. Tradition remains, of course, enshrined in beautiful buildings, carefully preserved customs, and among local families with deep roots in the land. However, with the composition of a community, the changes may be much greater than we imagine. Simon Barrington Ward tells of a village where he used to live in which only 3 or 4 of the original 150 inhabitants are left. Their places are taken by commuters 'who know little of the past or even of each other in the present'.[22] Even where a village is not engulfed in the urban sprawl physically, it may be psychologically.

The newest breed of First World rural-dweller is the occupant of the 'electronic cottage'. Micro-electronics and the information revolution is making possible the decentralisation of the workplace. More people are now able to earn their living at home. Alvin Toffler, in *The Third Wave*, waxes eloquent on the far-reaching social changes which the new technology is bringing in.[23] Whatever the longer future holds, it is already evident that people are coming back into the rural areas not to use them just for weekends or as dormitories, but as homes for working and for living. It follows that the rural locality, seen as a mission field, often contains not only more people, not only different people, but also people who at least potentially have a new commitment and contribution in the locality itself.

Decline and growth, conservatism and innovation: if that is the general picture in the First World village locality, what can be said about the local church or churches? These areas of the world are nearly all traditionally Christian. To what extent are they actively Christian?

A study on one Anglican diocese in rural England presents an overall picture of retrenchment and shrinkage. Leslie Frances, in *Rural Anglicanism*, shows that numbers of those confirmed (received into full adult church membership) have dropped in 1982 to a third of the level registered in 1956.[24]

Other negative trends in these Anglican parishes include reduction in the number of clergy, and Easter communicants as a proportion of adult population down to below 7 per cent. Against this he notes a significant rise in commissioned lay leadership. Most disturbingly, he observed that in all the churches studied virtually no midweek activities were provided for children and young people.

This is the bad news applying to one denomination in one area of one country. No doubt it has parallels elsewhere. However, in the midst of a situation in which many churches are struggling for maintenance, a few at least are growing vigorously. Where there is life and vitality evidence suggests that people will travel appreciable distances to share in it. What appears to be lacking is a coherent vision for the future of rural church life. Perhaps the church, like other organisations, supports its centres better than its outposts, and suffers from an urbanised leadership, relatively unaware of rural priorities. In Britain, after publication of *Faith in the City*, there was the call for a similar study of the social and spiritual conditions in rural areas. Now at last it is being implemented.

The missionary challenge

Before any other aspect of the First World rural missionary challenge can be tackled it is first necessary to cope with the constraints. The local church may be very small, with an elderly congregation. People who have lived in the district all their lives may be cautious, conservative, suspicious, or even intransigent. Those engaged directly in farming may have reduced their labour force down to the barest possible minimum and be working all daylight hours. Newcomers to the district may focus their interests elsewhere. Decline in public transport may restrict mobility to those who can afford cars. Such may be the reality against which any desire to see the spreading of Christ's kingdom will be tested.

To cope with constraints like these a ministry must be prayerful, credible, caring and coherent. Any new initiatives must focus upon venues where people customarily meet and involve things people are used to doing. The established rural population must be very sure of a new step before taking it. A response to the gospel may be worked out best in the sustained, unhurried and unpressured atmosphere of regular house Bible studies. For the rural evangelist and minister patience and consistency in approach to people are of primary importance.

These comments about an appropriate response to the difficulties of the situation reflect the conclusions of an English group called Federation for Rural Evangelism.[25] Certainly where populations are scattered, gathering large numbers of people in one place is scarcely feasible. Catering for the specialist needs of different age groups may also be very difficult; each may be represented by only ones or twos. Constraints there definitely are in rural ministry, but so are there opportunities. We should never forget that there has been a remarkable missionary history in rural Europe. We should take inspiration from the past. In some places preaching-crosses still stand where the pioneers proclaimed the gospel in the open air, illustrating it with the help of the carvings on the stone. What was done in those far-off days can, with modified means, be done again. And is; Peter Green, with his imaginative use of the sketch-board, is one evangelist modelling a contemporary approach which follows an ancient tradition.[26]

The missionary challenge is that we should cope with the present, take inspiration from the past, and anticipate the future. Christians with exclusively urban psychology may consider the rural areas to be of peripheral interest. Yet, if so, Christ has a special care for those on the margins and an identity with them. But again, looked at in another way, the rural areas should be less and less marginal to anyone's concern. Not only are they the essential base for food production but also, for a growing number, the context for a new way of life combining advantages of both city and countryside. Alvin Toffler believes "the electronic cottage could touch off a renaissance among voluntary organisations".[27] He lists churches among them.

There is no suggestion here that we should uncritically take our cues from secular analysts. The missionary challenge, though, requires of us that we should anticipate not only the changes dark with threat but also those rich with promise. A prospect of more people living together and working together in rural communities has great significance for those who long for the coming of God's kingdom. The old Celtic missionaries who carried the Christian message to the remotest habitations would scarcely have balked at a silicon cottage. May the gospel triumph in our day of rural opportunity as it did in theirs.

Local mission audit

A whistle-stop tour of six whole continents may be exciting or bewildering. A rapid exploration of six typical but contrasting localities may leave us aroused or bemused. Whatever the reaction, the object of the exercise is to learn a fuller obedience in mission. Nothing less than a global obedience is, I believe, enough. In one sense or another all Christ's followers are asked 'to go into all the world'. There is, however, no global obedience without local obedience. A primary and urgent question faces us: 'How do we work out our missionary obedience in our own locality?'

Of the six localities we have described some will be familiar and others will be strange. An attempt has been made to look at each from a missionary point of view. This perspective is important. If it does not occur to us that where we live is a mission field, it may not occur to us to engage in mission in it. We have also tried to discern, with the help of others, some of the challenges and priorities in mission which each typical locality presents. Of course no generalisations should ever be mechanically applied. The Holy Spirit has precise and particular plans for each place. How then do we discover them?

Mission Audit is the rather forbidding title of a Church of England Board of Mission and Unity booklet which approaches this very question.[28] Just as a financial audit examines the economic position of a company and assists in identifying future financial objectives, so a mission audit may help a church to see its missionary position more clearly and identify its goals in mission. If we are members together of a local church it is 'to ask ourselves if we are doing what we should be doing'. That, the booklet points out, 'is not faithless, but a duty akin to repentance. We can delude ourselves about what is actually happening both optimistically and pessimistically. Some objective measure should not be despised.'

To discover more fully what may be involved in such an 'objective measure' requires a study of *Mission Audit* itself. Full participation of church members, a shared sense of accountability to Christ, careful and effective information gathering on numbers of people inside and outside the churches, their attitudes and expectations, effective presentation of conclusions: all these things and more may be required. Ultimately new God-guided initiatives in local mission grow out of a congregation praying together, experimenting together, and discovering together the seal of God's approval for what they are doing.

None of these fundamentals, though, preclude the need for careful stocktaking and self-examination. Athletes, sports teams, companies undertake the most rigorous scrutiny of their performances. The church of Jesus Christ in its local mission has infinitely more serious responsibilities. Whether operating in First or Third World situations, in urban or rural areas, the local congregation has a unique and vital role. In carrying out its task the church should not be hazily casual but zealously clear.

6

Partners in Mission: Unbreakable Cords

Prior questions

In successive chapters we have argued that the crises of our time highlight the urgency of mission, the thrust of Scripture undergirds the meaning of mission, history teaches the lessons of mission, and the world in every continent and locality is the arena of mission. Now some basic questions confront us with renewed force:

How can we participate in mission in a way which squares with that of the patriarchs, prophets, apostles, and, above all, with that of Jesus Christ?

How can we take our place alongside those who have gone before us, and be worthy heirs of the missionary inheritance?

How, if at all, can we relate to the different continents and different kinds of localities today, and give and receive help from fellow Christians in these other places?

How, locally and across the globe, can we weave a Christian network which shows beautiful, just and loving relationships worth copying because they are better than the inter-connections of the secular world?

Four questions as big as these yield to a one word answer: partnership. No, not partnership! Surely there must be something more exciting than that? Yes, partnership! There is nothing more interesting, exasperating and exciting than partnership.

201

Fragments of memory: glimpses of partnership

... After the fierce heat outside, the air-conditioned atmosphere of the recording studio is decidedly chilly. Two middle-aged women and a man sit at the table, an all-angle microphone between them. Either from the cold or with a sense of anticipation, they shiver. On goes the light signal and on goes the broadcast.

'Amtena!' The tribal greeting reaches over the airwaves to a people who have never heard their own language issuing from their transistor radios before. Interspersed with their chat show about nutrition and care of newly weaned children is a recording from a local church music group, and a testimony of a man whose new faith in Christ has brought him release from a drink problem.

The chief speaker is a woman from that same tribe and the man, a pastor, is also a Mataco. The other woman is European but has spent more than half her life working with these people who are her friends. Many in the villages know all three. Even those who don't are glad to hear the message in their own words. As they say, 'If it's on the radio, it must be true.' ...

... The two men in the pick-up truck are of the same build and wear similar clothes and rope-soled shoes. Both are soft spoken, conscientious and intelligent. Each is in his thirties. The one at the wheel is the first among his people to graduate from secondary school, not far away. The other graduated from a distant university. For eight years now they have worked together, planned together, and prayed together.

The forest road, a straight cut made in the survey for petroleum, stretches through the shimmering heat haze into the distance. A column of dust plumes out behind the pick-up, covering its load of bagged seeds and fencing wire in a fine powder. The man driving has his mind on his invalid wife and the mischievous rumours circulating about him and other women. His colleague is weighing in his mind an invitation to share in another agricultural programme in a neighbouring republic. 'Will my friend cope with the pressures and responsibilities without my support?' ...

... Two very different men sit at a book-strewn desk in a cramped office. Without the windows and door open, the atmosphere under the tin roof would be suffocating. The bigger man makes an expansive gesture and launches into a commentary upon the ways of his people. 'We find it very hard to say, No! to our children.' His own had just appeared in the doorway, asking for money to buy freshly baked bread.

This comment doesn't appear to have any immediate relevance to the task in hand: the translation of Matthew's Gospel into the everyday speech of the tribe. The big man has, though, a kind of erratic brilliance. It was good that he should be appointed translator and the missionary his technical assistant and advisor. The one brings a fund of folk memory, philosophising, and fervour. The other brings a keen ear, an observant eye and the dryest sense of humour. 'Oh yes, where were we up to? Chapter 7 verse 9. "Which of you, if his son asks for..." What was I just saying about bread?' ...

The Bible and partnership

Partnership is not just a nice idea or a fashionable style for doing mission. It is, from a biblical standpoint, essential to mission itself. Several English words are used to translate *koinonia*, the basic New Testament word: partnership, fellowship, communion, participation. At root it is a sharing in something with someone or a sharing of something with someone. Thus it also gives the suggestion of generosity.

When Jesus was criticised by the Jewish leaders for healing a man on the Sabbath he responded by saying, 'My Father is always at work to this very day, and I, too, am working.'[1] This answer increased their hostility; it amounted to a claim that both Jesus and God, the Father, were partners in the same work. In fact the New Testament witness shows the one work of God in creation and redemption to be a partnership between Father, Son and Holy Spirit. We can say that the mission of God is carried out through a partnership among the Persons of the Trinity.

Moreover, from the New Testament it is apparent that this partnership extends further. The apostle Paul writes to the Corinthians, 'As God's fellow workers we urge you not to receive God's grace in vain.'[2] Evidently Paul sees himself as a co-worker with God, not of course implying that Paul's person is equal to that of his Lord, but rather that Paul's share in his Lord's service brings with it great intimacy with God. But there is no question here of some privilege unique to this apostle. Paul is as zealous to identify himself with others in his missionary service as he is bold to associate himself with Jesus. In the mission Christ entrusts to his infant church the divine fellowship overflows and the divine partnership includes the human participants.

The mission of Jesus Christ must be carried out as a partnership/fellowship exercise because partnership is in the very nature of God. We can even say that mission involves bringing people who were previously out of fellowship with God into fellowship with him. It is a contradiction then for mission to be undertaken by people who are out of fellowship with each other. Co-operation, sharing, generous appreciation, wide participation, these partnership qualities epitomise our New Testament inheritance.

Of course the Gospels and the Epistles are very frank in revealing the way that Christ's followers fail in their missionary partnership. The rivalries, disagreements and divisions are all reported. Mission is not brought to a halt when the partnership principle is injured; Paul can even be glad when the gospel is preached out of selfish ambition. However, in the same letter to the Philippians in which he refers to the rival preachers, the apostle makes his most moving appeal for partnership in mission, which is indeed humble, vulnerable Christ-copying 'fellowship with the Spirit'. Thus the Philippians are 'loyal yoke-fellows' who have 'laboured side by side' with Paul in the gospel. They are those who have expressed their partnership in Paul's missionary endeavour by sending him material support.

They have entered into his suffering, as Paul, himself, has experienced the fellowship of the suffering of Christ.[3]

For Paul missionary partnership was a very personal, intimate and local thing. No doubt he had learnt much about it in the vigorous and creative fellowship of the church at Antioch with its mixed membership of Jews and Gentiles. Paul could see, though, that partnership also had a vital application in the wider church. The collection by the Gentile churches of Macedonia and Achaia for the famine-stricken church of Judea was an act of Christian compassion which Paul eagerly encouraged. However, he saw its deepest significance not simply as an alleviation of immediate need, urgently important as that was, but even more as an act of partnership cementing together otherwise differing sections of the church. In Paul's eyes this was not a one-sided affair involving affluent donors and miserable recipients. Even in the emergency he could see a mutuality of giving and receiving in material and spiritual gifts.[4]

Partnership across the centuries

Perhaps it is not customary to think of the communion of saints as a missionary partnership but even so I believe we should do so. If we are Christians at all then it is due to a chain of missionary witness which has come down to us from the past. We benefit immeasurably from these missionary labours even though we may be totally ignorant of the identity of those who have shared in passing the faith on to us. If we are active ourselves in the mission of Jesus Christ, then, whether we are aware of it or not, we are entering into all that they sought to do in his service. Certainly that was my experience as a young missionary finding acceptance with tribal people because of their love for the old pioneers.

Mine was a happy experience and it was easy to appreciate brave and faithful men and women of the previous generation. Whether in general it is harder or easier to be on good terms with the church triumphant than with the church militant is a debatable point. What I want to emphasise from a missionary point of view is that it does matter how we think of generations that have preceded us. To ridicule, or worse, contemptuously dismiss their missionary efforts seems to me no better than to stoop to such attitudes with our contemporaries. There is a bond of fellowship to preserve even down the years. This is not to argue for an uncritical glossing over of their inadequacies and ineptitudes.

Instead of either of these mistakes what is urgently needed is a discerning and balanced appreciation of our missionary inheritance. Humility and generosity will be needed in this fellowship between missionary generations, as indeed it is between present colleagues. What a tragedy it will be if the radical stream in the church remains locked in its excessively negative estimate of mission and missionaries in the colonial period. How sad, too, if conservative Christians should remain partly blind to their failings. No doubt all of us need a humbler self-estimate, so essential to missionary partnership. How easily we in our generation could be the weakest link.

Local partnership now

The message of Christ and the apostles and the accumulated wisdom of our missionary forebears (not to mention their accumulated mistakes) demands that we should approach our present responsibility in fellowship with others. Our obedience in mission should be worked out with fellow Christians humbly, responsively, co-operatively. They require of us that we should turn away from competitiveness and personal ambition and espouse partnership. And this means getting on with people right where we are!

It would be hypocritical to recommend elaborate and impressive partnerships in mission across continents, between denominations, spanning geographical distances and racial diversities, and then be content with never more than superficial or barely patched-up relationships with people with whom we worship every Sunday, or fellow believers with whom we work every day of the week. Partnership must begin locally, if it is to begin at all.

This local imperative of partnership prompts me to write personally. I am a member of a staff team of a missionary training college. I work particularly closely with eight other colleagues. We are very fortunate to include two Indians among us, but otherwise we are all British. We share many interests in common. Thus far we have been spared any really furious disagreements. We share out our work tolerably well. All this put together though does not add up to more than a fraction of the potential of partnership in Christ.

All of us know that there is much more partnership 'land' to possess. We are gradually learning how to support each other more strongly, and, especially difficult perhaps, challenge each other more sharply. It is one thing to have a basic agreement in aims; it is another to see together a widening vision bright with God's glory. Ought we be satisfied with a lively and varied pattern of community worship when God may be leading us on to the kind of adoration and intercession marked by deep agreement on earth and grace overflooding from heaven?

Even among people who have the most in common, Christian partnership is not without its difficulties and challenges. There are always the God-given differences in character: the inward and the outgoing, the thinkers and the feelers, the planners and the plodders, the wrecklessly adventurous and the frustratingly prosaic. God knows we need each other. We sometimes think we do not, and find it hard to accept the contrasting traits. If we take our local partnership seriously then these things need to be worked through. And the rewards are great.

There is a special value and opportunity for like-minded Christians to work together, but missionary partnership is not confined to these alliances alone. The apostle Paul was not only committed to his immediate colleagues and to Antioch, his sending church, but also to a Christian community with a very different style and ethos at Jerusalem. His relationship with the Jerusalem church was never free from tensions, but it was never broken.

Dare I at this point return to the personal? The college in which I serve is part of a federation in which many different Christian traditions are represented and through which many things are organised ecumenically. I function here as an evangelical among Christians who in different degrees express their faith similarly and differently. In coming, this is exactly what I have felt called to do. My colleagues in the federation are generous enough to show forbearance over what they see as my Christian blind spots. I need to learn forbearance over what I may see as theirs. Of course superficial agreement covering real differences is worse than useless. Partnership requires us to disagree sometimes, and show goodwill always.

Both from a reading of Scripture and from a personal call I believe that local missionary partnership finds a place within it for the less alike Christians as well as the more alike ones. How this works out will be different for different people. However it works out there will be misunderstandings and frustrations. Anyone who tries to interpret one Christian tradition to another risks becoming a stranger to both. Even so our aim, where possible, should be to bridge even the polarisations with partnership, and in fellowship seek convergence upon Christ, to whom the Scriptures bear witness.

Global partnership now?

In tackling the theme of local missionary partnership I have written personally because I believe this to be a personal issue and a personal challenge to all Christians. I have seen at this personal level how a partnership approach can make the difference between fruitfulness and sterility. I think of how two former colleagues in Argentina, both gifted in evangelism, experienced a breakthrough in their church planting ministry when at depth they began praying and working together. There is no doubt that local mission thrives on local partnership, but what about global mission?

It would be easy to say that global mission depends upon global partnership, and then rush in with recommendations on how this partnership should be organised today. However, global partnership has all the difficulties of local partnership and many more besides. What is potentially very beautiful and fruitful may actually be distorted and stultifying. For the global partnership to work it must be a partnership of reconciliation, understanding, mutuality, prayer and suffering. Only then will it fully and truly be a partnership of reaping.

Partnership of reconciliation

Bishop Harry Moore, in the January 1987 issue of the CMS newsletter, writes about the question of black consciousness in Britain. He describes the pain and anger expressed by the black community in general and black Anglicans in particular: 'their sense of being pushed on one side'. He then very frankly admits his own mixed reactions to these expressions and his instinctive question: 'Why is he/she going on about black consciousness when we believe we are all one in Christ Jesus?'[5]

Harry Moore's gut reaction is one with which most, if not all, white Christians could identify. He can, therefore, speak for them and to them when he goes on to raise problems of a hidden sense of superiority and a need for a change of attitude and heart. This, he insists, will require an 'attempt to enter into the feeling of our fellow Christians who feel marginalised'. Sadly, many church members in Britain failed in doing this when the immigrants arrived in the 50s and 60s from the Caribbean. This failure led to a rift which is only now beginning to be healed.

When the relationships are played out on a world stage the divides may be even more alarming. The north-south division may appear unbridgeable. Simon Barrington Ward, commenting on the World Council of Churches conference at Melbourne in 1980, describes the assembly at one point as being 'locked into a rich/poor deadlock', bound into a false relationship with guilt on the one side and bitterness on the other.[6] Behind the outrage in this instance lay the colonial and military injustices of Latin America and apartheid in South Africa: evils in which professing Christians have been deeply implicated.

So is there no answer to these grievous wrongs and the effect they have upon relationships in the church worldwide? Even though it can be complicated and distorted by ideological presentations of the left or of the right, there is a massive and deeply injurious problem here. There is every reason for the distress and anger of oppressed people. But there is also a vital need that the Christians among them, in the words of Coptic Bishop Marcos, 'in the frenzy of their struggle... should not lose Christ'. The truth is Jesus, who bore the full weight of sin and suffering, can bring healing. No one else can: neither the sinned against, nor the sinners, nor those who by being part of the political system are implicated in the injustice.

But Jesus the Reconciler and Sin Bearer draws both the perpetrators, the victims and the accessories of these social evils into his redeeming embrace. He requires of them all something which is different yet the same; he gives them something which is free yet costly. In identifying with him and with his sufficient sacrifice they have to identify with each other. Even for those more sinned against than sinning there is a repentance. So too there is a far-reaching repentance required of those who have actively and violently misused their power. Even the compromised bystanders in the political arena are not allowed by Jesus to go groping around in a mist of guilt. They are to rework their relations and reorder their social and political lives with respect to justice.

So in Christ the global partnership is intact after all! The bonds are unbreakable! Because Jesus identified with all, sinned against and sinners, all have the possibility of identifying with each other. Through the grace of Christ all, black and white, military and revolutionary can see themselves in each other. They can say, 'If I had walked in that other person's shoes, I could have so easily done the same.' This is no trite formula; it requires a new kind of obedience, a shared exploration of faith, a costly entry into other people's worlds, a demanding co-operation in missionary service. Like all else, the global missionary partnership is the fruit of the reconciling dying of the Saviour.

Partnership in understanding

I repent so that I may understand. Christian understanding is never just a matter of mental gymnastics. Those who enjoy academic privilege have no monopoly of it; indeed they may suffer special handicaps. Christ's reconciliation which brings repentance also brings the kind of understanding required for Christian partnership in the world today.

What could be more important as a focus of concern for Christians in partnership across the world than the evangelisation of the 3,500 million who as yet do not profess faith in Christ? The critical value of the partnership of understanding is highlighted for me in a correspondence provoked by Dr Donald McGavran, the Church Growth pioneer, and his proposal for a 'giant step in Christian mission'. The Christian radicals responded to his letter by accusing McGavran of chauvinism, demanding that he should re-examine the way his North American culture distorts the gospel, and suggesting that his proposals would alienate more people from Christ than win to him.

Now there is nothing more salutary than to be told one's faults, but those who administer the treatment should receive the treatment. Radicals should welcome the opportunity to re-examine their own faithfulness to Christ's command to make disciples of all nations. They should ask what they have to learn from the riches even the genius of North American culture dedicated to Christ, as well as what they have to beware from American mistakes. The partnership of understanding is not cemented by strident demands that the other should do the repenting. Rather it requires the esteeming of the others more highly than ourselves.

Give-and-take partnership

'How can we truly be partners when one side is so strong and wealthy and the other is so poor and weak?'[7] This comment quoted by Robert Ramseyer, a Mennonite missionary leader, highlights a feeling common among Christians in both the

North and the South. It assumes that because the churches of the First World are rich in finances, have elaborately developed institutions, a highly trained ministry, and a long history, then their contribution to any missionary partnership must completely overshadow anything that the Third World churches might provide.

To attempt, as we have done, to look at the missionary situation in the different continents does not in fact present a picture of strength in the First World churches and weakness in the Third World churches. It is much more complicated than that. Instead there are some remarkable abounding strengths in the Third World and cringing, crippling weaknesses in the First. But still the idea persists that we (in the North) have much to give them (in the South) and they have little to give us. How then do we achieve the breakthrough to the kind of give-and-take partnership we both need so much?

Robert Ramseyer believes that we, as Christians, need whole new attitudes: an understanding that 'we are strangers and pilgrims even in the lands of our birth'. He continues, 'Only as we achieve a measure of personal detachment from what we have always considered our native socio-cultural settings do we become capable of perceiving both our own needs and the resources which God provides to and through our fellow Christians.'[8] In simpler words, we need to take off our cultural blinkers and then we will discover how much our Third World brothers and sisters have to offer and how fully their gifts match our needs.

'I want missionaries to take their appointed place in the church. I want them to exercise the authority that is given to them and to submit to the authority of those under whose oversight they work.' In making this comment recently, Archbishop Olufosoye is reflecting upon an emerging give-and-take partnership between Anglicans in Nigeria and Britain. The Nigerian Church has such obvious strengths and the British Church such obvious limitations that the old unequal relationship can be a thing of the past. Missionaries can therefore take their place alongside nationals much more naturally and less self-consciously, giving and receiving guidance the same as anyone else.

This balanced interdependence is an ideal for partnership. It doesn't happen automatically or easily. Malcolm Warner of the Church Missionary Society, through his experience of churches in Asia, suggests a whole series of steps from dependence, through independence, to interdependence. Three of these he expresses as, 'We want you, because we need you to do what we can't do' (dependence). 'We don't want you, because we don't need you, because we can do what we have to do' (independence). 'We want to welcome you so that we can discover that we need each other.' James Sarpei, a Ghanaian, enlarges upon this last stage, 'Then we shall want you as you want us, I hope, essentially for ourselves.'

Partnership in prayer

If the churches grasp the full potential of give-and-take partnership, then we can anticipate a very fruitful increase in the movement of missionary helpers between different regions of the world. There is no question though of a sort of global musical chairs with everybody moving to somewhere else. And in any case even the most mobile missionary can only be in one place at a time. So global partnership must contend with the constraints of distance. Something which leaps over the longest distance is prayer.

Prayer confronts not only the problem of distance but also of weakness. What could appear more innocuous and inconsequential than a prayer diary and a sheaf of prayer letters? Yet these aids to prayer can assume immense significance because of the potential of prayer itself. Prayer is a way of standing shoulder to shoulder with people thousands of miles away. Through prayer impenetrable barriers against the advance of the gospel can be pierced. The transforming relationship with God cemented with prayer can transform other relationships however difficult or distorted. Prayer can empower anyone; even the most physically restricted invalid can have an adventurous worldwide missionary role through intercession.

The fact that God is well able to change the world through the prayers of his people doesn't of course make prayer any easier. Missionary intercession can still appear a chore. To meet to pray for the advance of the gospel in another part of the world may come very low on our priorities. Yet, as a powerful way of weakness, prayer has no substitute. It is an indispensable part of missionary support. To be the focus of intercession is to be carried forward on a strong current, sails filled with a favourable wind. For the exposed missionary a prayer partner is a partner indeed.

Partnership in suffering

Imagine for a moment that instead of a link through a page of typescript we were actually imprisoned together and under threat of torture. The communication between us would take on a new dimension of directness and urgency. If we survived the experience at all with our faith intact, then we would have learnt a very great deal: not least about what the apostle Paul calls the fellowship of Christ's sufferings.

The quality of this fellowship or partnership in suffering is such that it reveals the authentic things and relegates the secondary things. As a boy, I remember reading a collection of letters written by Christians imprisoned and condemned to death by Hitler. Some of these prisoners were Roman Catholic, some were Protestant, some were lay people, others were ordained. With these differences and many more, their letters still bore a striking similarity. Most remarkably they all breathed a spirit of joy. Deeply embedded in the fellowship of suffering is the secret of how very different people can be fashioned as one.

Partnership of reaping

The Bible promises that those who sow in tears shall reap in joy. A missionary partnership which is forged in suffering will be sealed with fruitfulness. Such an affirmation is true to Scripture and surely to be believed. Even so, the pain of suffering is such that any good result may seem totally remote in the moment of trauma. Physically at least, suffering may even break the partnership. I think of Johannes Ludwig Krapf, pioneer missionary to East Africa. Only months after their arrival on Mombasa Island Krapf's young wife and infant child were dead.

In the face of this tragedy, he had a vision of a chain of mission stations stretching from East to West across the continent. Fruitfulness out of suffering? Perhaps, but a different kind of testing came with the years of hard journeys, discouragement and loneliness. Krapf made few converts; the first was a crippled man. There was to be a rich harvest of both suffering and success in East Africa, but during his years of service this pioneer saw plenty of the former but little of the latter.[9]

In spite of appearances, the story of Johannes Krapf serves as an example of the partnership of reaping as well as the partnership of suffering. It underlines the fact that so often the two are inseparable. It emphasises the delays, the small advances, the large reverses, the frailty of the human body and the limits of the human understanding. And at the end of the heroic but apparently ineffective endeavour—what? Today there are literally millions of Christians in Kenya, Tanzania and Uganda. Are they the harvest of one young couple? No, they owe their faith to a fellowship of many witnesses, yet the Krapfs take their place among them. In losing a family they helped to found one.

Structures for partnership

It seems a pity to end with structures. If 'partnership' at first sight appears a dull idea, then 'structures' must be positively petrifying! Those with little sympathy or contact with missionary organisations may jump to this conclusion, and those within them may be sometimes tempted to agree. And yet there is another side to this question. Think of the human body. Consider the perfect, intricate construction of the rib cage and the hidden diaphragm. How would the breath of life enter that body without those structures? How will a life-giving partnership in Christ's body be built up and sustained without a suitable framework and skeleton? Mission requires partnership; partnership requires structures.

Already, though, we have seen enough to know that any old partnership and any old structures will not do. There is a need for quality structures matching a quality partnership. The authentic features of the Christian *koinonia*, or partnership, we have described as reconciliation, understanding, mutuality, prayer, suffering and reaping. Clearly an organisational framework cannot produce these results of itself. The structures can and do, however, stifle the desired relationships or allow them to grow. They can help Christian partnership to have a beautiful shape or a very ugly one.

The structures of partnership in mission must also fully relate to the present realities of the six continents. Structures need to be developed to channel the immense contribution that the African churches could now make in world mission. Europe, with its urgent need for help in re-evangelising the continent, requires receiving structures to match its sending structures for mission. Missionaries from one country have access to some of their neighbouring countries and are denied entry in others. The international combinations of partnership need to maximise the possibilities of access and entry, which in a politically divided world are not getting easier. Likewise the international flow of money is free in some directions and impeded in others. In the most ingenious ways financial partnerships can facilitate mission. On the other hand wide differences in material wealth between churches can also complicate partnership. Where these inequalities occur and where cultures differ a missionary organisation may be needed to help make the link and act as interpreter. Good partnership should secure ways of helping local churches meet the challenge they face without taking their responsibility out of their hands.

Many of the illustrations I give for what partnership represents are drawn from Anglican sources, but there are others, as letters I receive from missionary colleagues in other missionary agencies bear out. I know less about partnership structures of other churches, but I hear of Western missionaries working under the direction of Asian colleagues in the Indonesian Missionary Fellowship, their presence seen as 'a witness to the universality of the Christian gospel'. Relationships in Papua New Guinea mean (as one missionary tells me) that Christians there 'feel for and feel with Christians in the West'. In yet another letter, one missionary wrote: 'The (Western) missionary places himself at the disposal of the church leadership' in Thailand. Such glimpses of a mutual and fruitful partnership are all taken from wider sources than Anglican and can surely be matched with others from all over the world.

Attempting, as best I can, a balanced view, I offer a ten-word specification for a framework of partnership: thoroughly adaptable, primarily personal, consistently loyal, essentially functional, ultimately dispensable.

Thoroughly adaptable Only the Holy Spirit has a monopoly function in Christian mission. No church, council of churches, or missionary institution, however good its way of working or however representative it may claim to be, can operate a sole and exclusive basis of partnership. Even from New Testament times no such monolithic structure existed. Instead there have been a multiplicity of organisations adapting to constantly changing situations in the world. For the sake of partnership they must do this, and for the sake of partnership they must relate adaptably and Christianly to each other. The complete organisational design is in heaven, not on earth; the many terrestrial missionary bodies have to keep adapting to their Spirit-prompted, but still partial, understanding of it.

We can therefore affirm the value of many different attempts to bring together different churches and mission agencies: united missions in Nepal, Sudan and Tunisia, other co-operative ventures encouraged by the Evangelical Missionary Alliance, also the missionary arm of the World Council of Churches. No structure should necessarily exclude another, all should adapt to change around them, none should pretend to be all embracing.

Primarily personal A missionary organisation may have specialist functions which deal with finance, communications, and material resources of many kinds. Essentially, though, mission is by people and for people, and a structure is as good or bad as the interpersonal relationships that it makes possible. In mission 'efficiency' should never be allowed to weaken the network of friendships in Christ nor the degree of accountability. Vinay Samuel and Chris Sugden, in *Partnership for Mission: A View from the Two Thirds World*, raise important questions about the functioning of some newer relief and development and missionary organisations, comparing them with more traditional missionary societies.[10] They argue that where the sustained, on-the-ground contact, traditionally provided by the long-serving, local language-speaking missionary, is missing then the accountability of the agency to those among whom it works may be seriously weakened: so too may be the level of mutual comprehension.

The older missionary societies have many good things to learn from the newer organisations, but in the process they should never weaken the value they place upon human relationships. The Church Missionary Society with its slogan 'People with a Purpose' sees itself in these terms: as funding a relationship. This priority is good and right; mission is primarily personal.

Consistently loyal Relationships are not made in a day; languages are not learnt in a week. Partnership structures certainly should facilitate the 'coming and going', but they also need to support the 'staying'. Only ephemeral relationships in mission can leave people very insecure. In the West we are used to a 'here today and gone tomorrow' style of living. People from other cultures may set great store by a new relationship and feel betrayed when it is prematurely broken. If money is involved in a missionary partnership, the quality of relations between partners becomes not less but even more important.

Simon Barrington Ward recounts an occasion when his Pentecostal hosts in a rural area of the Sudan gave thanks that 'those who first began the work here are even now coming back to share in its fulfilment'. Through a troubled history CMS has maintained its work in this region of Africa. The continuity of its involvement gives it a special, though by no means exclusive, value.

Essentially functional The more traditional mission agencies are usually strong on their loyalties, but they need to be watchful over their continuing usefulness. Their relationships with the churches they serve may be time honoured but otherwise not noticeably fruitful. Some forms of partnership are graciously impeccable: a kind of ecclesiastical diplomacy with a missionary flavour, but appear to issue in nothing more significant than the struggling survival of the institutions themselves.

Undoubtedly partnership is not just for partnership; nor should structures be for structures. There is a kind of ecumenical partnership which is so bureaucratic and self-absorbed that it strangles any useful action. The calling of a new missionary does not necessarily have to be the climax of a long and tortuous negotiation between churches and mission agencies. There must also be a place for an agile response to the urgings of the Holy Spirit.

Summing up their views on structures for mission, Vinay Samuel and Chris Sugden have this to say: 'Authentic partnership is actually between two crippled partners—the blind and the lame—who cannot go on a journey unless the lame person provides eyes for the blind and the blind person provides legs for the lame. That partnership is not worked out by sitting and talking about it. It is worked out by setting out on the journey.'[11]

Ultimately dispensable Lastly, I am prepared to believe that there will be some generously handsome plaques in the New Jerusalem commemorating the missionary societies I know and love, but I don't expect the heavenly post to be delivering their subscriptions, regulations, or committee agenda. The structures serve their time. Some continue a little longer than they should. At best they are mother of pearl; the costly stones of *koinonia* love outprice them.

7

Learners in Mission: Together on the Road

Casualties

It is a November afternoon on an 'overspill' estate in the industrial wastelands. In the fading light the box outline of a high-rise block marks out grey against grey. Look closer. Half the flats are empty: their windows smashed and their walls damp and rotting. Why are they so depressing and so derelict? Ask the young mother living on the first floor, where the lights are still burning. The flats were built in her lifetime and like her they seem prematurely old. Her TV set flickers out its message, advertising goods she cannot afford. Her two-year-old cries, and she cries inwardly. Her man has deserted, unemployed and unable or unwilling to stay in the hellishly frustrating confines of their home...

... It is one minute to midnight and the heavy tropical air is tainted with the smell of chicken blood. The dejected figure of an undergrown youth sits on the mud floor of a shadowy patio with his back resting against the adobe brick wall. In the centre of the confined space there's a low altar stained with candle wax, and the blood, some fresh, the rest dark and dried. The boy's eyes widen with fear and his face twists with horror. He is retching now, as if trying to vomit out something inside him: something poisonous, ugly and terrifying. 'Help me!' he screams...

... It is mid-morning and bright April sunshine is streaming through attractively curtained windows of the hospital ward in the south coast resort. A middle-aged man lies between immaculately laundered sheets on one of the beds: his complexion is blotchy but his breathing is easier now. 'Whatever made him want to do a thing like that?' muses the male nurse, glancing at the man, at a stomach pump and then at the man. 'He had it made. That was his car outside the hotel. If I had money like that, what wouldn't I do with it?' As if in response, the patient quietly groans...

The casualty list in a fallen world is endless and heart-breaking. A succession of lives precious and full of potential are cruelly damaged and in constant jeopardy. Where are the modern 'Samaritans' ready to help those left injured by the modern 'robbers'? It is the responsibility of the church to share in bringing the healing, saving love of Christ to the millions hurting themselves and being hurt physically, socially, spiritually. How, though, can the church respond to such a volume of need?

Can the whole body move?

In our search for an answer to this question we have focused on partnership: its qualities and structures. But who will engage in the partnership? Who will work seriously and co-operatively in Christ's mission? What proportion of the one and a half billion people in the world who identify themselves in some way or other with the church of Jesus Christ will be committed to serve others in his name? Are the 20,000 Christian denominations and service agencies effective instruments of mission or do they major on their own maintenance and survival? What about the 100,000 institutions worldwide founded and controlled by Christians? And is it enough that there should be three million lay and ordained paid workers engaged within their own countries and a quarter of a million sent abroad?[1]

The whole church committed to Christ's whole mission: is that a compelling vision or an idle dream? The authors of *Not*

Strangers but Pilgrims affirm their belief that 'Christian faith is of its very nature missionary'.[2] A welcome emphasis on mission is coming out in more and more pronouncements of the churches. How can good intentions be translated into reality and action? What solid and practical steps can be taken towards awakening, equipping and mobilising the whole body for the very purpose for which it was conceived?

Missionary discipleship

If more members of Christ's church are to become actively committed to Christ's mission then there needs to be a more conscious encouragement of missionary discipleship. Discipleship means obeying, following, learning and serving. In the way Jesus called his first disciples these things combined together and took place along the road. So for us a willingness to be mobile is also part of our missionary response, usefully described as missionary discipleship.

Missionary discipleship is for you and for me, indeed for all believers everywhere. But wait! Church membership embraces every age from infancy to dotage, every personality type from showman to recluse, every degree of intelligence from mastermind to moron. Is all this variety of people to be trained for mission and engaged in it? Yes, missionary discipleship should be pitched as wide as that. God delights to use the very weakest agents as well as the strongest. I know of some housegroups run by elderly people, some with failing health, who have drawn to Christ elderly neighbours. Nothing merits the name of mission more than this wise spending of the last years.

But there is another difficulty: many Christians do not think of mission as something that applies to them and to their locality. Instead they think that mission is done by other kinds of people and in other parts of the world: something perhaps heroic and spectacular. Those who think like this need to see that the humble act of crossing the street to share the love of Christ can have as much missionary meaning as crossing the sea. Nothing is too small to have significance; even a smile can break a barrier down and let the gospel in. As one nurse said of an old lady who kept her radiance longer than her reason, 'A face like that makes it easier to believe in God.'

Let us hold on to this ideal of every believer being a missionary disciple. At the same time we must adapt our approach to the changed conditions of our locality and the wider world. On the one hand it is becoming harder for the traditionally sponsored missionary to enter more countries of the world. On the other hand there are fewer uniformly Christian or 'safe' areas, so more than ever local believers need to be equipped for the kind of front-line evangelism and social action that previously might have been thought of as happening only overseas.

For such reasons it is no good being hooked on the stereotypes of yesterday. We need new categories of missionaries for our own day. I believe that at least six kinds can be distinguished. The first and most numerous I would call the *global locals*. Our Lord does not send everyone to the opposite end of the world. Instead he calls the majority to pursue their mission within a fairly limited radius of where they were born. Even Jesus was restricted in that way! The 'global locals' should have a strong missionary motive in their local outreach and service, coupled with a sympathetic understanding of the missionary challenge their fellow believers are facing in some other parts of the world. Many folk, for many good reasons, are tied quite closely to their localities. This does not prevent them from being equal partners and kindred spirits with those who travel the world. After all, it may take as much to climb the local barriers against the gospel as it does the more exotic ones.

The fact remains though that between two and three billion people live beyond the sphere of influence of local churches and at least three quarters of these are resident in countries closed to the free passage of the traditional missionary. Part of the answer to this massive contemporary challenge must surely be to raise up in increasingly substantial numbers another kind of mission agent. Various names have been used: tent-makers, non-professional missionaries. None is perfect, but let's try another: *passport missionaries*. This does not mean that they have 'missionary' on their passports. Instead these agents of the gospel have passport skills or a passport profession: a secular job which enables them to enter countries or areas which do not welcome 'official' missionaries. Among their business or social friends and acquaintances there they can share the knowledge of Christ and in time nurture small groups of new believers.

These technicians, engineers, scientists, teachers, linguists, business people, nurses or doctors will use the access their training gives them to people who need to receive the gospel. Those looking towards this kind of service may deliberately seek to acquire the training and experience which will give them a 'passport' into otherwise inaccessible parts of the world. In a special sense these missionaries will be unstoppable. Even in restrictive countries their work will be legal and their witness hard to proscribe because it is informal. Tetsunnao Yamamori calls for 100,000 of such 'new envoys', who could play a crucial part in the conversion of people who would form 'Christ groups' in the unevangelised half of the world, the members of which would then share the gospel with their own countrymen.[3]

Passport missionaries do already and will increasingly complement the work of traditional missionaries, but they will not supersede them. There will still be a vital role for people officially sent by churches or mission agencies (from whatever part of the world they are allowed out) and officially received by churches or agencies (wherever they are allowed in). These official missionaries will not necessarily be the evangelistic pioneers, though their evangelistic motivation and readiness should be undiminished. Their most characteristic contribution may now be in reinforcing the global partnership in mission. The CMS has adopted *mission partner* as the name it gives to members of its missionary personnel. Ideally these should be resource people linking churches to which they go to churches where they come from.

For the passport missionary the overseas contract is likely to be of limited duration. Similarly the mission partner may be required to make a specific contribution and then be replaced by a national colleague. Sooner or later for either there comes the demanding challenge: 'Missionary, don't go home. Move on!' Some will quite literally move on to yet another sphere of overseas service. There is nothing easy about a second or third major adaptation. Others will go home, to their home country. There is nothing easy about that either! Nor will their return mean an end of missionary service. In a world in which increasingly people of other cultures are not only across the water but also across the street the returned missionaries have insights and skills which are more important than ever. Whether young or old these *veterans* should be fully used by churches especially in multi-cultural areas. They may have a language, a cultural sensitivity, a theological insight which is just what the local churches need in order to minister to their neighbours.

This list of missionary categories may appear to be moving in the direction of the specially gifted people. That end of the spectrum may also include *underground missionaries*, those who may be called to witness in countries where the Christian religion is actively supressed by government. After all, Christian mission is not limited by official permission. Then, too, young people need opportunities for short term service, acting as *missionary apprentices*. But our list really does include everybody, so mention must be made of the *unconscious missionaries*. Infants, little children, the elderly and infirm, even the mentally handicapped can be part of the missionary witness of a church alive to mission because it is alive to the generous, outreaching, barrier-breaking love of God. These people can be the special agents in breaking the barriers and reaching the 'unreached', though at the time they may have little conscious knowledge of the part they are playing.

Missionary discipleship represents a kind of lifelong service which adapts to the contingencies of the modern world and which offers a valued role to all God's people. This surely is the God-approved standard, but in a church which has a chronic tendency to lose its missionary character there is always the gap between the ideal and the reality. What then in soberly realistic terms are we asking for? Precisely this: that through an infectious commitment, a Spirit-fed enthusiasm, and a deliberate extension programme, a multi-plying number of Christians may become effective and active in different kinds of missionary service, some of which we have described.

Mission is a long road and the travellers on it are a very mixed band. Some go far and fast, others progress much more slowly. How can such a variety of people best learn the way ahead? We can scarcely build a missionary training college on every street corner. Instead I commend five features of a com-prehensive missionary discipleship programme.

Community commitment Both the local congregation and the missionary training college, and indeed the theological seminary, should be communities of missionary commitment. What was so superbly true of von Zinzendorf's communities, in which every member played such a dedicated part (the craftsman every bit as much a missionary as the traveller he supported), should be effective today. Through the friendships and the frictions, the discipline and the discovery, such communities, especially those that are mixed racially and socially, can turn defensively isolated Christians into expan-sively adventurous ones.

Members of local churches no less than missionary training colleges need to be committed to each other in encouraging missionary vocations. It is a miracle of grace when someone previously oblivious of other churches and areas of the world, or indeed of the needs of local people outside the congrega-tion, becomes actively interested in them. This can be as hard won a breakthrough as an offer for overseas work. Both can come as the result of prayer in the local church family. The congregation should also prayerfully identify the different kinds of roles that different members may be called to fulfil. The 'global locals' can play a part in picking our potential 'passport missionaries' or 'apprentices'. 'Veterans' can be affirmed.

Adventurous encounter 'Love the Stranger', is both a book title and Bible verse.[4] It is essential to Christian mission and cannot be learnt academically. The stranger must be encountered face to face. He or she can't just be plucked off the shelf of a public or college library. There is no substitute for the fumbled greeting, the unclear expectations, the unscrambled misunderstandings and the emerging friendships. People in local congregations have to be encouraged to move outside their circle of people to the other kinds of people beyond. So do those undertaking more specialised Christian training. In each case the ability to befriend people different racially or socially from themselves is vital.

A very good place to meet people of another culture is in their own community. Local church members and missionaries in training need to go out to where these communities are. The meeting and the action needs to be on the spot, and so does the reflection. A vital missionary ability, whether for the local witness or the world traveller, is to discover how God's word speaks to a particular situation. This must normally require that action and reflection keep close together. Personally, I am very thankful to be based in Birmingham, rich in the variety of its human groups, and in the opportunity it gives for meeting the stranger. Some participating in training with us are off the college campus altogether, living instead in multi-cultural Sparkbrook.

Many-coloured worship Of all the encounters important in missionary discipleship none can compare with encounter with the living God. This undoubtedly is the most 'adventurous' encounter of all. With missionary commitment should come an expectancy that God will meet with us afresh in our personal prayers and our communal worship. There is nothing better than worshipping the Creator and Redeemer of every tribe and tongue with a good sprinkling of them represented. Of course Anglo-Saxon order, Latin American fervour, Asian harmony, and the swaying, overflowing exuberance of Africa do not automatically mix. But, put at its lowest, it is fun to try to make your offering to God like the others do. At its highest, it is reminiscent of Pentecost and a foretaste of heaven.

People who are 'travelling on' in mission not only hit the high spots in prayer and worship but also the low. To get out of a rut we need to be faithful to doctrinal loyalties but willing to experiment with new forms. We will need to sink deeper roots into God when we come to the exposed places.

Study in depth and by extension As a part of our Christian and missionary calling we need to love God with our minds. Within its limits this book sets out a mental framework helping us to engage deliberately and intelligently in mission. That is our reason for examining the global crises, seeking the biblical answer, and developing a missionary world-view.

It is not a Christian idea that some people have minds and others do not. Thinking about mission is something everyone can do. New converts are rightly encouraged to join Christian nurture groups. From the outset these can be used to open people's eyes to the missionary opportunities in the locality and in the world. New Christians are specially good 'missionaries'; they are more likely to break new ground in outreach for their local church than long established members. If a mission audit is carried out as many as possible in a congregation will be engaged in a study of local openings for the gospel and barriers against it. Together they will discover how the riches of Scripture speak directly to their situation, and, with the Spirit prompting them, they will identify their next step in mission.

A special contribution of the missionary training centre will be teaching of Old and New Testament with deep insights into the culture of the people who first received God's revelation in Christ. These centres also need to bring together insights and resources from many parts of the world. The new things God is doing in one place are full of instruction and encouragement for those in another. Mission is a science demanding many skills practical and theoretical: theology, languages, communications, religions, social analysis, as well as the business of living and moving from place to place. We must bring many resources together to help prepare resource people for the church in the world.

Vigorous steps should now be taken to increase the interchange between missionary training colleges and local churches. Out of the demands of a dynamic missionary situation in Guatamala began TEE, Theological Education by Extension. It is high time that something discovered through mission should be fully applied in preparation for mission. Increasingly, mission training centres must become extension centres. International teams should be sent out from them to teach, encourage and assist local churches in their missionary understanding and engagement. It will not be a one way process though; the specialists will learn much from the local practitioners.

An exciting possibility exists for such extension programmes to operate between two or more nations. Among the most significant developments in recent mission history is the growth of the emerging missions, mission agencies in Latin America, Asia, Africa and Oceania. The abounding vitality and substantial commitment of these groups is described in Laurence Keyes' book, *The Last Age of Missions*.[5] Already Third World and First World churches and mission agences are launching important co-operative ventures. There is scope for these to have a training dimension and, applying the extension approach, mixed teams can alert local congregations in the countries concerned to entirely new missionary horizons.

No one should imagine that missionary training is just an academic exercise of interest to a few specialists only. Missionary discipleship can embrace everyone. It is something which involves heart and mind, hands and feet. To be fully mobile for mission is to have 'feet fitted with the readiness that comes from the gospel of peace'.[6] 'Mission is the overflow of a great gift, not the carrying of a great burden.'[7] Commitment is by no means cost free, though. People come on to this road with wounds from the past and may need inner healing for the continuing journey. In the course of service they may be 'Honourably Wounded'.[8] Neither international nor local mission is free from severe strains.

Disciples rewarded

No account of missionary discipleship would be complete without reference, though, to one of its greatest rewards. This approach to life brings us in touch with a wonderful mixed company of God's people. They will be of all ages and colours of skin. They will have come from vastly different backgrounds and passed through totally different experiences. The common bond will be Jesus, Saviour and Lord. It is with all these saints that 'we have power to grasp how wide and long and high and deep is the love of Christ'.

If on our missionary road we are able to keep company with tribal people they will show us a new way of belonging to each other and to those who have gone before us. If we let them, they will break down our individualism. Once we are in their confidence, they will share how God meets them in dreams and vision, how with the spirit world such an immediate reality the Holy Spirit performs miracles of healing and deliverance. With them we shall be more at home in the unseen world.

In a special way the gospel is good news for the poor and oppressed. It is a great privilege to journey with them. They teach another dimension to freedom in Christ: a power to overcome crushing political and social disadvantages; power to recover self-respect having been ground down and despised. In their experience Jesus saves the sinned against as well as sinners.

These brothers and sisters, and especially those who speak and write for them, may carry much pain and anger. The gospel does not bypass this but neither is it trapped in the anguish. Others in the missionary church may come from places with an all-pervasive religious tradition and ancient culture. For them their countries' long search for a great harmony will have found its unique fulfilment in Jesus Christ. Their art of living in consecrated simplicity will be a blessing to fellow Christians wherever they are from.

From the West we also have good things to share and bad things to shed. We may have an asset of orderly administration, or developed art, science or technology. We may have the liability of making our faith a private affair when it should be applied in public. The Western gods of reason and material securities may hinder and haunt us. We can help others on the missionary road, and they can help us, especially if they know a more companionable, Spirit-sensitive, miracle-expectant way.

Missionary discipleship, in company with Christ and his people, teaches missionary theology. By no means a 'no go' area for ordinary folk, 'theology is God in dialogue with his people in all their thousands of different situations.'[9] 'Since theology is the knowledge of the living God, every believer is a theologian.'[10] It is with very different brothers and sisters that we are shown remarkable new depths of meaning in God's word. There are riches there illuminated by insights from all over the world, but monopolised by none. That is also part of the blessing of going with people of other cultures along the way of Christ.

But what about those derelict lives we glimpsed at the beginning? For whom would Jesus be more concerned than for the despairing mother, the demon-possessed youth or the suicidal man? Christ's way of missionary discipleship in all its richness offers no prospect of selfish reward; the blessing is for sharing with those whose hope is gone.

8

Mission in the Last Days

The key to the future

'The march of time has not been towards a far-off eternity, but along the margin of that mysterious ocean, by which it must be engulfed at last, and into which, fragment by fragment, the beach it treads is crumbling.'[1] Words of G.A. Chadwick, an old commentator on Mark's Gospel, illuminate a deep truth: that throughout what seems a long history the missionary church has been living on the edge of eternity. When the New Testament writers affirmed, 'These are the last days,' they were not betraying a mistaken perspective and a naive belief that Christ would necessarily return within a few months or years. Rather, they were describing the essential character of a period which began in their lifetime and has continued into ours. At different stages in history the beach has no doubt appeared firmer and the waves more distant from the walkers' feet. But at other times the sinking sand and the thunderous waves have been more starkly apparent.

We are living at just such a time of heightened awareness of the impending future and of the last things: the ultimate issues of life and death, time and eternity. Ours is a period of accelerating change and accumulating crises. It becomes more and more difficult in almost any sphere of life to work out what to do in the present solely on the basis of past experience. Increasingly people are being required to anticipate the future and act in new ways in response to unprecedented challenges. In being true to its missionary calling the church should never have ceased to be a forward-looking body. But what exactly do we look forward to? In terms of Chadwick's picture, what is the beach like ahead of us, and what will be that last great inrush of eternity that will sweep it away? Something which happened less than six weeks after Jesus rose from the dead gives the key to the answer to these questions.

A little cluster of Galileans stand on the rounded summit of a hill outside Jerusalem, gazing into a cloud suffused with an intensely beautiful, yet fading brightness. With the group oblivious of their approach, strangers come alongside them straddling the stony path along the ridge. They break the awed silence. 'Why are you standing looking up into the sky? Jesus, who has been taken up from among you, will return. Just as you have seen him go, so will he come again.'

By thus recording the event of Christ's ascension and the testimony of the angels, the Scriptures point us to a humanly unknown but divinely ordained calendar date when Jesus who rose in glory will return in glory to judge the living and the dead and to inaugurate new heavens and a new earth. This moment of unveiling must be the pivot upon which our Christian and missionary thinking about the future must hinge. We look forward to God's final intervention: the axe is at the root of the tree; the whistle is in the referee's lips; the photographic paper is in the developer and the image about to emerge.

Crisis of responsibility

As the angels of the Mount of Olives were quick to point out to the first disciples, such a time is not one for prolonged sky-gazing. Jesus' last act among his followers before he ascended had been to give them his missionary commission and blessing. When they were clothed with God's power, they were to preach repentance and forgiveness of sins in Christ's name to all nations. Then, 'he lifted up his hands and blessed them.'[2]

How important it is now for us to enter both into that blessing, and into the urgency of the task in which we will be blessed and outside of which we forfeit our well-being in Christ. Earlier Christ had said, 'This gospel of the Kingdom must first be preached to all nations, and then the end will come.'[3] So for us Christians the crisis situation around us is also a crisis within us: a crisis of responsibility. Through our words, our actions, our attitudes and through the very people we are, we must proclaim God's kingdom. God's rule confronts the world in a new way and demands that people should recognise the values and follow the way of his Son.

The dimensions of this crisis of responsibility are overwhelmingly large. Although there are more people than ever who have responded to the gospel there are proportionately more people still who are yet to respond. Further, this response of faith in Christ as Saviour is made substantially more difficult by the compromised witness of churches and nations identified as Christian. Over the years our appeal to both Muslims and Jews has been severely harmed by inconsistencies and even atrocities. The resistance to the gospel on the part of many belonging to the great world religions and, indeed, Western ideologies and materialism can only be overcome by Christ-inspired words backed by Christ-transformed lives. In a world near to despair the potential response to such witness is great, but the cost is great; Christians must be prepared to pay with their lives. Otherwise at a time when more people have more difficulty in hearing the good news of Christ, yet need it most urgently, they may be betrayed by those privileged to bear his name.

Talk of betrayal is hard to write about and discomforting to read. We know that our own personal failures with family, friends and neighbours match the inconsistencies of witness of the church on the world stage. We need the comfort of Scripture if we are to go on facing forward. On even a short reading, this Bible comfort, though deep, is by no means soft.

Forward into the last days: Scripture points the way of mission
We find in the Book of Revelation that the word of the risen Christ to seven representative churches of the first century

province of Asia was 'Repent.' His most common charge against them was that of idolatrous compromise. They lived at a time of turbulence and faced the ultimate issues of life and death, and, whether at the centre or on the edge of the modern whirlwinds, so do we. Also, whether recognised or not, there is idolatry among Western congregations. World poverty raises sharp questions about stewardship of resources in the richer churches. The nuclear threat and the arms race force us to look at the basis of our security and loyalty, as Christians. The millions of those unevangelised challenge us to examine our evangelistic obedience. Often the church finds itself too closely conformed to its surrounding culture and so unable to demonstrate Christ's different way.

So Jesus says again, 'Repent! In these crisis days, I want you to follow me very closely.' My understanding of what this means includes five things: all the following are indispensible items in our crisis equipment.

Biblical wisdom There is a story of two theological students who wanted to know whether their very learned Old Testament lecturer said his prayers in Hebrew. They paused outside his door at what they thought was the right time and were amazed to hear the old man repeating, 'Gentle Jesus meek and mild, look upon a little child.' On a night when all the nuclear powers were on full nuclear alert and the world appeared poised on the brink of the abyss, that is indeed a good prayer. We have to admit that even when we have thought our hardest and worked and prayed our hardest we are still little children dwarfed and largely powerless before the forces that evil may unleash. Wisdom teaches what we can do and what we can't do. It also recognises what the Lord can do: meek, yes, but also mighty.

Yet wisdom has a special value at times of uncertainty. In a rough sea correct steering is critically important. As we look ahead and number our days, Scripture tells us to 'apply our hearts to wisdom'. Unlike Greek wisdom, biblical wisdom is very practical. It is concerned with the business of making workable plans. It is free from the extremes of reaction and counter-reaction. Instead it discerns a good way through life's dilemmas. Guided by this kind of wisdom, human action is encouraged but human pride is held in check; without the fear of the Lord, there isn't even the beginning of wisdom.

Let us focus upon one issue: what light does wisdom throw upon international security and the nuclear threat? Are not Christians divided on what response to make, and sometimes overtaken by events? Humbly we have to admit that we are, and humbly we recognise with the authors of *The Church and the Bomb* that, 'There are no simple solutions to the problems created by nuclear weapons, no risk-free policies.'[4] It can scarcely be wise to underestimate the violent abuse of power which individuals and nations have repeatedly committed throughout the course of history. Yet even against potential aggressors the increasing costs of maintaining military sanctions need also to be carefully weighed. An accident-prone and high-risk military security, with its appetite for scarce resources, is already jeopardising economic, social and environmental security. Military budgets around the world are consuming wealth equivalent to the income of one and a half billion of the world's poor. Stability cannot be built upon a process which is as destabilising as this.

Is there such a thing as a missionary perspective on this difficult issue? I dare to say there is. The missionary experience is an international experience, and the missionary knows what it means to live under a wide range of different types of government. He or she knows the best that can be expected and the worst and the ambiguities that operate everywhere. The missionary has seen how the church flourishes or survives under all kinds of political regimes. Above all, engagement in mission introduces us to Christ's international family. We have a special loyalty to these our brothers and sisters. We have a general loyalty to all humankind, for whom Christ died. The missionary's loyalty to his own nation, though real, comes third.

The mission of Jesus Christ strengthens, I believe, our internationalism and qualifies our nationalism. In the fluctuations of international policy, Christians who learn from the missionary experience, will be seeking to increase human contacts and reduce the levels of threat between power blocs. We are well represented on both sides of the East-West divide. If it is clear that respectively we are unwilling for the sacrifice of lives in the other 'camp', then it will be that much harder for our governments to follow policies threatening the mass destruction of civilians.

Prophetic action It is one thing for Christians to be able to discern a good and wise response to a crisis situation, but then comes the question: What do we actually do? Oh yes, there are little things we can try, but aren't they trivial? Surely, a frenzied activism isn't the answer any more than an armchair resignation? What can we do, small as we are?

This problem faced the prophets. Many of them lived at crisis points in history. What could odd-job man Amos be expected to do about the rotten religion and morals of a whole nation? And what kind of a hearing might unshaven Elijah, fresh from the desert, expect to receive in the cosmopolitan and idolatrous court of King Ahab? Jeremiah was just a boy in a country parsonage when he was charged to deliver an impossibly stern message to the deluded rulers of the capital. These prophets faced up to their moment of crisis, and confronted their own and other nations with God's command. To do this they had not only to grasp hold of God's message, but God himself. Clinging to him, they could contemplate a staggering assignment, and enter the action. In God, their words, their acted signs, their political interventions, though humanly weak, had power.

So we in our crisis world are to be prophetic. God who is just requires justice in international trade. God who is generous, demands generosity in international aid. God who is wise condemns the folly of wasting upon arms and affluence the resources that could sustain life for the poor. Words such as these must be said persuasively, repeatedly, even inconveniently. Vested interest will ensure that many ignore them. Yet words that are in line with God's word can never completely fail.

Prophecy, though, is more than words. When the Babylonian armies were already besieging Jerusalem and Jeremiah was under arrest for predicting the capture of the city, he purchased a parcel of land in his native Anathoth, quite unprotected from the invading army. In obedience to God, Jeremiah didn't just verbally declare God's promise of eventual restoration, he acted upon it practically. A weak and apparently irrational action supported that prophet's lonely stand. Those who seek to uphold prophetically the demands of God must similarly be prepared to match action with words, even when the actions may appear incongruously weak. The actions may include donations, changes in lifestyle, membership of organisations, non-violent political protest. These need not be frenzied. They must be utterly consistent. The whole direction of our lives must speak for God.

Apocalyptic realism 'If disaster must come, let it come only when men and women have done all they can to avert it.'[5] This sentence from *The Church and the Bomb* strikes a solemn chord. Faced with different threats, God requires us to do all that he gives us to do. But suppose evil is still not restrained? Then what?

The apocalyptic literature of the Bible gives a remarkable answer to the question about how to live when the tides of evil are sweeping everything before them. The Book of Daniel recounts how faithful Jews exiled in Babylon responded to imposed idolatry. Refusing to comply with the state religion and under threat of execution by burning, Shadrach, Meshach and Abednego answer King Nebuchadnezzar by saying, 'If we are thrown into the blazing furnace, the God we serve is able to save us from it, and he will rescue us...but even if he does not...we will not serve your Gods.'[6]

The 'but even if not' is crucial; it is the bottom line. Even in the worst event there is to be no betrayal of loyalty to the living God. Stubborn faith does not balk at a super-heated furnace. Christians, of all people today, need to be able to look straight into the nuclear gun barrel or at whatever other menace human evil may invent. There is a calm realism which sees all the dangers and yet refuses to place any idolatrous reliance on securities which threaten others.

In times of overshadowing evil the biblical anticipation of 'apocalypse' is neither escapism, nor resignation, but realism. It means a realistic recognition that the powers of evil may wreak havoc on the earth. Thus far in his mercy God has preserved the 'Fragile Peace'.[7] We will use every day he gives us to spread the gospel peace. By God's grace we will work prayerfully, intelligently, strategically. But the day may come when we can no longer actively work, but only faithfully endure.

Resurrection hope 'The choir sang, "Christ is risen from the dead... " In the midst of unending anguish Easter had dawned again.' In a CMS newsletter written in 1985 Simon Barrington Ward describes Easter in Beirut: the shelling, the deaths of children, the bitter grief, and in a church sharing the tragedy of its neighbourhood, the resurrection worship.[8] There is in the experience of Christians an essential link between the brink of despair and the doorway of hope. Those who have suffered most know this best.

It was Jeremiah, the prophet of doom, who learnt to call God, 'Thou Hope of Israel.' Isaiah's vision of stern judgement is also a vision of soaring hopefulness. In his missionary service in the province of Asia Paul had to be unbearably crushed and despair of life itself in order to learn to trust in God who raises the dead. 'On him,' he declared, 'we have set our hope.'[9] There is a logic-defying law that as the crisis deepens, so the hope expands. In its teaching on the last things the Bible indicates a final manifestation of evil, but also holds out the prospect for a substantial advance of good.

And this is a missionary vision. The New Testament looks beyond the initial rejection by Israel of her Messiah to a time when she will turn to him. It also anticipates a period when Satan is bound, when evil is held in check and when the influence of those faithful to Christ is powerfully extended. It is the missionary church which keeps this hope alive. Those active among Jews know at first hand the heartbreak in the relations between the two communities. Yet they retain a proper missionary optimism. Indeed in days of crisis new congregations of Messianic Jews are being formed. Who knows what may result from the resurgence of Christian faith in Soviet Russia? Think of the blessing that will flow when the zealous faith of Islam is increasingly surrendered to Christ.

Apostolic witness Our attempted overview of mission has shown us a world of promise and a world of menace. We have traced the master-plan of the Servant through Scripture and into history. We have seen opportunities missed and opportunities grasped. Continents and localities appear before us as mission fields each in their different ways full of difficulty and encouragement. In Christ we can model a way of partnership which knits together a fragmented humanity. And in case we imagine that not all of us are invited to follow Christ in missionary discipleship, he says to us, as he said to the apostolic band: 'When the Holy Spirit has come upon you, you shall be my witnesses.'[10]

Apostolic witness is Christlike. It does not erect barriers against the gospel; it breaks them down. All witness, whether conservative or radical, catholic, evangelical, orthodox or charismatic, must be judged by the apostolic standard. Only the Holy Spirit makes apostolic witness possible. It is when the life-giving Spirit comes that, as William Barclay says, 'the tired, lack-lustre, weary defeatedness of life is gone, and a surge of new life enters us.' The powerful Spirit enables a person 'to do the undoable...face the unfaceable and to bear the unbearable'. By the creative Spirit 'our dishevelled, disorderly, uncontrolled lives are moulded...into the harmony of God'.[11]

Now Jesus speaks to you and to me. In his love and through the power of his Spirit, Christ is offering to resolve our inner crisis of guilt and indifference and invite our co-operation, weak as it is, in his creative and redemptive purpose. We have the opportunity of saying yes to Jesus and yes to his mission. My 'yes' is nothing to be proud of, but will you add yours? Our days are in the truest sense last days. It is right for us to spend them in an enterprise incomparably great in its scope and prospect. As the end approaches we may expect a climax both in the opportunities and the cost of this calling.

The final unveiling

We come back to the staggering challenge of it all. The storm is gathering and the harvest is ripening. In the churches this is no time for wordy confusion or cold criticism. Rather, as together we face a test of daunting proportions, we must warmly encourage each other. In his day of crisis the writer of the Book of Revelation introduced himself, 'I, John, your brother and companion in the suffering and the kingdom and the patient endurance'.[12] How much his fellow Christians needed such brotherly companionship: deep sharing both in the trials of persecution and in the victories of the kingdom.

And finally because of what the risen Christ gave to him, John was able to give to them an incomparable gift for witness in the last days: an unveiling. Following John, they could enter into 'the sphere of spiritual reality, where the masks are off and both good and evil are seen for what they really are'.[13] Though symbols may be mysterious, the total picture is clear: the glory of God's throne, the vindication of the slain Lamb, with those who have been cleansed through his blood, the warnings and the judgements upon rebel people and powers in a sin-spoilt world, the cosmic conflict, and the perfect recreation. All this is the reality behind these our critical days. On the last of them Jesus will return in person and in glory, and then the unveiling will be complete.

Notes

Chapter 1

1. *The Gaia Atlas of Planet Management*, p16, Editor Norman Myers, Pan Books, 1985
2. *The Church in Response to Human Need*, p11, Editor Tom Sine, MARC, 1983
3. *The Gaia Atlas of Planet Management*, p232, Editor Norman Myers, Pan Books, 1985
4. *The Gaia Atlas of Planet Management*, p138, Editor Norman Myers, Pan Books, 1985
5. *World Military and Social Expenditures 1986*, pp6, 12, Ruth Leger Sivard, World Priorities Inc. 1986
6. *The Gaia Atlas of Planet Management*, p242, Editor Norman Myers, Pan Books, 1985
7. *The Church and the Bomb* p58, Hodder & Stoughton, 1982
8. *World Military and Social Expenditures 1986*, Ruth Leger Sivard, World Priorities Inc., 1986
9. Archbishop Robert Runcie preaching at an open air service in Oxford in 1984
10. *The Gaia Atlas of Planet Management*, p258, Editor Norman Myers, Pan Books, 1985

Chapter 2

1. Colossians 1:16
2. Genesis 12:3
3. Genesis 13:14; 15:5
4. Exodus 3:1–6
5. Exodus 3:7 and 9
6. Isaiah 6:8
7. Isaiah 33:17
8. Isaiah 14:26, 27; 46:11
9. Isaiah 19:25
10. Isaiah 6:7; 45:22; 65:1, 2; 55:2; 43:25; 1:18
11. Isaiah 42:1–4
12. Isaiah 53:2; 50:6; 9:6; 53:3
13. Isaiah 53:11, 6, 8; 52:15
14. Luke 1:38
15. Luke 2:25–35
16. Mark 10:45
17. Matthew 28:19, 20
18. Luke 4:14–21; 7:1–10; 17:11–18
19. John 1:14; 12:23; 1:5

Chapter 3

1. Acts 2:14–41
2. Acts 6:7
3. Acts 8:1
4. Acts 9:3, 4
5. Acts 10:44–48
6. Acts 13:2
7. Acts 19:17
8. *The First Advance*, p99, John Foster, SPCK, 1972
9. *A History of Christian Mission*, p54, Stephen Neill, Penguin Books, 1964
10. *A History of Christian Mission*, p53, Stephen Neill, Penguin Books, 1964

11. *A History of Christian Mission*, p44, Stephen Neill, Penguin Books, 1964

12. *Evangelism in the Early Church*, p47, Michael Green, Hodder and Stoughton, 1970

13. *A History of Christian Mission*, p42 Stephen Neill, Penguin Books, 1964

14. *The First Advance*, p41, John Foster, SPCK, 1972

15. *A History of Christian Mission*, p55, Stephen Neill, Penguin Books, 1964

16. *Men of Vision*, pp26–30, John Foster, SCM Press, 1967

17. *A History of Christian Mission*, p69, Stephen Neill, Penguin Books, 1964

18. *The First Advance*, p121, John Foster, SPCK, 1972

19. *The Ecclesiastical History of the English Nation*, Book II ch.1, Venerable Bede

20. *The Ecclesiastical History of the English Nation*, Book I ch.xxiii, Venerable Bede

21. *A History of Christian Mission*, pp74–77, Stephen Neill, Penguin Books, 1964

22. *Setback and Recovery*, p61, John Foster, SPCK, 1974

23. *A History of Christian Mission*, p106, Stephen Neill, Penguin Books, 1964

24. *The Ecclesiastical History of the English Nation*, Venerable Bede

25. *The Arabs: A Short History*, Philip K. Hitti, Macmillan, 1968

26. *A History of Christian Mission*, p116, Stephen Neill, Penguin Books, 1964

27. *A History of Christian Mission*, p137, Stephen Neill, Penguin Books, 1964

28. *Setback and Recovery*, p80, John Foster, SPCK, 1974

29. *New Movements*, p85, Alan Thomson, SPCK, 1976

30. *Setback and Recovery*, pp40–51, John Foster, SPCK, 1974

31. *A History of Christian Mission*, p165, Stephen Neill, Penguin Books, 1964

32. *A History of Christian Mission*, p170, Stephen Neill, Penguin Books, 1964

33. *A History of Christian Mission*, p179, Stephen Neill, Penguin Books, 1964
34. *A History of Christian Mission*, p208, Stephen Neill, Penguin Books, 1964
35. *A History of Christian Mission*, pp217, 219, Stephen Neill, Penguin Books, 1964
36. *Dynamics of Spiritual Life: An Evangelical Theology of Renewal*, p36, Richard F. Lovelace, Paternoster Press, 1979
37. *Zinzendorf, the Ecumenical Pioneer*, p91, A.J. Lewis, SCM, 1962
38. *Count Zinzendorf*, John R. Weinlick, Abingdon Press, 1956
39. *Zinzendorf, the Ecumenical Pioneer*, pp116, 117, A.J. Lewis, SCM, 1962
40. *Zinzendorf, the Ecumenical Pioneer*, p98, A.J. Lewis, SCM, 1962
41. *William Carey*, p97, F. Deaville Walker, SCM, 1926
42. *William Carey*, F. Deaville Walker, SCM, 1926
43. Proclaim the Good News, pp7, 8, Jocelyn Murray, Hodder & Stoughton, 1985
44. *A History of Christian Mission*, pp259, 260, Stephen Neill, Penguin Books, 1964
45. *A History of Christian Mission*, pp274, 275, Stephen Neill, Penguin Books, 1964
46. *A History of Christian Mission*, pp 293, 294, Stephen Neill, Penguin Books, 1964
47. *A History of Christian Mission*, p333–336, Stephen Neill, Penguin Books, 1964
48. *Unquenched Flame*, p184, Phylllis Thompson, Hodder & Stoughton, 1983
49. *A History of Christian Mission*, pp424–427, Stephen Neill, Penguin Books, 1964
50. *Concise Dictionary of the Christian World Mission*, p75, Lutterworth Press, 1970
51. *Concise Dictionary of the Christian World Mission*, p568, Lutterworth Press, 1970

52. *A History of Christian Mission*, p393, Stephen Neill, Penguin Books, 1964
53. *A History of Christian Mission*, pp393–396 and 545, Stephen Neill, Penguin Books, 1964
54. *World Christian Encyclopedia*, pp783, 784, David Barrett, Oxford University Press, 1982
55. *World Christian Encyclopedia*, pp782, 785, David Barrett, Oxford University Press, 1982

Chapter 4

1. *World Christian Encyclopedia*, pp806, 413, David Barrett, Oxford University Press, 1982
2. eg *The Gaia Atlas of Planet Management*, Editor Norman Myers, Pan Books, 1985
   World Military and Social Expenditure, Ruth Leger Sivard, World Priorities Inc., 1986
3. *World Christian Encyclopedia*, pp866, 867, David Barrett, Oxford University Press, 1982
4. *World Christian Encyclopedia*, p782, David Barrett, Oxford University Press, 1982
5. *A Humanist in Africa*, p22, Letters to Colin Morris from Kenneth Kaunda, Longmans, 1966
6. *A Humanist in Africa*, p20, Letters to Colin Morris from Kenneth Kaunda, Longmans, 1966
7. *Africa in Crisis*, p8, Lloyd Timberlake, Earthscan, 1985
8. *Christianity, a World Faith*, p142, Lion Publishing, 1985
9. *The Primal Vision*, p151–152, John V. Taylor, SCM Press, 1963
10. *A Humanist in Africa*, p72, Letters to Colin Morris from Kenneth Kaunda, Longmans, 1966
11. *Henry Martyn, Confessor of the Faith*, p242, C.E. Padwick, SCM, 1922
12. *An Introduction to Asia*, p61, Jean Herbert, George Allen and Unwin Ltd., 1965
13. *An Introduction to Asia*, p29, Jean Herbert, George Allen and Unwin Ltd., 1965

14. *Mahatma Gandhi*, pp66, 19, B.R. Nanda, George Allen and Unwin, 1958
15. *World Christian Encyclopedia*, p798, David Barrett, Oxford University Press, 1982
16. *An Introduction to Asia*, p61, Jean Herbert, George Allen and Unwin Ltd., 1965
17. *An Introduction to Asia*, p42, Jean Herbert, George Allen and Unwin Ltd., 1965
18. *The Sadhu*, p54, Streeter and Appasary
19. *World Christian Encyclopedia*, pp783, 394, 134, David Barrett, Oxford University Press, 1982
20. *Christianity, a World Faith*, Part 2, Ch.4, Lion Publishing, 1985
21. *Christianity, a World Faith*, p206, Lion Publishing, 1985
22. *U.K. Christian Handbook*, p5, MARC Europe, 1986
23. *The New Nomads*, p15, Barney Milligan, WCC, 1984
24. *The New Nomads*, Barney Milligan, WCC, 1984
25. *To Live among the Stars*, pxi, John Garrett, WCC, 1982
26. *World Christian Encyclopedia*, pp802, 803, David Barrett, Oxford University Press, 1982
27. *I have a strong belief* Leslie Boseto, Unichurch Books, 1983
28. *The Island Churches of the South Pacific*, p80, Charles W. Forman, Orbis, 1982
29. *America*, Alistair Cooke, BBC 1987
30. *The Story of Religion in America*, p28, Sweet, Harper, 1930
31. *Winds of God*, p24–5, Rodney Booth, WCC, 1982
32. *Winds of God*, p42, Rodney Booth, WCC, 1982
33. *America*, p274, Alistair Cooke, BBC, 1978
34. *Winds of God*, p60, Rodney Booth, WCC, 1982
35. *The Americans and Civilisation*, p380, Darcy Ribeiro, E.P. Dutton, New York, 1972
36. *America*, Alistair Cooke, BBC 1978
37. *The Americans and Civisation* Darcy Ribeiro, E.P. Dutton, New York, 1972
38. *World Christian Encyclopedia*, p783, David Barrett, Oxford University Press, 1982

39. *Christianity, a World Faith*, p220, Lion Publishing, 1985
40. *Christianity, a World Faith*, Lion Publishing, 1985
41. *A Vision of Hope*, Ch.2, Trevor Beeson and Jenny Pearce, Collins, 1984
42. *World Christian Encyclopedia*, p6, David Barrett, Oxford University Press, 1982
43. *God's New Envoys*, p11, Tetsunsao Yamamori, Multnomah Press, 1987

Chapter 5

1. *Come out the Wilderness*, p18, Bruce Kenrick, Collins, 1963
2. *World Class Cities and World Evangelisation*, David Barrett, New Hope, 1986
3. West Midlands Planning and Transportation Sub-Committee Notes on Deprivation in the West Midlands County, 1986
4. The Report of the Archbishop of Canterbury's Commission on Urban Priority Areas, *Faith in the City*, pxvi, Christian Action, 1985
5. *World Class Cities and World Evangelisation*, p17, David Barrett, New Hope, 1986
6. The Report of the Archbishop of Canterbury's Commission on Urban Priority Areas, *Faith in the City*, pxv, Christian Action, 1985
7. *Come out the Wilderness*, p24, Bruce Kenrick, Collins, 1963
8. The Report of the Archbishop of Canterbury's Commission on Urban Priority Areas, *Faith in the City*, p384, Christian Action, 1985
9. The Report of the Archbishop of Canterbury's Commission on Urban Priority Areas, *Faith in the City*, pxvi, Christian Action, 1985
10. *Christianity, a World Faith*, p322, Lion Publishing, 1985
11. *Come out the Wilderness*, p208, Bruce Kenrick, Collins, 1963

12. *A Tale of Three Cities*, David Bleakley, CMS, 1985
13. Case Study, Wheaton '83 Consultation, David Hewitt
14. *Ten Growing Churches*, p189, Edited by Eddie Gibbs, MARC Europe, 1984
15. Case Study, Wheaton '83 Consultation, p14, Graham Cray, 1983
16. Case Study, Wheaton '83 Consultation, p2, Waldron Scott, 1983
17. CMS Newsletter, J.V. Taylor, February 1968
18. CMS Newsletter, J.V. Taylor, February 1968
19. *People in Rural Development*, p115, Peter Batchelor, Paternoster, 1981
20. CMS Newsletter, Simon Barrington-Ward, November 1982
21. *People in Rural Development*, Peter Batchelor, Paternoster, 1981
22. CMS Newsletter, Simon Barrington-Ward, October 1985
23. *The Third Wave*, p210, Alvin Toffler, Collins, 1980
24. *Rural Anglicanism*, Leslie J. Francis, Collins, 1980
25. Federation for Rural Evangelism, 9 White Rock Road, Hastings, E. Sussex, TN34 1LE
26. *The Contribution of Open-air Preaching to the Rooting, Reformation and Revival of the Church in Britain*, Peter Green, M.Th. Thesis, National College of Divinity
27. *The Third Wave*, p220, Alvin Toffler, Collins, 1980
28. *Mission Audit*, General Synod Board for Mission and Unity, 1984

Chapter 6

1. John 5:17
2. II Corinthians 6:1, I Corinthians 3:9
3. Philippians 4:3, 10, 14
4. II Corinthians 8:14
5. CMS Newsletter, Harry Moore, January 1987
6. CMS Newsletter, Simon Barrington-Ward, October 1980
7. *International Review of Mission*, Robert Ramseyer, January 1980

8. *International Review of Mission*, Robert Ramseyer, January 1980

9. *Proclaim the Good News*, pp95, 96, 125, 235, Jocelyn Murray, Hodder & Stoughton, 1985

10. *Partnership for Mission*, Vinay Samuel, Chris Sugden, Asian Trading Co-operation, Bible Churchmen's Missionary Society, 1983

11. *Partnership for Mission*, Vinay Samuel, Chris Sugden, Asian Trading Co-operation, Bible Churchmen's Missionary Society, 1983

Chapter 7

1. *World Christian Encyclopedia*, pp3, 18, David Barrett, Oxford University Press, 1982

2. *Not Strangers but Pilgrims* – Report of the Swanick Conference on an Inter-Church Process, September 1987, p10, British Council of Churches

3. *God's New Envoys*, Tetsunsao Yamamori, Multnomah Press, 1987

4. *Love the Stranger*, Roger Hooker and Christopher Lamb, SPCK, 1986

5. *The Last Age of Missions—A Study of Third World Missionary Societies*, Laurence Keyes, William Carey Library, 1983

6. Ephesians 6:15

7. *Mission in Christ's Way*, p32 Lesslie Newbigin, WCC, 1987

8. *Honourably Wounded*, Marjory F. Foyle, MARC Europe, 1987

9. *The Urban Christian*, Ray Bakke, MARC Europe, 1987

10. Jurgen Moltmann. Spoken at an address he gave in Buenos Aires in 1976

Chapter 8

1. *The Gospel of St. Mark*, p356, G.A. Chadwick, Hodder & Stoughton, 1889

Stoughton, 1889
2. Luke 24:50
3. Matthew 24:14
4. *The Church and the Bomb* Hodder & Stoughton, 1982
5. *The Church and the Bomb* Hodder & Stoughton, 1982
6. Daniel 3:16–18
7. *The Cross and the Bomb*, ch.1, A Fragile Peace, Graham Leonard, Mowbray, 1983
8. CMS Newsletter, Simon Barrington-Ward, May 1985
9. II Corinthians 1:10
10. Acts 1:8
11. *Matthew*, Vol.1, p41, William Barclay, The Saint Andrew Press, 1956
12. Revelation 1:9
13. *I saw Heaven Opened*, Michael Wilcock, IVP, 1975